DAWN
OF THE
MIDDLE
AGES

DAWN OF THE

MIDDLE AGES
MICHAEL GRANT

BONANZA BOOKS
NEW YORK

CONTENTS

This 1986 edition is published by Bonanza Books, distributed by
Crown Publishers, Inc., 225 Park Avenue South, New York,
New York 10003, by arrangement with McGraw-Hill Book
Company.

Manufactured in Italy

Library of Congress Cataloging in Publication Data

Grant, Michael, 1914—
    Dawn of the Middle Ages.

    Reprint. Originally published: New York:
McGraw-Hill, 1981.
    Bibliography: p.
    Includes index.
    1. Middle Ages—History.   I. Title.
[D117.G7 1986]   909′1   86-15644
ISBN: 0-517-62510-5
h g f e d c b a

Art Director: CHARLES WHITEHOUSE
Editor: DAVID BAKER
Managing Editor: FRANCINE PEETERS
Designer: INGRID REINECKE
Picture Procuration: ZORKA NEVOLE
Production Manager: FRANZ GISLER
Graphic Artist: FRANZ CORAY

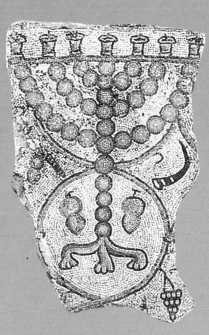

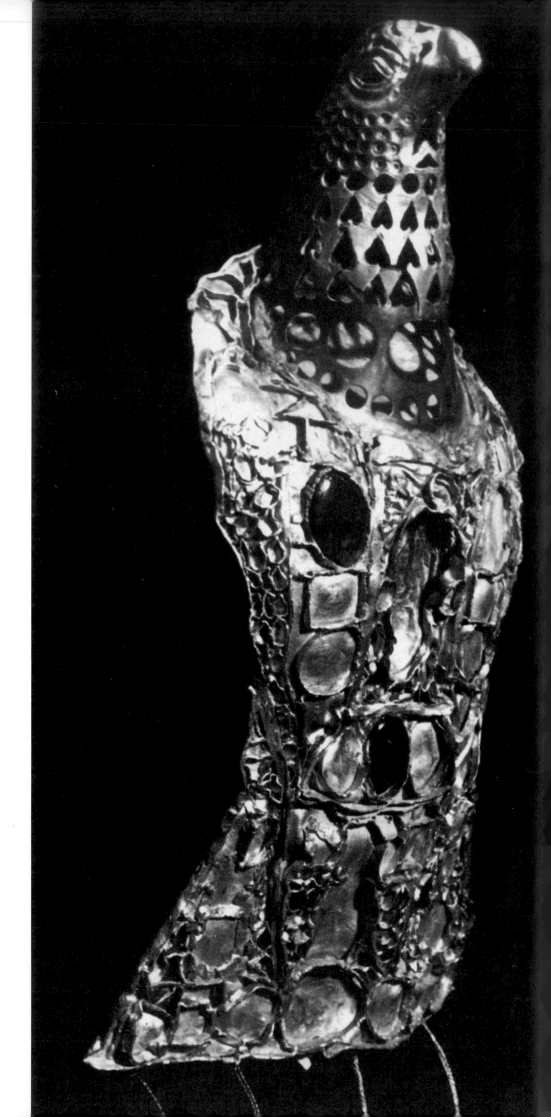

*An able Goth wants to be
    like a Roman;
only a poor Roman
    would want to be like a Goth.*

Theodoric, King of the Ostrogoths in Italy

*You are the salvation
    of the whole world; rightfully do
all other peoples look up
    to you with respect, knowing that you
are unique.... Our kingdom
    is only an imitation of yours,
a copy of the only true empire on earth:
    and because we imitate you,
we stand above all other peoples.*

Theodoric, writing to the Byzantine emperor
Anastasius I, A.D. 508/509

THE AGE CALLED "DARK"

The epoch following the disappearance of the western Roman empire is one of the most exciting, varied, and creative in the history of the world. These centuries witnessed astonishing, overwhelmingly important developments and events.

This was the rise of a new world, of many new worlds: the dawn of a new age—with the well-known proviso that in history no *entirely* new beginning is ever possible, since, consciously or unconsciously, there is always a deep connection with what has happened in the past: and the peculiar interest of the dawning of the Middle Ages—the ages that extended between the ancient and modern world—lies in this continually and subtly changing balance between old and new, with the old always there, but the new sometimes very new indeed.

When people call other tracts of time the Age of the Greek City State, the Age of the Roman Empire, Renaissance, Reformation and so on, they are looking at those periods from a culturally and geographically restricted point of view: that of the western world. The same is true of the term "Dark Ages," which, applied to the epoch described in this book, is the least satisfactory designation of all.

To begin with, the phrase is ambiguous: it can mean either that the epoch is dark because backward and uncivilized, or that it is dark because we know too little about it. But the first interpretation stems from an attitude that is once again too parochial, and excessively orientated toward the classics—the assumption that once the western Roman empire was no more, then everything, everywhere became dark and barbarous and dreary. That, however, as we shall see, is far from the truth: indeed it

is better to speak of the "transformation" of the empire rather than its fall. Besides, once again, such a title could at best only apply to a limited region of the globe, namely western Europe and the western Mediterranean area, since those were the only territories that had belonged to the western Roman empire.

But in any case, whatever view may be taken about the disappearance of that empire, there were other great areas of the world, during the early Middle Ages, which could not by any stretch of the imagination be regarded as "dark" in the sense of barbarous or sluggish. Was the period dark, then, in the other sense of the word—because it is obscure, because we know so little about it? As before, the question bears an occidental, classical, literary bias. For in the west, during this epoch, it is true that there were many fewer (and less elegant) historical and informative writers to draw upon than there had been in ancient Greek or Roman times. And for America and most of Africa our information is unfortunately too limited for any connected account to be worth the attempt. Yet, once more, this does not apply to other parts of the world—in China, for example, the situation was quite different. And in Europe, too, we can nowadays rely on a variety of archaeological and art-historical techniques that were unavailable to those who used to complain that the age was obscure and dark.

Nevertheless, in spite of all the information that we can derive from these more recently exploited sources, one must admit that there do remain huge gaps of darkness in our knowledge. True, reflection suggests that for all other ages too, at least before modern times, our understanding is inevitably deficient and

The brilliantly fashioned works shown on these pages belie the sentiment of inferiority evoked in the quotation at left. In Anglo-Saxon England as in other Germanic kingdoms the manufacture of multicolored jewelry was widespread. A splendid example of this art is provided by the seventh-century Kingston Brooch *(above)*, from Kingston Down, Kent, now in the Merseyside County Museum, Liverpool.

Opposite: Eagle brooch from the Visigothic "Treasure of Athanaric," a hoard of twenty-two gold objects found at Pietroassa (or Petrossa) in Rumania, fourth century. A spectacular example of the jewelry, frequently concentrating on animal forms—at every stage between naturalism and abstraction—which was one of the most remarkable (and for all its echoes of earlier styles) most original contributions of the Germanic peoples to the art of the early Middle Ages.

Diverse Germanic invaders from the mainland were drawn in successive waves to the British isles, where the process of Christianization soon began. In the cross-currents between Germanic and Celtic elements, the kingdom of Northumbria became a major center. Missionaries spread the religious and artistic influences of Britain and Ireland to the continent.

The hardy peoples of Scandinavia took quite early to the sea. Attacks on Britain and other countries along the coastline of continental Europe were followed by commercial and colonial ventures by land and river deep into the interior of Russia. The Vikings emerged as a dynamic, often menacing force, with enormous capacities for expansion.

The Slavs, originally from the western Ukraine, experienced unparalleled increases in population during this period, but so far failed to develop social or political instructions capable of attaining national independence. Three main groups of East, West, and South Slavs developed in Russia and Poland, Central Europe, and the Balkan peninsula respectively.

The Germanic invaders who had shaken the Roman empire founded new states in western Europe. The Franks emerged in France and Germany as the most powerful Germanic people, and soon developed an imperial state that could, for a time, offset the rising power of the Papacy.

Division was to be the lot of the Iberian peninsula for several centuries, as the Islamic forces took and held most of the land and the Visigothic state withdrew to the northern area of Asturias. The Moslems in Spain broke away from the Arab empire to create an independent kingdom centered at Cordoba, which became one of the principal cultural centers of Europe.

By far the richest, strongest, and most stable state of the western world was the Byzantine empire, with its fortress-capital at the imposing city of Constantinople. Despite wave after wave of attack by Sassanian Persians, Bulgars, Arabs, Turks, and others, this bulwark of Christianity held firm (except for a single brief interval) throughout a whole millennium.

After the Romans' suppression of two major revolts in the Holy Land, the Dispersion of the Jews throughout the Mediterranean area and the Middle East increased greatly in dimensions. Tolerated (even if tightly controlled) in some countries, they were severely persecuted in others. By the end of the fifth century their scholars had completed the monumental commentary of the Talmud.

The years between A.D. 476 and 814 have posed a problem for generations of historians who sought a clear, appropriate, and convenient label to characterize the period. It has been referred to as an age of great migrations, an age of faith, the birth of European civilization, the postclassical period, and of course as the "dark ages." All are less than adequate, some are complete misnomers. As this map and its commentary suggest, the age was one of activity, change, and enormous diversity—all of which resist easy characterization. These centuries witnessed a great deal of violence, as various

peoples vied for control over territories and the minds of their inhabitants. But constructive developments also abounded, not just in the realm of the arts but also in the elaboration of governmental and religious institutions, the emergence of important ruling dynasties, and the foundation of wholly new nation states. The period was conspicuous for its dynamic interplay of many forces, warlike and peaceable alike; and there were great movements of population. These changes and accomplishments had momentous results that are still felt in east and west today.

From Mecca in Arabia, in the course of the seventh century, Mohammed created the new religion of Islam, a mixture of Jewish and Christian influences, with a powerful stress on monotheism, a simple ethic, and a crusading zeal that inspired its believers to seek military conquests. Within three generations they had branched out from the Middle East across all of north Africa and into Spain.

Hordes of Avars, Bulgars, Khazars, White Huns and Turks—nomadic horsemen belonging to the Turanian (Turkish) language group—moved from central Asia westward into Europe, and eastern into China and India, forming loosely organized states and bringing great numbers of people under their sway.

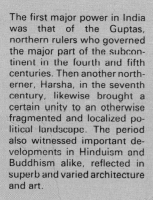

The first major power in India was that of the Guptas, northern rulers who governed the major part of the subcontinent in the fourth and fifth centuries. Then another northerner, Harsha, in the seventh century, likewise brought a certain unity to an otherwise fragmented and localized political landscape. The period also witnessed important developments in Hinduism and Buddhism alike, reflected in superb and varied architecture and art.

Instability in northern China was followed by the strong, centralized rule of the short lived Sui dynasty and the three centuries of T'ang rule that followed. China became the largest and most powerful state in the world, and a rival to Byzantium as the greatest center of civilization, producing outstanding poetry, painting, and sculpture, and many technical innovations. By the eighth century, too, centers in Japan were brilliantly reflecting Chinese styles.

patchy—there is a great deal that is not and cannot be known. Still, for the period discussed in the present book this patchiness is quite particularly notable.

In this tomb lies the body of Charlemagne, the great and devout emperor, who most splendidly did increase the kingdom of the Franks and govern them happily for forty-seven years. Hie died at age seventy in the year of our Lord 814 on the fifth day before the Calends of February [28 January].

Inscription at Aachen

The authoritarian, pyramidal structure of early medieval society is reflected not only in our historical sources but in the artwork of the period. While showing the common man in group scenes, usually employed in day-to-day work which seemed to define him, the artists, not unnaturally, glorified their leading personages. *Right:* Ivory diptych of an eminent churchman from Ravenna, early fifth century (Museo del Duomo, Novara). *Above right:* Eleventh-century illuminated manuscript painting depicting St. Benedict of Nursia (ca. 480–547), the most important figure in western monasticism, with an abbot. The work is from the Monastery of Monte Cassino, founded by Benedict in 529.

The two lower pictures: Detail from an ivory jewel case (Palazzo Venezia, Rome), showing a shepherd piping; and work in a vineyard, detail from a manuscript illumination (Bibliothèque Nationale, Paris).

Indian literature was not very historically minded, Yang Hsien-chih and Li Tao-yüan were historians of outstanding significance. It is these rays of light shining through the penumbra that make the epoch a profoundly rewarding challenge to all who would seek to solve some of the pressing questions it raises. It is necessary, first of all, to create some sort of chronological framework, to establish the

There were, for example, a few outstanding historians, for example Procopius at Constantinople, Gregory of Tours in Merovingian France, and Bede in England, and other authors, too, who throw conspicuous light on the epoch, notably Cosmas the explorer, Boethius, Cassiodorus, Benedict, Isidore of Seville, and the compilers of the Koran and the poetry and law of the Arabs and Irish. Moreover in the far east, although the rich

approximate course of events in the various regions. To shelve all dates and landmarks in favor of general trends, although such a procedure is well regarded today, will not in itself give the feel and quintessence of the age: it must also be seen how the various situations unfolded—in other words, we must detect the sequences of events that made the epoch what it was. Obviously, "events" are hard to define, since even if one can be sure that something

nating over events as happily obsolete—because we have seen such appalling men of power in our own times: so that once again it seems cosier to see general tendencies as the history-producing agents.

Yet these tendences, however powerful and inexorable, were often given a sharp twist and fresh direction, even a complete reversal, by a single individual. Indeed, he or she could still

"happened," its character looks quite different according to your political views, or according to whether, for example, you were a general or a private soldier. Now, the viewpoints and activities of the generals (and other leading figures) of the time are, inevitably, more important than those of other ranks in the effects they exercised upon history. Many of us would like to regard the nineteenth-century theory of the admired Great Man domi-

do the same today, if such a man or woman could be found—as the electors to great offices of state seem to be hopefully aware. But in the steeply pyramidal, authoritarian societies of the epoch between the fifth and eighth centuries, one of the few certain ways in which anything could get done at all was by the initiative of a single, potent, gifted, often violent personality at the top: men such as Mohammed or Charlemagne.

The period covered in this book was an age which produced art forms of bewildering diversity. Much depended not only on the geographical area, but on the historical era. Thus the Byzantines created many great objects of religious art and artifact, only to smash most of them later after a radical change in church doctrine, Iconoclasm. And this was an age of great migrations and conquests, so in many cases we find forms blended from two or even more different cultures: pagan and Christian scenes engraved on the same piece of wood; Moslem mosques built on the floorplans of Christian churches. It is possible only to give the merest hint of this multiplicity and diversity in the illustrations on these two pages.

From Bulgaria: the head of a Saint, a detail of a sixth- or seventh-century wall painting. Regional Historical Museum, Shumen.

From the Roman, soon to be the Byzantine, empire: sardonyx relief showing Constantine I the Great (306—337), refounder of the city of Byzantium as Constantinople, with his family. Stadtbibliothek, Trier.
From Persia: a rich manuscript illustration, of later date, showing the Sassanian emperor Khosrau (Chosroes) II (591—628) engaged in combat against a usurper. Bibliothèque Nationale, Paris.

Besides, at the lower, broader end of the pyramid, it was very hard for people to influence history at all, except with extreme slowness over an extended period. It was even much harder than it is today. For the multitudes of the poor were very poor indeed, living at the bare level of subsistence, or below it. In most countries the gap between the poor and the rich is still startlingly large in our own times. In the dawn of the Middle Ages, taken all in all, it was a great deal larger still: that is why, in order to see how the history of the epoch evolved, it is necessary to study the

"great" powerful man in relation to society, and in action. And another remarkable contrast to be seen in this same early medieval period was geographical in character. There was a difference of extraordinary dimensions between the prosperity, civilization, and stability of some countries and the poverty, backwardness, and instability of others. That too is by no means unfamiliar today. Yet, the contrast was even more glaring, if possible, in the early Middle Ages. The prominent countries will have to engage our attention; many of the others, despite every effort by archaeologists, must still go unsung.

Wherever practicable, I have tried to rely on pictures of the art and architecture of the period to supplement what can be learned from written sources. And here again, we have further conspicuous proof, if any were needed, that this period cannot be considered a Dark Age. On the contrary, it was a time that saw the production of astonishing masterpieces, an epoch that produced the church of Haghia Sophia at Constantinople, the mosaics of Ravenna, the Dome of the Rock at Jerusalem, the Great Mosque of Cordoba, the jewelry and gold work of the Germanic kingdoms, the Books of Durrow and Kells, and the flourishing, diverse arts of China and India. Bearing in mind the implications of these early Middle Ages upon the periods that lay ahead, I have sometimes looked forward from them—beyond the early ninth century at which the book is supposed to end—so as to refer, by comment or illustration, to events and developments that were still to come.

From Ireland: the St. John's Crucifixion Plaque (left): bronze decoration for a (wooden) cover of a Bible, late seventh century. National Museum of Ireland, Dublin.

From Germany: gold brooch set with sardonyx and glass, and a silver ring with almandines (far left): examples of the intricately manufactured Germanic jewelry of the fourth and fifth centuries. Stadtbibliothek, Trier.

From Scandinavia: the boss of a shield (below left) made of iron and bronze coated with tin by a highly skilled Swedish smith in the seventh century. Statens Historiska Museum, Stockholm.

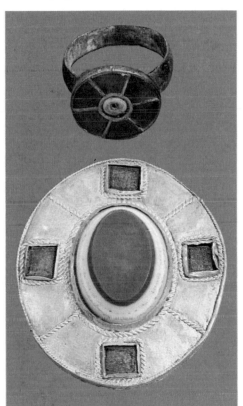

From China: highly decorated pottery cup (above). Made in the seventh century under the T'ang dynasty, which reunited the whole of the country in conditions of great prosperity and culture.

From eastern Europe: part of the treasure of ninth-century goldware found at Nagyszentmiklós (Banat, Rumania). Of Bulgarian manufacture. Kunsthistorisches Museum, Vienna.

From the rising of the sun, to the shore of the sea where it goes down again, all hearts are full of grief. Alas is me! Franks, Romans, and all Christian peoples mourn, bent down with sorrow. He was the father of all orphans, pilgrims, widows, and virgins. The Frankish kingdom, though it had to suffer much harm before, has never known so great a pain as in the moment of laying in the ground the most worthy, most eloquent Charlemagne. O Christ, take the pious emperor into your holy dwelling place among your apostles.

By an Irish monk in Bobbio, in northwest Italy

13

JUSTINIAN I   THEODORIC   ATTILA

The dawn of the Middle Ages (476–814) was a period marked by the careers of many great leaders, in a diversity of countries and cultures. A few of the best-known figures of the age are illustrated by way of example here, though it must not be forgotten that the list could be extended to include at least as many more—notably in China and India, which experienced equally remarkable rulers.

The emperor Justinian I (527–565) is considered the most brilliant ruler in the history of the Byzantine empire. His reign was particularly famous for its military conquests, under his generals Belisarius and Narses, who restored to the empire many German-held territories formerly controlled by Rome: north Africa (533–534), Rome itself (536), northern Italy (538–540), southern Spain (550–552). Great building programs were also initiated, the most celebrated being Haghia Sophia in Constantinople and the churches of Sant'Apollinare in Classe and San Vitale at Ravenna in Italy. His law compendia were another major achievement: to the historian Edward Gibbon, "The vain titles of the victories of Justinian are crumbled into dust, but the name of the

The first major Germanic leader to establish a kingdom in Western Europe after the fall of Rome was Theodoric (ca. 471–526), known (like Justinian I) as the Great. Theodoric became founder of the Ostrogothic kingdom of Italy. The Ostrogoths, the eastern branch of the Gothic people, had migrated from Scandinavia to the Ukraine and thence made their way westward to invade the Roman world. Upon succeeding his father as king, Theodoric had first fought a series of wars against the eastern Roman (Byzantine) empire before launching his offensive on Italy in 488–489. In 493 he overcame and killed another Germanic ruler, Odoacer (who had unseated the last of the western Roman emperors in Italy in 476), and became sole ruler of the country. He established his capital at Ravenna, and went on to conquer Sicily and parts of Dalmatia and Germany. His rule in Italy was stable and peaceful, an attempt at a synthesis between Roman and Germanic elements. In his respect for Roman institutions, Theodoric paid homage to the Byzantine emperor and adopted Roman law codes for his Germanic population. But the Ostrogoths were Arian Christians—members of the sect excoriated as a heresy by the ecclesiastics of Rome and Constantinople—and no truly successful integration of Germanic peoples with Roman imperial institutions was achieved. The coin above depicts Theodoric on a gold medallion, early sixth century, Museo Nazionale delle Terme, Rome. The king's mausoleum at Ravenna, a composite of different styles and influences, is shown below.

'The Scourge of God,'' Attila (ca. 434–453) is one of the most significant forerunners of the Middle Ages, though the results of his career were not permanent. For a time, he succeeded in forming a large state under the Huns in central Europe, by conquering many rival barbarian groups. He terrorized the eastern Roman emperor Theodosius II with the aim of extracting tribute payments, but waged violent, destructive campaigns throughout the Balkans between 441 and 450. Then, however, the eastern emperor Marcian in 450 refused to grant concessions or pay tribute, and Attila turned his attention to the West. But when he invaded Gaul, the Roman general Aetius, assisted by Visigoths under their king Theodoric I, defeated him on the Catalaunian Plains (Châlons-sur-Marne) in 451 and drove him back across the Rhine. He returned the next year to invade Italy, destroying the city of Aquileia. But then, after a meeting with Pope Leo I, he suddenly withdrew. He planned to renew his attacks on the eastern empire; but then, suddenly, he died. This Renaissance medallion (above) from the Certosa di Pavia is an imaginary depiction of Attila.

legislator is inscribed on a fair and everlasting monument.'' He is seen above on a gold coin (solidus) issued during his reign. The marble head shown here (Castello Sforzesco, Milan) has been believed to portray his dynamic and controversial wife, Theodora, whose irregular past remained a subject of scandal.

KHOSRAU I

MOHAMMED

GREGORY THE GREAT

CHARLEMAGNE

One of the foremost Persian kings, Khosrau (Chosroes) I (531–579) governed the Sassanian state during its period of greatest strength, brilliance, and geographical expansion. The Sassanians, who had succeeded the state of Parthia in the third century, were formidable neighbors first to the Romans and then to the Byzantines. Khosrau succeeded his father, Kavadh I, who was removed because he had caused anger by abandoning the state religion, Zoroastrianism, for a Manichaean cult. On coming to power, Khosrau restored the official Church and began a long reign which earned him the name Anushirvan ("of the immortal spirit"). Military campaigns against the Byzantine emperor Justinian I, interrupted by several armistices, lasted until a fifty years peace was declared in 561. But in 573 fighting was resumed, against Justin II, and negotiations to end it were not complete when Khosrau died. On his eastern frontier, he had made contacts, first friendly and then hostile, with the new power of the Turks. Persian contacts also extended to China and India. Khosrau reordered the social structure of his huge kingdom, introducing a fair and durable system of taxation. His enlightened court at Ctesiphon on the Tigris became a haven for Athenian Neoplatonist

philosophers in exile. But only seventy-three years after his death, the Persian empire, weakened by renewed wars against the Byzantines, was totally destroyed by the armies of the Arab caliphate. The relief (above) showing the king on his throne is engraved in rock-crystal in a gold dish known as the Cup of Solomon. The coin below is a Sassanian issue depicting a fire-altar.

The prophet and founder of Islam, Mohammed (A.D. 570–632) was born in Mecca, in western Arabia, a town that was already established as an important religious and trading center. Orphaned as a boy, raised as a shepherd and camel driver living in close proximity to the Bedouin, he became established as well-to-do merchant after his marriage to a wealthy widow, Khadija, many years his senior. His vocation dates from the year 610, when he reportedly had a visitation from the angel Gabriel who commanded him to preach the word of God. His monotheism reflected both Jewish and Christian influences (both religions enjoyed considerable support in Arabia), and his preaching, as reflected in the Koran, bears many traces of these links. As soon as Mohammed began to widen his circle and preach publicly (in 613), he fell foul of the Meccan leaders and had to leave the city. In 622 he arrived in Yathrib (Medina) this journey is referred to as the Hegira, or emigration—and from this base he waged a war which enabled him to return to Mecca (630), where he ordered the pagan shrine of the Kaaba to be converted into a Moslem sanctuary. During the remaining three years of his life he extended his control over the whole Arabian peninsula. After his death, the conquests begun in Arabia were soon widened to the neighboring countries of the Near East. The imaginary portrait of Mohammed shown above is a detail from a fourteenth-century Persian manuscript (Edinburgh University Library). The late eighth-century Koran text below is from Arabia (British Museum, London).

St. Gregory I the Great (ca. 540–604) rose to the imperial rank of prefect of the city of Rome and then became a monk; he was subsequently elected to the papacy in 590 at a critical time in the history of Italy and of the Church. His moral efforts to rally the Italian populace, and stem the tide of Lombard and other invasions, also enabled him to establish the secular basis of the papacy, which, largely through his efforts, became the prestigious institution it would remain throughout the Middle Ages and beyond. A critical development under his pontificate was the encouragement and establishment of monastic life, on the Benedictine model, as a major ally and instrument of the papal Church. Gregory also began the revival of Christianity in the British Isles by sending Augustine as a missionary to Kent in 597. His diverse and prolific writings, dealing with many points of faith and morals, earned him the title of Fourth Doctor of the Church. No authentic likenesses of Gregory are known, but the portrayal above is a detail from an ivory plate (Kunsthistorisches Museum, Vienna), and he is seen below on a detail from a thirteenth-century illumination (Biblioteca Apostolica Vaticana, Vatican City).

In 768 Charles the Great, that is Charlemagne (742–814), and his brother Carloman shared the kingdom of their father Pepin III the Short, and on Carloman's death (771) Charlemagne took over the whole kingdom. A series of forcible annexations which enormously extended the Frankish dominions included the subjugation of the Saxons (772–785, 793–797), the Lombards (773–774), and the Avars (791–796, 802–803), as well as a minor conquest in Spain (778) which became the subject of the Song of Roland. Pope Leo III crowned him emperor in Rome in 800, thus fatefully reviving, in the west, the imperial title which had fallen into abeyance since the fifth century. Charlemagne established his principal residence at Aachen, Germany, in the center of his realm, and through counts, bishops, and travelling envoys sought to

control the varied territories of his empire. His realm became the basis of the Holy Roman Empire which continued for many centuries in German lands. The emperor is depicted above on a tenth-century copy of a drawing of the previous century (Palazzo dei Musei, Modena). The spear which was supposedly used by Charlemagne, "the holy spear," is shown above.

15

THE BYZANTINE EMPIRE

Constantinople—"New Rome," earlier called Byzantium—succeeded, as a city and an empire, where Rome had finally failed. This stronghold on the Bosphorus commanding entry to the Black Sea remained for many centuries the preeminent city of the western world and the seat of the far-flung Byzantine empire, incontestably the greatest political organism of the West in the years following the collapse of the western Roman empire. The emperor Justinian I's codification of Roman law provided a bridge from antiquity to modern times by handing down to European nations the basis for their legal system. The eastern (Orthodox) branch of the Christian church dominated the life of the Byzantine empire to an extent rarely or never achieved by any church elsewhere, successfully combating a whole series of deviationist "heresies." It was the Church, too, which nourished and stimulated the glorious Byzantine culture and civilization. Where Rome had its lofty domed Pantheon, Constantinople boasted the awe-inspiring Church of the Holy Wisdom (Haghia Sophia). As a military power, the Byzantines enjoyed a durable success. They served as an eastern bulwark against Islamic incursions in Europe until the fifteenth century—by which time their empire had outlived its western Roman counterpart by an entire millennium.

*I declare confidently
      that although hostile barbarians
may rise briefly against
      the Roman Byzantine empire
to correct us for our sins,
      yet through the strength of Him
who maintains us the empire
      will remain undefeated
—if no one hinders the expansion
      of Christianity.*

Cosmas Indicopleustes

Byzantine art, a rich and subtle blend of
Greek, Roman, and oriental elements,
reached its zenith in the mosaic. This example
(opposite), a mosaic of Jesus as the Good
Shepherd, in the mausoleum of Galla Placidia, Ravenna, Italy, shows strong Byzantine
character, and gives an idea of the appearance of all those mosaics in Constantinople itself which have not survived.
The relief *(left)* depicts Ariadne, wife of the Byzantine emperor Anastasius I (491—518), the
first eastern emperor to start his reign after the
western empire had ceased to exist. Bargello
Museum, Florence.

THE FALL OF THE ROMAN WEST

For centuries the Roman empire was a going concern, extending over a vast area from Britain to the Sahara Desert, and from the Atlantic Ocean to Iraq. Yet by the third century A.D. it was already gravely threatened by external pressures.

For then, at one and the same time, the long Rhine-Danube border was beset by unprecedentedly menacing incursions from many German tribes, and at the other extremity of the frontier, across the Euphrates, Rome's only large-scale neighbor, the feudal Parthian state, was replaced by the infinitely more formidable kingdom of the Sassanian Persians. Owing to the difficulties of guarding both the

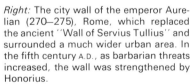

Battle between Romans (including an emperor on horseback) and German invaders, from a sarcophagus in the Museo Nazionale delle Terme, Rome. These reliefs date from the third century, when the threats to the empire's northern frontier became acute; at the same time, the Sassanian Persians superseded the Parthians and constituted a menacing foe in the east.

Right: The city wall of the emperor Aurelian (270–275), Rome, which replaced the ancient "Wall of Servius Tullius" and surrounded a much wider urban area. In the fifth century A.D., as barbarian threats increased, the wall was strengthened by Honorius.

northern and eastern frontiers at the same time, the empire was eventually divided into two administrative parts, under imperial colleagues (A.D. 364). Beyond the eastern borders, two large German principalities had taken shape, the Ostrogoths in the Ukraine, and the Visigoths in Rumania. However, the non-German, partly nomadic Huns, living beyond them on the steppes, broke through into the territories of these two states in the years round A.D. 370. The Ostrogoths collapsed, and 200,000 Visigoths fled across the Danube. Theodosius I permitted them to stay. They could live under their own rulers, but must supply soldiers and farm workers to the Romans, thus becoming the first of a series of German peoples of allied, "federate" status.

The German pressure now switched to the west, where the emperor Honorius (395–423) moved his capital (which had hitherto been at Mediolanum, the modern Milan) to Ravenna for the sake of his personal security. Most of Gaul had to be surrendered to invading tribes early in the fifth century; Rome was temporarily overrun and sacked by Alaric; and the Visigoths and another German people, the Vandals under their brilliant leader Gaiseric, seized north Africa (439)—from which Rome

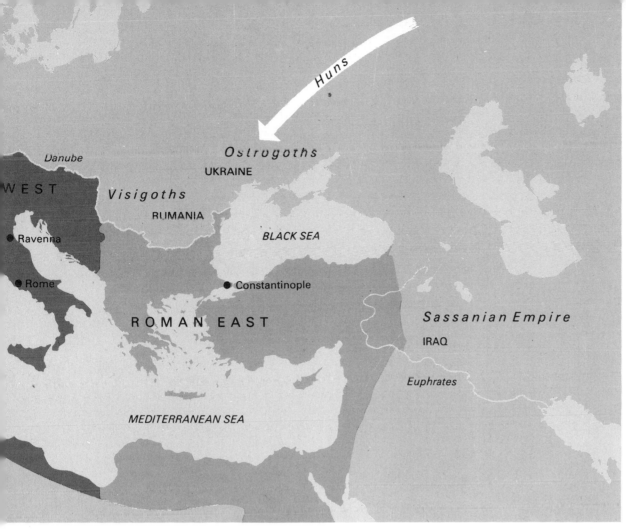

Huns

Danube

Ostrogoths
UKRAINE

WEST

Visigoths
RUMANIA

● Ravenna

BLACK SEA

● Rome

● Constantinople

ROMAN EAST

Sassanian Empire
IRAQ

Euphrates

MEDITERRANEAN SEA

Beset by invasions along its northern and eastern frontiers since the third century A.D., the Roman empire was definitively divided, in the year 364, into two zones. While the east, administered from Constantinople (Byzantium), held together for another thousand years, the western empire could not withstand the pressures of invading peoples, including Visigoths and Ostrogoths who were themselves displaced by Huns arriving from eastern Europe. Those invading from across the Rhine included Vandals, Suevi, Franks, Alans, and Burgundians. These comprised a mass of loosely confederated peoples speaking dialects of the Germanic language group, already greatly mixed racially and in terms of cultural development. Those nearest the Roman frontiers had become familiar with agriculture and stock-breeding.

All was not primitive "barbarian" darkness among these Germanic peoples, as witness this elaborate silver fibula, a work of the fourth century A.D. found in a warrior's grave at Vermand, France. The fibula (or brooch) bears engraved designs of gold and niello—a black alloy of silver, lead, copper, and sulfur. Jewelry of this

had been accustomed to acquire most of its grain. Within another decade Gaiseric had become the first German leader to convert former imperial territory into a completely independent state; while Attila the Hun (d. 453) established an enormous state in central Europe, from which he mercilessly raided the western Roman empire. Pressures on the Romans continued to multiply until, in 455, Gaiseric captured Rome, and in the course of two weeks of occupation carried off a great deal of loot. The Roman court of Ravenna now depended on its German commander-in-chief, Ricimer. But he was killed in 472 and four years later another German, Odoacer, decided to request from the western empire, within Italy itself, the federate status and land grants which other Germans had been awarded in Gaul and elsewhere. When his claim was rejected, he forced the last western emperor, Romulus Augustulus, to abdicate (476), and accepted the office of "king" from

kind was one of these peoples' most noteworthy contributions to western art. The "barbarians" introduced a number of innovations to Europe: butter, rye bread, furs, felts, trousers, skis, staved barrels, the wooden-framed saddle, and apparently the heavy wheeled plow (some of these inventions having been first acquired from more easterly peoples).

Left: Reconstruction drawing of the fortifications along the empire's northern frontier, in Rhaetia (Austria-Switzerland). The final breach of such defenses in the fifth century sealed the downfall of the western empire.

19

his own troops. And this is traditionally regarded as the date when the long declining western Roman empire finally fell.

These events, however, do not tell the whole story. The western empire could have withstood its external foes if it had still possessed sufficient internal strength. But the stability of earlier times had been fatally undermined from within by a variety of factors.

The first was the preposterous frequency with which emperors lost their thrones and lives to their rivals; usurpers were a constant threat, requiring costly defensive operations. Another problem was the numerical weakness of the imperial armies, due to the increasing

tion to the estates of the great noblemen. These refugee tenants became virtual serfs, not unlike the tied, feudal labor of the Middle Ages that lay ahead. As for the noblemen, they were magnificent personages, too magnificent, very often, to give much obedience to the emperors, which meant that the needs of the empire, in terms of defense and authority, suffered again. The poor, then, were ruined, and the rich went their own way unchecked. As for the classes in between, taxation and oppression virtually wiped them out. The Church also helped to undermine the old Roman patriotism, by placing another authority above the emperor himself.

Battered from without by invaders, the western empire was also beset by deep-seated, progressively worsening internal problems. Roman society became more and more polarized between rich and poor, as the noble classes consolidated their power. The official shown on this sixth-century ivory diptych *(below),* with the goddess Rome laying her hand on his shoulder, still holds the ancient office of the consulate, reserved for the privileged group. Heavy taxation proved catastrophic to the Roman middle class: the stone relief *(above right)* from Noviomagus (Neumagen, Germany), third century A.D., shows the counting of tax money. It was, above all, the small-scale artisan (terracotta relief of a blacksmith's shop, *right*) who finally became crippled by ruthless taxation.

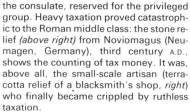

failure of the western government to enforce conscription. It was mainly from the so-called "free" rural population—on whom the empire's main industry, agriculture, depended, since slaves had become fewer—that the huge taxation needed to support the soldiery had to be extorted. However, the people were too impoverished to pay, either in cash or in kind. And thus it was impossible to find and mobilize enough troops.

This oppressive situation also revolutionized the structure of society. For when farmers and laborers became destitute, they fled for protec-

End of the western Roman empire: The army, composed of Germans living within the empire, got out of hand. In Italy, their leader Odoacer *(far left)* removed Emperor Romulus Augustulus *(left)* in the year 476 and claimed the title of king for himself. Italy became one more Germanic kingdom.

Who can find words to describe the enormity of our present situation? Now when the Roman commonwealth, already extinct or at least drawing its last breath in that one corner where it still seems to retain some life, is dying, strangled by the cords of taxation as if by the hands of brigands, still a great number of wealthy men are found, the burden of whose taxes is borne by the poor; that is, very many rich men are found whose taxes are murdering the poor. Very many, I said: I might more truly say all . . .
The rich have thus become wealthier by the decrease of the burdens that they bore easily: while the poor are dying of the increase in taxes that they already found too great for endurance. So the vaunted remedy most unjustly exalted the one group and most unjustly killed the other. To one class it was a most accursed reward and to the other a most accursed poison.

Salvian

This marble statue depicts a late Roman consul, around the year 400, in the traditional toga, holding aloft the *mappa* symbolizing his status and power—the power not of his office, which was titular, but of the rich men whose wealth remained dominant.

And yet everything might still have been well, or at least tolerable, if the western and eastern Roman administrations had managed to cooperate with one another. But all too often they proved unable to do so. The results were disastrous—above all, for the western empire, which was being so rapidly undermined from without and within. Moreover, it had missed an enormous psychological opportunity. When tens of thousands of Germans were brought in as federates and employed as soldiers, a fruitful partnership with them would not have been impossible. For, at first, these Germans had no desire whatever to destroy Roman civilization, but only to be given a share of its benefits. Yet from the Roman side they met with incomprehension, racialist contempt, and exploitation. And so in due course, by way of return, Germans of the stamp of Gaiseric the Vandal stopped talking about coexistence and passed to the counterattack —with success.

CONSTANTINOPLE

Constantine I the Great (306–337) took two decisions that altered the history of the world. He made Christianity the dominant religion of the Roman empire, and he refounded the town of Byzantium on the Bosphorus—the channel linking the Sea of Marmara and the Black Sea. This city, under its new name of Constantinople, was destined to be the unrivaled center of the western world.

A little more than forty years after his death, Constantinople became the permanent residence of the eastern Roman emperors, who continued to rule there, with only a brief intermission, for more than a millennium, until 1453. They also continued to call themselves Romans, though Greek increasingly superseded Latin as their language. According to the terms current today, they were at first the rulers of the eastern Roman empire, and then—from the fourth or fifth or sixth century A.D. onward—of the Byzantine empire in its place: which in turn greatly influenced many countries beyond all its borders.

In November of the year 326, the emperor Constantine I the Great visited Byzantium and marked out the boundaries for the new city, New Rome, or Constantinople, which was rebuilt within four years. This tenth-century mosaic portrait *(below)*, over the door of the Church of the Holy Wisdom (Haghia Sophia) at Constantinople, shows Constantine offering his city to the Virgin Mary.

The city was nearly surrounded by water. The main approach by land was through the Golden Gate *(above right)* to the west of the city. Erected by Theodosius I in A.D. 380 as a Triumphal Arch outside Constantinople, in the following century the gate was incorporated in the wall of Theodosius II.

Right: The female figure depicted on this leaf of an ivory diptych is the city-goddess of Constantinople (a fifth-century work, now in the Kunsthistorisches Museum, Vienna). Although Constantinople was Christian from the outset, it was nevertheless personified as a goddess, just as pagan cities had been before it.

Throughout by far the greater part of this immensely long period Constantinople was probably the finest city in the world, and certainly by far the finest in Europe. Its situation, on a triangular peninsula at the extremity of the continent, was superb. On one side it faced the Sea of Marmara, and on the other the Golden Horn, a deep body of water which could hold a large number of ships and protect them from currents and winds. The Golden Horn is an arm of the Bosphorus, the narrowest sea-crossing between Europe and Asia, which enabled Constantinople to dominate the great trade route between the Black Sea and the Mediterranean. Moreover, the rapid tides swirling through the Bosphorus guarded the city from naval assault. From the land side too, massive fortified walls made Constantinople almost impregnable, so that for many hundreds of years, despite sieges and scares, the city never fell to a foe. It was also ideally located for the defense of the empire, since its rulers could supervise the Danube and Euphrates frontiers at one and the same time. The

The land is water, and the water land,
The ocean blossoms, ships sail on the sand.

*Anonymous Byzantine description
of Constantinople*

Of holy relics I need only say
    that it contained more than all
Christendom combined; there is no
    estimating the quantity of gold,
silver, rich stuffs and other valuables....

Villehardouin

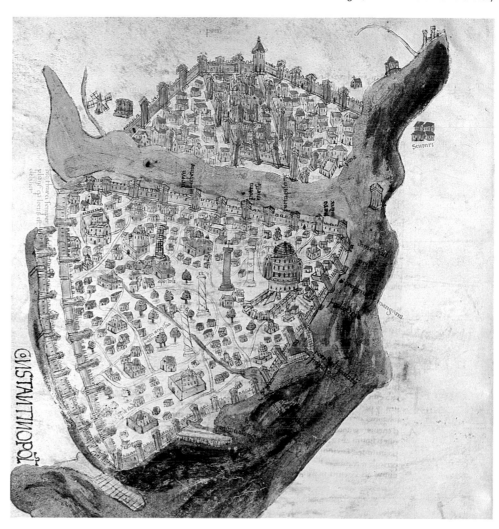

local water supply was excellent, and except in grain, the citizens were self-supporting. Wealth and culture flowed in from west and east alike; but the greatest strength of the place lay in the immediate proximity of Asia Minor (Anatolia), the empire's indispensable reservoir of soldiers, sailors, and natural resources.

Containing a population of ca. 500,000 by A.D. 500 (later, temporarily, decreased by plagues), Constantinople had also become, by that time, the economic and commercial as well as the political capital of the empire. Its riches were founded on the state ownership of mines, factories, domains, and cultivation, and on an elaborate system of taxes. Local industries included the production of many luxuries, notably silks, brocades, jewelry, and ivory and enamel work. The city's varied amenities proved an irresistible magnet for traders, merchants, bishops, monks, theologians, scholars, adventurers, mercenaries, ambassadors, and princes.

True, the climate was harsh and damp, the

23

Unlike the leading cities of the west, Constantinople remained impregnable against its attackers for century after century. Shown at right is the great city wall built by Theodosius II (A.D. 408—450), in a reconstruction drawing as it looked then and *(far right)* in a photograph of the actual ruins. The towers on the embankment reached a considerable height, and beyond them on the outside ran a line of battlements and dug-out fenced trenches (right side of drawing).

The Church of Sts. Sergius and Bacchus, Constantinople *(above)*, built under Justinian I in 526—537 as part of his ambitious construction program for the city. The dome, an octagon in a quadrilateral without pendentives, is a less ambitious variant of the form of construction that was reaching its climax, at the same time, in the Church of the Holy Wisdom. The minaret at left is an addition by the Ottoman Turks: the church became a mosque under their rule.

stench of the tanners' quarter was as famous as the scent of the perfume bazaar, and shattering epidemics recurred all too often. But the survivors, forming themselves into parties of Blues, Greens, and Reds, which represented different political, religious, and social interests, consoled themselves with the races in the Hippodrome, attended by the emperors and their courts. The victors' triumphs were identified with the Triumph of the unconquerable Christian monarch.

A gorgeous enclave in an age which, because of it, could never be described as "dark," Constantinople was the rampart of Europe, safeguarding the sum of what Mediterranean human beings had achieved up to that time, and protecting its empire from eastern and northern perils alike. The west had fallen, or was in the throes of violent transformation. That this did not happen in the east, for better or worse, was due, in no small part, to the unshakable permanence of Constantinople.

The sixth-century Byzantine author Cosmas Indicopleustes predicted that the empire would survive all hostile barbarian invasions so long as Christianity continued to flourish. One could in fact argue the inverse: it was the continued well-being of the empire and its capital city which enabled western Europe to remain Christian.

Below: Water supply was a vital necessity in this growing city which reached a population of half a million by the year 500. The aqueduct of Valens *(below left)* was begun in A.D. 368, using stone from the city of Chalcedon (Kadiköy) which had unsuccessfully rebelled. It carried water to a large reservoir in the city, the Nymphaeum Majus. Ten of the present arches of this aqueduct are the work of Ottoman sultans. The picture at right shows the columns of the Basilican Cistern at Constantinople, built by Justinian I in the sixth century. Its 336 columns, each 24 feet (more than 7 meters) high, support brick vaults over an area of more than 400 by 200 feet (ca. 125 by 65 meters), capable of holding enormous quantities of water against siege or drought.

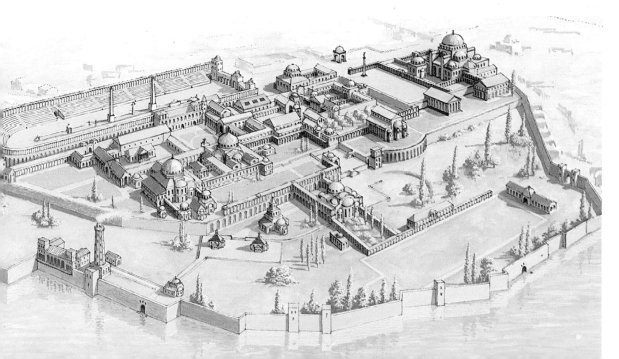

Left: Modern reconstruction of Constantinople in its heyday: Haghia Sophia at upper right (one of the few structures from the period now surviving), the hippodrome upper left, imperial palace at center, with several domed churches also visible. The model represents the eastern point of the peninsula on which the city stands, with water on three sides. In comparison to an ancient city such as Rome, in Constantinople today there are extremely few ancient buildings to be seen.

WHY THE EAST DID NOT FALL

In addition to the unique role of Constantinople, there were other significant reasons, too, why the eastern empire did not fall. For one thing its provinces were much less vulnerable to external attack, owing to their geographical situation. The western empire had to defend the long fronts of the Rhine and upper and middle Danube, the eastern empire the lower Danube sector only. For on its further, eastern flank its neighbor was Sassanian Persia, a civilized power with which there were some periods of peace or, at worst, cold war. Furthermore, if the western emperors were driven back and forced to recoil from any part of their Rhine and Danube frontiers, they

collect a far larger amount of taxes than the incompetent, oppressive government of the west. Moreover, the elderly Anastasius I (491–518), himself a former palace official, successfully rehabilitated the finances of the eastern empire by far-reaching currency reforms and methodical measures against waste.

The eastern territories he controlled were more populous and better cultivated than those of the west. And it was not only their economic conditions that were better. For the internal political situation of the eastern empire was also far more stable. In contrast to the perilous and costly proliferation of usurp-

The contrasting political situation in east and west is clearly apparent in this map of the Mediterranean area as of about A.D. 500. The west was henceforth fragmented, occupied by a series of Germanic peoples at various stages of cultural development. In the east, the Sassanian Persian state offered a border, and the fortifications and social conditions of the empire were also conducive to order and continuity.
Invasions in the east were generally fought off successfully, as this cameo (above) from Yugoslavia indicates; one of the emperors is seen triumphing over barbarians. National Museum, Belgrade.

Right: Byzantine soldiers, with spears and round shields, in the field: from an illuminated manuscript, Bibliothèque Nationale, Paris. The army of the eastern empire was strong enough to wage successful campaigns under Belisarius in the sixth century, regaining considerable territory that had fallen to invaders in the west.

had no second line of defense and the attackers could penetrate straight into Italy and Gaul. No enemy, on the other hand, could force his way, either by land or sea, into the Byzantine heartland round the Sea of Marmara. Besides, owing to this comparative absence of external pressures, the eastern empire, after its first admission of the Visigoths in the later fourth century, did not have to receive nearly so many German settlers and federates.

Moreover, the structures of the two governments differed significantly. In the west, the noble landowners, many of whom were men of great wealth, made only a trifling contribution to the expenses of army and administration. The eastern empire, on the other hand, could rely on the old, extensive middle class which peopled its ancient Greek communities; this class had for centuries provided a professional civil service which was able to

My opinion is that, although we may save ourselves by flight, it is not to our interest. Every man that sees the light must die, but the man who has once been raised to the height of empire cannot suffer himself to go into exile and survive his dignity. God forbid that I should ever be stripped of this purple [the royal robe], or live a single day on which I am not to be saluted as Mistress.... For my part I like the old saying: the empire is a fine winding sheet.

The empress Theodora during
the rebellion of 532 in Constantinople
(Gibbon, after Procopius)

ers in the west, the occurrence of these nuisances in the east was rare and unimportant. Popular uprisings were rare, and could be promptly quelled (as in the ruthless crushing of the Nika riots in 532, when Theodora, quoted at left, persuaded Justinian to stand firm rather than flee). And the social policies of Constantinople were relatively enlightened, especially in provisions of amenities for the poor.

Thus the eastern emperors were much less plagued by both external and internal menaces than their western colleagues. The ecclesiastical divisions in their midst, it is true, were just as sharp, and sometimes sharper. But these problems they were able to surmount, because the other hazards that transformed the west affected them so much less acutely.

Two city walls in Asia Minor (Turkey), the region that was the Byzantine empire's principal reservoir of military manpower and wealth. *Above left:* Ancyra, modern-day Ankara, capital of Turkey. In Byzantine times Ancyra was the capital of a province *(theme),* and since the eighth century the headquarters of an army 8,000 men strong. *Right:* The city wall of Dara (now in southeastern Turkey). Built by Anastasius I (491–518) for the defense of the Mesopotamian frontier, the town became one of the principal centers of the empire's eastern defenses. The outer wall was added by Justinian I, whose general Belisarius defeated the Persians there in 530.

THE WEST
RECONQUERED

Survival of the eastern empire did not, however, mean peace and tranquillity. Justinian I (527–565), the most famous Byzantine emperor of the whole age, was also among the most warlike. His entire reign was marked by massive, protracted, and enormously costly military operations in east and west alike. On the eastern frontiers a long peace with the Sassanian Persians was shattered and fighting went on for many years. After the leading Byzantine general, Belisarius, had won considerable successes, King Khosrau (Chosroes) I of Persia made peace in 532–533. War broke out again in 540, when Khosrau attacked Syria and Armenia. However, Belisarius and

others partly retrieved the situation, and a fifty-year truce was concluded in 561.

Byzantium also turned its sights toward the west. For Justinian, himself from a Latin-speaking province, considered it his duty to recover the territories of the vanished western empire. And his conviction of this responsibility was intensified by the subjection of so many of the Catholic inhabitants of those lands to the German successor states, whose rulers followed a brand of Christianity (Arianism) that he deplored as heretical.

First of all Belisarius overcame the Vandal kingdom of north Africa, with only five thousand cavalry, in an astonishingly speedy campaign (533–534). The last Vandal ruler, Gelimer, was forced to submit and the imperial authority was restored along practically the entire Mediterranean coast, although another fifteen years of ruinous warfare were necessary to bring the native populations effectively to heel. A disputed succession had been one of Justinian's original excuses for intervening in north Africa, and he used a similar pretext in order to recapture a strip of southern Spain from the Visigoths (552–555), thus reasserting imperial control of the Straits of Gibraltar.

Most important of all, however, was his reconquest of Italy, by the suppression of its Ostrogothic kingdom. Profiting once again from convulsions in the enemy's royal house, he sent an army overland through Dalmatia, while Belisarius created a diversion by launching a naval attack on Sicily (535). The Ostrogoths soon appeared to be overcome; Ravenna was captured (540) and became the center of the reestablished Byzantine government in Italy. Yet the financial rapacity of its administrators and soldiers made them very unpopular, and the Ostrogoth Totila,

This gold medallion of Justinian I was issued in A.D. 534–535 to celebrate the reconquest of North Africa from the Vandals by his general Belisarius. The emperor is shown in full armor on horseback, guided by Victory carrying a trophy. The inscription reads ''Salus et Gloria Romanorum,

Con(stantinopoli), ob(ryziacum)''—''The salvation and glory of the Romans, issued at Constantinople, pure gold.'' The original found at Caesarea in Cappadocia (Kayseri, Turkey) has disappeared, but the photograph is taken from a cast in the British Museum, London.

Justinian I's reconquests in the west, in the years 533–562, brought the Byzantine empire to its fullest expansion. Belisarius first took all the Vandal territory in north Africa (533–534), and then Visigothic lands in Spain (552–555), while the struggle for Italy took more time (535–562). None of these reconquests proved permanent.

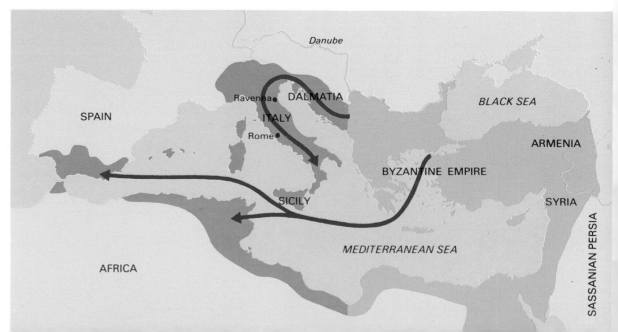

A splendid relic of Justinian's golden age, this Byzantine gold pectoral (breast ornament) attached to a necklace is decorated in niello and dates to the sixth century A.D. The centerpiece contains an imitation of an imperial coin or medallion, with a botched inscription, and round it are fourteen other coin portraits. Metropolitan Museum, New York.

Below: Chieftain's or king's helmet, a sixth-century example from Stössen, Germany; of the "Spangenhelm" type. This helmet form probably derives ultimately from a Near Eastern, perhaps Iranian, source. Some twenty of these helmets have been found at sites ranging from France to Hungary; they may come from a single workshop (perhaps at Ostrogothic Ravenna).

declared king in 541, succeeded in driving them all out and recapturing almost the whole country. In 552, however, a new Byzantine commander, the seventy-five-year-old eunuch Narses, appeared on the scene, and Totila was defeated and killed. Within the next ten years all resistance was stamped out. But meanwhile Rome had lost its aqueducts, destroyed by the Ostrogoths, and the prolonged wars had left Italy in a state of devastation.

Nevertheless, this huge series of operations, in various western countries, had been crowned by total military success. Exploiting the vast resources and skills at his disposal, Justinian had judged his timing rightly and struck precisely when the various German kingdoms were already unstable or crumbling. As a result, he had recovered a Roman empire embracing almost the whole of the Mediterranean world. This served the useful purpose of strengthening his position at home. Yet it had been a ruinous process, not only to the local inhabitants but to the imperial exchequer as well—and the revival of the old order was not backed by sufficient manpower or popular Byzantine support. Moreover, the emperor's massive military enterprises in the Mediterranean countries—coinciding with enormously costly operations against Persia—had meant that the Danube frontier was partially neglected, so that Slavs and Bulgars were able to make deep and damaging inroads. And the reconquests did not prove lasting. Only three years after Justinian's death, substantial parts of Italy were lost once again, to German (Lombard) invaders—against whom the Ostrogoths would have been a useful buffer. Ravenna itself fell to the Lombards later on, in 751; and long before that time north Africa and southern Spain, too, had ceased once again to be imperial possessions. With hindsight, then, Justinian's mighty recovery of the west proved a failure—a nostalgic move to revert to the conditions of an early epoch: conditions which could not, in fact, be effectively revived.

Left: Cross-shaped baptismal font of the sixth century A.D. excavated at Kelibia near Carthage (Tunisia, north Africa). The mosaic in the basin depicts a fish, emblem of Christianity, and above it is the cruciform monogram XP (Christus) and the letters alpha and omega, the beginning and the end. The font was dedicated to St. Cyprian, bishop of Carthage, martyred by the emperor Valerian in 258. Carthage was the second city of the west, and the devotion of Cyprian and the talent of Tertullian had made it a center of Latin Christianity. It became the Vandal capital, but in 533 Justinian's general Belisarius entered Carthage unopposed.

JUSTINIAN
AND HIS LAWS

Justinian I achieved his most lasting fame as a codifier of laws. Like other Byzantine emperors after him, he inherited from the Romans a deeply rooted instinct of legality. Yet when he came to the throne he found the law of his empire in a very confused state. It consisted of large, mixed masses of Latin regulations, divided into two categories known as the Old and New Law. The former included formal legislation and senatorial decrees of Republican and early Imperial date, and the pronouncements of jurists during the same epochs. The New Law comprised the edicts and other measures promulgated by emperors during the last three or four hundred years.

This material had never been collected together in its entirety before, and this was the vast, massive, and immensely valuable task that Justinian set himself and his lawyers.

First, he appointed a commission which, after fourteen months of work, published a code *(Codex)* of all past imperial regulations that were judged suitable to remain in force (529). Next, he established a further commission, sixteen members strong, presided over by the eminent Tribonian. He instructed them to read through all the writings of every authorized jurist of the past, and to excerpt (and edit) all the contents of these works that seemed to be of permanent value. The result of their labors, comprising more than nine thousand extracts, was published as the *Digest* or *Pandects* in 533; its preservation of the opinions of the greatest legal experts in Roman history is obviously of the first importance. Soon afterward, an elementary handbook (the *Institutes*) followed, and then a revised edition

Justinian I, 527–565 *(right),* enriched his age with military victories, imperial expansion, art treasures, and great buildings, but the laws he handed down from antiquity have proved his most durable contribution. This portrait of Justinian is from a mosaic in the church of Sant'Apollinare Nuovo, Ravenna (built by the Ostrogothic king Theodoric). Although Byzantine mosaics served mostly religious aims, the emperor and his court sometimes appeared, since he was God's earthly representative and Church and State were inextricably interlinked.

This elaborate cross *(below)* was presented by Justinian's successor, the emperor Justin II (565–578), to the Basilica of St. Peter, in the Vatican region of Rome. It is an early example of the remarkable embossed or repoussé jewelry at which Byzantine craftsmen excelled. The capital from the Church of the Holy Wisdom, Constantinople *(below right),* bears the monogram of Justinian I at lower right.

of the *Codex,* which has come down to us and provides historians of the Roman empire with a quarry of inestimable value.

These works do not constitute a systematic, scientific code. But they sum up and adapt Rome's entire legal experience, reducing a mass of preexisting material into a manageable and usable form; two thousand books had been excerpted, and three million lines reduced to a hundred and fifty thousand. Next, Justinian's Corpus of Civil Law was completed by the collection of *Novels,* the numerous ordinances which he himself had issued during the course of this reign, introducing changes in the law at many points. Unlike the other works in the Corpus, the *Novels* were almost all published in Greek, though Latin versions were made for the use of the empire's western provinces.

It is understandable that the emperor should describe the result of all these endeavors as a "holy temple of Roman justice." They were

lasting, too. With a few subsequent additions, the Corpus remained the standard lawbook of the Byzantine world; and, at the end of the eleventh century, its study was actively revived at Bologna in Italy. It was a code that reflected a commonsense philosophy of life, based on a sturdy belief in the traditional patterns of society. That is to say, like so many other codifications throughout the ages, it was a support for conservatism—the expression and confirmation of a social order in which everyone had and knew his or her place. However, the Corpus also embodied an element of wishful thinking, for it depicted the imperial government as it should be rather than as it was. For even Justinian could not avoid the Nika riot or revolt (532), the worst explosion of popular disorder in Byzantine history, in which two of the circus factions, the Blues and Greens, rose up against extortion and religious oppression, crying "*Nika!*" (Victory). The revolt frightened the emperor into establishing an autocracy of unending vigilance, presided over by "the ruler who never sleeps."

Though he knew how to choose the right helpers, Justinian habitually took too much upon himself. Nevertheless, the reign of this stocky, ugly, shrewd, religious peasant was one of those periods when truly momentous events and achievements are stamped with the personality of a single man. Yet Justinian, for all his wily diplomacy, was not always farsighted; and he was fortunate in having the support of a wife who was cleverer, stronger, and crueler than himself—namely Theodora, a former ballet dancer, symbol of a society in which, as in ancient Rome, women had a substantial part to play.

The age of Justinian is illuminated by two remarkable men: a great historian and a great traveler.

The historian was Procopius, born at Caesarea Marittima (Israel) in about A.D. 500. He became an adviser and aide of Justinian's general Belisarius, whom he accompanied on campaigns in Persia, North Africa, and Italy (527–550). It is not known when he died.

His most important work is the *History of the Wars of Justinian.* While dealing faithfully with this great series of military campaigns, he also covers a much broader canvas, allowing comprehensive room for political and other events of many kinds (and including a supple-

of valuable information, mingled this time with adulation of the emperor.

His *Secret History,* however, provides a great surprise. It covers most of the period dealt with by the *History,* but from an entirely different standpoint. Far from praising Justinian any longer or even being merely a little lukewarm and detached when the emperor is under discussion, the *Secret History* subjects him to a continuous barrage of violent and scurrilous attacks, introducing every kind of abusive gossip and scandal. The work was completed in about 550, but cannot possibly have been published before the emperor's death in 565. Procopius, who had a strong his-

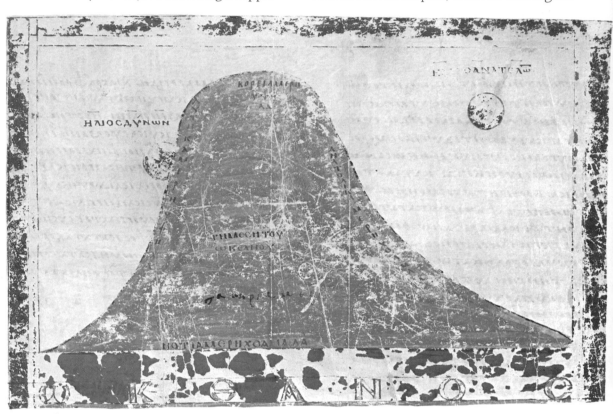

ment to bring the story up to date, as far as the year 553). Writing in clear and lucid Greek, the historian possessed a genuine determination to get at the truth, and subject to a certain bias in favor of Belisarius, took special pains to be accurate. The attitude of the work to Justinian and his government displays a cool detachment. Procopius' judgment was acute and intelligent, and he knew a lot about military affairs. About many matters he had first-hand knowledge. When he had not, he was able to enquire from those who had; and in addition he employed written sources in the Greek, Latin, and Syriac languages. In most respects, his *History* is remarkably reliable, worthy to rank among the most important of its classical forerunners. A shorter work, *On Justinian's Buildings* (ca. 553–555), is also full

torical conscience, must have been plagued by a feeling that, for safety's sake, his earlier works had not been as critical of Justinian as they ought to have been; and now he was trying to set the record straight.

Which version is right? Both, up to a point, since Justinian was far from infallible, and eventually became little short of a tyrant. Yet he had remarkably impressive achievements to his credit, and the pent-up fury of the *Secret History* bears the marks of exaggeration and special pleading.

A contemporary of Procopius was Cosmas Indicopleustes ("sailor to India" or "of the Indian Sea"), whose *Christian Topography* (ca. 535–547) is one of the world's most fascinating travel books. Cosmas, a merchant of Alexandria, journeyed to the ports of the Red

The Byzantine historian Procopius wrote glowing accounts of the reign of Justinian I *(top)*, followed by a cynical, critical account of the emperor some years later. This gold medallion of Justinian, dated 534–535, is the obverse of the one shown on page 30. The victorious emperor appears with halo, jeweled diadem, and spear. The sixth-century Byzantine marble head *(above)* is considered by some to portray Justinian's wife Theodora (ca. 500–548), who was the subject of some scandal. A ballet dancer from early childhood, and later famous as a prostitute, she was reputedly the daughter of a circus bear-keeper. The empress exerted a strong influence on her husband and guided his reign through serious crises.

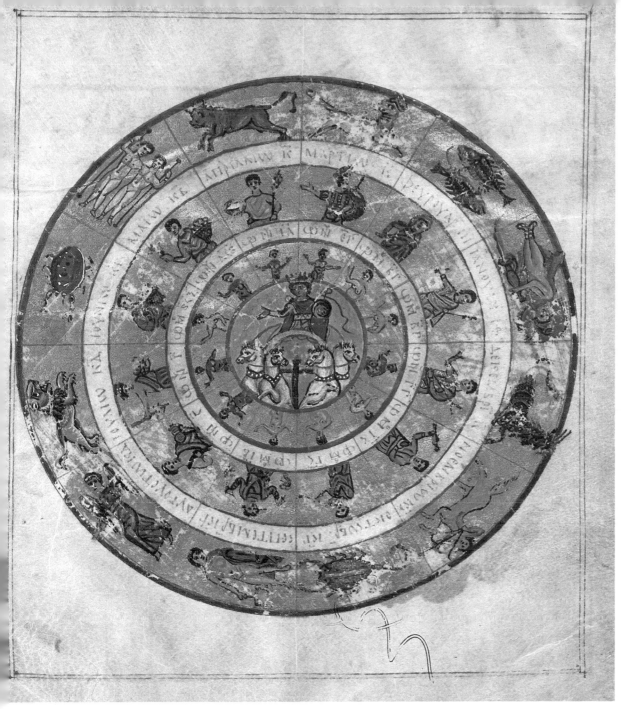

Left: The zodiac, illustration from the standard second-century text, which greatly influenced Cosmas, Ptolemy's *Mathematical Collection* or *Almagest.* The painting is from a Vatican manuscript of Ptolemy's work, dated between 813 and 820, a very rare example of figure painting executed during the Iconoclastic period. Helios (the Sun) is shown at center with his chariot and white horses, surrounded by the signs of the zodiac and other figures.

The manuscripts of Cosmas' work, all probably imitated from a single original copy, are decorated with two sets of illustrations: secular pictures (as opposite page) executed in the classical style, and religious scenes *(two illustrations above)* exhibiting a more monumental and Asiatic appearance. These two pictures show episodes from the life of St. Paul, including (upper picture) the stoning of St. Stephen. All the paintings on these pages are from manuscripts in the Biblioteca Apostolica Vaticana, Vatican City.

Sea, east Africa, and the Persian Gulf; and he described India and Ceylon, though whether he actually visited those countries is not clear. Although special geographical knowledge was outside his scope, his vivid descriptive narrative provides a mass of arresting information about trade and much else. He was also a keen and inquisitive observer: taking note, for example, of albatrosses. He also took care to copy inscriptions of the Ethiopians, of whose expedition against the Yemen he was an eyewitness. And he adorned his manuscripts with secular and religious pictures, of which copies survived.

Cosmas' work provides impressive testimony of the impact made on the world by Justinian's empire, of which he attributed the commercial success to the magnificent imperial coinage. He also saw the Christian religion as a significant contributor. For like so many of his contemporaries, Cosmas was profoundly interested in theology. The results of this preoccupation, however, were disastrous, since it led him to heap scorn on the theory that the earth is spherical, and to maintain that the Tabernacle of Moses was a replica of the universe in every detail.

Meanwhile, another, entirely separate, distinguished literature was also appearing on the northeastern borders of the empire, in the Armenian language.

IMPERIAL CRISIS

During the half-century following the death of Justinian, the empire ran into trouble on every side. In 568 the Lombards invaded and occupied large parts of Italy. From the north, the nomad Avars constantly invaded the Balkans and extorted subsidies, while hordes of Slavs poured into the peninsula as well. To the east, there were severe struggles against Sassanian Persia, until the energetic emperor Maurice (582–602) established relations on a more stable basis. Maurice also reorganized the Italian and north African provinces of the Byzantine empire by combining the military and civil authorities in each region—with military leaders in charge.

Then Heraclius (610–641), perhaps the ablest of all Byzantine rulers, founded a new dynasty. Taking over the throne at a perilous time of external attack and internal anarchy—when there was even talk of having to move the capital to Carthage—he seemed at times, notably at the beginning and end of his

while fending off an Avar attack on Constantinople itself, took the offensive against the Persians in three brilliantly successful campaigns (622–628), which were long remembered as the great war of Byzantine history. All the invaded territory was won back, the True Cross was recovered, and the setback to the Persians was disastrous. But Heraclius, too, was so greatly weakened that he could do nothing to hold up the terrible Arab advances which followed immediately afterward and engulfed the entire Middle East, detaching Egypt, Syria, and Palestine forever.

It was the gravest blow that Byzantium and Christianity had ever sustained, forcing the empire into a state of precarious defensiveness that lasted for a quarter of a millennium. All the same, this enforced limitation of its eastern regions to their Greek-speaking core may eventually have been a blessing in disguise, since this was at least more or less homogeneous—and defensible.

The flame-throwing technique known as Greek Fire *(below)* made use of a mixture of quick-lime, petroleum, and sulfur, squirted at ships through siphons. The illustration is from an illuminated manuscript of Scylitzes. This was the Byzantine empire's most important contribution to military science. Under Constantine IV Greek Fire played a major part

in defeating the first siege of Constantinople by the Arabs (674–678), whose ships were set on fire off Cyzicus on the Sea of Marmara. The bronze coin *(right)* shows Constantine IV Pogonatus ("the Bearded"), who repulsed the caliph Moawiya from the walls of Constantinople, thus beginning the process which checked the advance of the Arabs toward the west.

reign, to have no firm grip of the situation. Yet between these two periods, at the height of a new Persian crisis, he deployed his resources in the most effective manner possible, and by his enormous efforts saved and reshaped the empire.

Soon after his accession, Persian invaders captured Jerusalem—along with the remains of the True Cross—conquered Egypt and Armenia, and advanced into the heart of the empire in Asia Minor. Heraclius, however,

The formidable Constans II (641–668) bore the brunt of this Arab aggression, and despite recurrent crises still found time to check the Slavs in the Balkans. They were under the suzerainty of Bulgar invaders, who formed a dangerous state that even the energy and statesmanship of Constantine IV (668–685) proved unable to suppress. However, he triumphantly beat back a prolonged siege of Constantinople (674–678) by the Arab caliph Moawiya I. That epoch-making success was

achieved by the Byzantine navy's weapon known as Greek Fire, a mixture of quick-lime, petroleum, and sulfur, propelled by pumps or siphons to incinerate the enemy fleet. Invented by the Syrian refugee architect Callinicus, this was the most devastating application of technology to warfare throughout the entire period; it started the world's military technicians on the track of the ever more combustible mixtures that they have been concocting ever since.

Thus relieved from the menace to his capital, Justinian II "Slit Nose" (685–695, 705–711) blocked both the Arabs and the Slavs, and continued a policy of settling the latter in Asia Minor by wholesale transplantation. It was also the same emperor, it is now believed, who issued the Farming Law. Agriculture was by far the major industry of the Byzantine empire, as it had been of the Roman empire before it, and according to the code of instructions contained in the Law its basis was no longer the large agricultural estate worked by serfs but a rural commune of freehold lots owned by "free" peasants. That is to say, they were no longer tied to a private master but bound directly to the imperial treasury, from which they received grants of land subject to the hereditary obligation of military service. Meanwhile the system of large provinces, in which the military and civil power was combined under army domination, had been extended, and the empire was now divided

into six great provinces virtually on a permanent war footing; particular emphasis was placed upon Asia Minor, which remained the principal recruiting ground of the Byzantine army. Thus despite grim crises and economic recessions, the emperors of the Heraclian dynasty had guided the Byzantine world into a new epoch. The empire had moved from its earlier to its middle period—from the ancient to the medieval world—and the system now established remained in force for five hundred years.

Like the besieged warriors depicted in this Byzantine manuscript painting *(above)*, Constantinople offered valiant resistance to the far-ranging Arabic armies, as well as those of neighboring Slavs. The Byzantine victory over the Moslems in 674–678, like the Arab defeat by Charles Martel at Poitiers, France, in 732, marked a crucial turning point in the history of Christian western Europe. Justinian II "Slit Nose" (successor to Constantine IV), whose portrait appears on the coin *(above right)*, consolidated the empire's defense against Slavs and Arabs. On its other side this coin bears the bust of Jesus Christ, a remarkable innovation.

AN EMBATTLED EMPIRE

The new dynasty founded by the soldier-adventurer Leo III (717) was known as Isaurian, after a region of Asia Minor, but the family probably came from northern Syria. These successive rulers, while by no means attractive personalities, possessed great ability and resolution: and Leo III, who came to the throne at a critical time of menacing Arabs and unmanageable Byzantine nobles, was a leader whose reforming hand became active in every sphere of government. Of his policy of overturning religious images something will be said later. More constructive was his legal handbook, the *Ecloga,* not written in Latin, which was now scarcely used any longer, but in Greek which was the language of the empire. The work summarized Justinian's *Corpus,* adapted it to contemporary needs by recognizing popular usage and custom, and influenced the future development of Byzantine law, as well as the legislation of the Slavs which was derived from it.

For Byzantium, the eighth century was marked by several crucial turning-points. Its

The threat on the empire's eastern borders, which was to continue for some time to come, called for massive defenses. The fortress of Cotiaeum in Phrygia (Asia Minor), now Kütahya in Turkey, was typical of these. The entire region of Asia Minor assumed ever greater strategic defensive importance, and was defended in depth

against Sassanian Persians and Arabs as a bulwark protecting Constantinople. Though the core of the Byzantine empire held intact, there were losses on the periphery—first of all in the newly reconquered Italy, and later in the eighth century in the Balkans.

position in Italy suffered from new Lombard aggressions. Against the Arabs in Asia Minor, on the other hand, a historic victory was gained. In 717 the army and fleet of the caliph Suleiman appeared before Constantinople, which was blockaded throughout the especially severe winter that followed. For a year the outcome hung in the balance. But finally, with the aid of Bulgar and Khazar allies, the siege had to be called off. Thus for a second time the full force of the Arabs' might had been stopped at the gateway of Europe, and in their subsequent retreat through Asia Minor they suffered shattering losses.

The Byzantines' fleet had played a decisive part in these successes, and so had the technical

efficiency of their cavalry-based army (strengthened by numerous fighting men imported from Armenia); but in the last resort it was high morale, among service men and civilians alike, that had enabled the empire to prevail. At the further extremity of Asia Minor, Leo III was now able to establish a stable frontier, which a combination of force and diplomacy kept intact for the next two hundred years.

Freed from the immediate menace of the Arabs, Constantine V (741–775) was able to adopt an aggressive demeanor toward them, while at the same time successfully checking the Bulgars on his other frontier, having enlisted the Khazars against them by marrying their chieftain's daughter. A complex, violent, and purposeful personage, of considerable intellectual boldness and subtlety, Constantine V was not only a keen admirer of secular music, boys, and demonology, but also a first-class soldier and outstanding financier and administrator. Next, at the end of the century a remarkable woman, Irene, dominated affairs for twenty years. But the diminishing role of Constantinople was displayed in 800 by the coronation of Charlemagne as "emperor" at Rome.

In the sixth century the population of the Byzantine empire had perhaps been seventy million. But this total was greatly reduced by a series of bubonic and other plagues of eastern origin, among which an outbreak in 745–747 proved particularly severe. Great social changes also occurred during the same period. At its outset, the Byzantine world still possessed its ancient urban centers with cultural traditions of their own, and a ruling class of the old type endowed with a traditional Greek education. But very soon, as Justinian I expelled the pagan teachers from the once famous schools of philosophy at Athens, this classical élite was fading away. The empire found itself ringed around with many enemies who declared the need for a united Byzantine front, and a new, simplified society arose in which the ancient divisive boundary between aristocratic and popular culture was blurred and a different sort of community with novel, nonclassical, sensibilities began to take shape. The culture of the man and woman in the street was for the first time the same as that of their rulers. However, by the eighth century a new aristocracy had appeared on the scene, in which the great landowners from Asia Minor, imbued with the military tradition, played a prominent part.

But the possession of these new conquests
(Africa and Italy) was transient
and precarious,
and almost a moiety of the Eastern empire
was torn away by the arms
of the Saracens. Syria and Egypt
were oppressed by the Arabian caliphs,
and after the reduction of Africa,
their lieutenants invaded and subdued
the Roman province which had been changed
into the Gothic monarchy of Spain.

Edward Gibbon

This bronze statuette, said to have come from Istanbul (Constantinople), now in the Metropolitan Museum of Art, New York, was made in the fourth or fifth century A.D. There were two types of Byzantine cavalry, light *(foederati)* and heavy *(cataphracti)*, mostly from Asia Minor. This rider was probably a heavy cavalryman. A group of Byzantine cavalrymen are portrayed *(above)* on this manuscript painting of Scylitzes (Biblioteca Nacional, Madrid). The cavalry, so essential to the empire's total military effort, used spears and battle axes.

39

THE BYZANTINE SYSTEM

One of the strangest of Byzantine phenomena is the emperor's undisputed divine power which persisted throughout all the vicissitudes and crises of a turbulent history. The emperor was the source of all authority throughout his empire, "the animate and living law," against whom there was no appeal: nor was there any machinery for modifying his views or actions. He, personally, made all appointments and dismissals, down to provincial governors and regimental commanders. He was surrounded by religious ceremonial following the calendar of the Christian year, in which time, place, words, dress, and gesture were all minutely specified, hallowed by custom, and closely coordinated with the ecclesiastical liturgy, so as to mirror the splendors of heaven itself.

"An autocracy tempered by assassinations" (C. Diehl), the Byzantine political system, though it accorded the emperor near-exclusive authority, was not without its hazards. This miniature (below) depicts a leader being dragged into the hippodrome, after he was executed by a rival's supporters.

Right: This illustration of an Old Testament scene, from a manuscript of the sixth century, features clothing styles of the contemporary Byzantine aristocracy. The painting shows the meeting of Joseph with Potiphar's wife, in Egypt (Genesis 39: 7–20).

Thus the entire official life of the Byzantine court was passed in a kind of ballet of ritualistic movements, in which the emperor appeared as the image of majesty and justice, and his empress as the exemplar of beauty and mercy. Now the Byzantines did not, generally speaking, employ the armed forces as active instruments of foreign policy unless this seemed absolutely necessary. For such purposes, instead, their favorite weapon was diplomacy, the science of managing foreign powers and especially "barbarians." The highly flexible methods of Byzantine diplomacy, greatly developed by Justinian I, included the encouragement of unfriendly relations between one foreign country and another, the conferment of honorary titles and decorations on foreign princes who toed the line, the hospitable reception of political refugees, the arrangement of royal marriages, the dazzling of envoys by sumptuous ceremonies, and above all the disbursement of large sums of money. As an emperor later remarked to a German ambassador at his court, "We have gold, and with this gold we shall rouse all peoples against you and break you like an earthenware vessel."

The vast sums of money needed for these and other purposes were raised by an elaborate and rigorous system of taxation—founded on the all-important land-tax supplemented by indirect dues—which made Byzantium the most highly taxed country in the world. As for the money itself, the Byzantine standard gold

*There are two main gifts bestowed
    by God upon men: the priesthood
and the imperial authority. Of these the
    former is concerned with
things divine, the latter with
    human affairs. Proceeding from
the same source, both adorn
    human life. Nothing is of
greater importance to the emperors
    than to support the dignity of
the priesthood so that the
    priests may in their turn
pray to God for them.*

Justinian, Sixth Novella

Black Sea, and Trabzon (Trebizond) and the Crimea on its southern and northern shores respectively, became important outlets for this eastern carrying trade, while western commerce passed from Jewish (formerly Syrian) hands to the Italian coastal cities. Byzantine trade was organized through guilds in which every branch of industry formed a corporation of its own. Although liable to abuses, the system assured quality, eliminated middlemen, and checked price increases and overproduction. The state itself owned all mines, many factories, and huge domains, which made its rulers the richest in the world.

The infrastructure for this semi-monopolistic regime was provided by a uniquely professional, tenacious, and all-pervading civil service, part of an important middle class. At the

Opposite: Flora, goddess of spring, on an early Byzantine tapestry. Textile manufacture, with flourishing and individual branches in various regions, was one of the most notable and successful features of Byzantine art. Although Flora was a pagan deity, she was retained in Christian iconography and handed down as a beloved figure in medieval art and literature: she appears, for instance, in Dante's earthly paradise, at the top of the mountain of Purgatory.

The *solidus,* or gold coin, created by Constantine the Great, remained the standard currency in the Christian world for many centuries. The example here depicts Leo III (717–741), founder of the great new Isaurian dynasty. The inscription is still in Latin—very soon to be superseded by Greek.

Chinese ladies preparing a length of newly woven silk. A painting on silk, A.D. 1082–1135, but based on an older work by Chang Hsuan, a court painter active between 713 and 742. Beginning in the sixth century, the Byzantine empire traded with the Far East by way of the Silk Route and the Spice Route.

coin, the *solidus* created by Constantine the Great, had established a standard which mirrored the country's prodigious financial stability and was maintained unchanged for seven centuries. Because of the coin's unfailingly reliable, undebased weight, it passed everywhere as a valid medium of exchange, and from the ninth century onward, under the name of "bezant," was virtually the only gold piece in the entire Christian world.

It was an invaluable aid to the commerce which was one of the Byzantine empire's greatest sources of strength. From the sixth century onward two great lines of communication, the more northerly Silk Route and the Spice Route further south, linked Constantinople with the Far East. Subsequently the

lower end of the economic hierarchy, despite oppression here and there, the Byzantine peasantry was better off than any other in the medieval world.

The tradition that the Byzantine empire was an effete and degenerate institution, representing only a feeble survival from the empire of the Romans, was greatly fostered by that most eloquent of historians, Edward Gibbon, and still lingers on today. But it is based on misleading biases in favor of the old western empire that had gone. True, the eastern empire was not by any means perfect. Yet insofar as the dawn of the Middle Ages was glorious, it owes very much of its glory to Byzantium.

BYZANTINE CHRISTIANITY

The earliest known icon of the Virgin Mary (sixth or seventh century): a rare survival from the period before the Iconoclasts, or image destroyers, decimated the great patrimony of Byzantine art. The work is found in St. Catherine's monastery, Sinai, where the finest and most numerous early Byzantine icons are to be seen. The Virgin is shown enthroned with the Child, between Sts. George and Theodore.

Early Byzantine churches were often built around a central floor-plan (cross or octagon, for example) as well as in the western rectangular basilica form. The interior of the Church of Sts. Sergius and Bacchus, Constantinople, reconstructed to the orders of Justinian I, is dominated by the central dome (an exterior view appears on page 26).

Constantine's conversion of the Roman empire from paganism to Christianity (306–337) exercised a greater influence than any other event, or series of events, on the centuries that lay ahead—and bore abundant fruits in Byzantine society.

And yet, at the time when Constantine accorded the Christians' faith his overwhelming official support, their community had possessed no political or social or economic power. The emperor's motives in making this surprising move have been unendingly discussed and disputed. Although a cruel, unscrupulous, and disagreeable man, Constantine continually felt an impulsive need for a divine, transcendental companion and sponsor. For a time the Sun-God, who for a century or more had been receiving almost monotheistic reverence from the population of the empire, was his choice. But this cult, even when supplemented by the appealing divine figure of Mithras, was unable to satisfy the need felt by Constantine and so many other persons for a personal savior. No pagan cults, and not even Judaism (despite all it shared with Christianity), could offer a personal god who dramatically intervened here on earth to save human beings—as Jesus Christ was believed to have done.

Christianity offered a ruler certain more worldly benefits as well. Constantine and his counselors must have formed an increasingly strong conviction that, despite the relative weakness of the Christians, they alone possessed, at least potentially, the efficient, cohesive organization, and the universalist ("Catholic") aims and claims, that might eventually be able to weld together all the various conflicting peoples and classes of the empire in a single, all-embracing unity. It was in the belief that this process should be accelerated—if necessary by strong measures—that Constantine went on to launch a massive, and increasingly intolerant, missionary drive. By this act of faith and policy he transformed the world.

The intensely holy position of the Byzantine rulers, as the representatives of God and Christ on earth and Defenders of the Faith, endowed their regime with a religious character such as no other Mediterranean or European state has ever possessed. Christianity had come to dominate every aspect of thought and life, every kind of human activity, and every mode of reasoning. Indeed, Church and State, so firmly united by Constantine, became scarcely distinguishable. The "Orthodox" ("right-minded") Church of Christ on earth (its distinction from "Catholic" still lay in the future) was allied to the administration in a pattern of harmony (symphonia) and mutual support: the Church worked through the power structure, and as a power structure in itself. Its character as a national institution was expressed by its synods or general Councils, summoned by the emperor and presided over by himself or his lay deputies. A regulation known as the "Nomocanon in Fourteen Titles," accepted by one of these Councils (692), shows in detail how the secular and ecclesiastical authorities worked in unison and interdependence, each indispensably, inseparably, and inextricably supplementing the other.

Under the emperor himself, the principal representative of the Church in Constantinople was its archbishop or patriarch, who virtually became a permanent minister of the government. The emperor could always control the election of the patriarch, and conversely, from the mid-fifth century onward it became the practice for each successive ruler, on his accession, to be crowned by the patriarch of the day. This did not, however, mean that the patriarchs conferred the imperial office; it signified rather that emperors ruled by the grace of god. The patriarchs were usually docile enough. But they also had several means of resisting the secular power, means which they employed in emergencies; for they regarded themselves, and were regarded, as the keepers of the empire's conscience.

The emperors and patriarchs who directed these two interlocking forces of State and Church shared the profound conviction that both institutions alike were eternal and unique. The Byzantine mind saw the empire as the direct and only terrestrial reflection of God's heavenly kingdom, willed by Him, protected by Him through the agency of the imperial throne, and specifically sanctified by the Incarnation. It might be a pale, earthbound reflection, because of the people's sins. But it must continually seek to realize its ideal, for it was the providential scheme of human society, and therefore, potentially, of the entire inhabited world *(oikoumene)*. over which in God's good time it would achieve universal Christian rule.

Orthodox popular devotion centered on the celebration of the Eucharist. Mystery of mysteries, and sacrifice of sacrifices, in which the invisible God dramatically revealed Himself to the faithful, the Eucharist was a triumph of Byzantine originality. As in the ceremonials of the court that were so closely related to it, every gesture and word had its own solemn, emblematic significance. In a society where religious, political, and aesthetic life were indistinguishably blended, this resplendent act of divine worship gathered together and united the highest conceptions of art, theology, poetry, and above all music, the great new idiom of sixth century thought and feeling. The monodic music of the Byzantines, with its novel notation, has not come down to us; probably it incorporated a kind of recitative. But we have eighty antiphonal hymns out of the thousand composed by Romanus the Melode, a converted Jew from Beirut, whose dramatic, heartfelt, crystalline writing is perhaps the greatest Christian hymnography of all time.

In this totally spiritual civilization, a large part of Byzantine literature was inevitably devoted to the Christian faith. In particular, the sixth century was the golden age of Lives of the Saints. Triumphs of middle-brow culture, read by the entire population, they display a deep sense of the horror of sin, exhale an air of overwhelmingly emphatic and credulous piety, and provide an excellent picture of how people were expected to think and feel—and of how, no doubt, these people truly thought and felt.

ORTHODOX MONKS AND NUNS

A vital and integral part of this all-pervasive Byzantine religion was monasticism. Already in the later years of pagan Rome, ascetic remoteness from everyday anxieties and troubles, and the withdrawal into solitary contemplation, was increasingly regarded as a desirable ideal and way of life. Then, in the third century A.D., came the founding of the Christian monastic movement, deep in the wastes of Egypt—one of that country's most remarkable gifts to the world, and one of the outstanding achievements of eastern Christianity, expressing all that was best and worst in it.

The reputed founder of monasticism was St. Antony, whose imaginative *Life,* written by Athanasius, bishop of Alexandria (ca. 295–373), became a best-seller. St. Basil, bishop of Caesarea in Cappadocia (ca. 330–379), gave eastern monasticism its definitive form, composing rules for the monastic communities he organized in Asia Minor, the ear-

Monastic life, in the Byzantine tradition based on the example of St. Antony, was considered to be a life apart, rather than one based on service in and to the community. Thus the monastic communities often became autonomous societies with a complex of buildings serving diverse

needs. One of the greatest and most revered monastic foundations of the Byzantine world was the monastery of Qala'at Sem'an in Syria *(above),* a vast complex covering many acres, shown in a drawing made in 1862. The large basilica (one of four) is seen on the left.

liest such rules we possess, full of common sense and moderation. From that time onward, monasteries and convents spread throughout the Near East and flourished remarkably in the Byzantine empire. Soon after 500 there were nearly seventy monastic centers in Constantinople alone, and another forty at Chalcedon (Kadiköy) just across the Bosphorus; two centuries later as many as a hundred thousand monks and nuns were living under Basil's rule. Their monasteries were self-governing, under superiors exacting rigorous obedience, men whom even the emperor and patriarch could scarcely keep under any sort of control.

True, these institutions proved allies to the bishops in the field of social services, and their leaders served as counselors to the laity. Nevertheless, the primary purpose of Byzantine monastic life was not pastoral, or charitable, or educational, or social. For the monks and nuns were, above all else, intended to serve God by working for their own individual perfection and salvation. They divided their time between prayer, study, manual work, meals, and sleep, but the essential feature of their lives was the daily performance of the divine liturgy. All the same, despite this concentration within their own walls, it was they, above all, who were revered by the people as providers of the intercessions with God that were so urgently demanded: it was the monks

and nuns who, in times of disturbance or famine or plague, were relied upon to mediate between the stricken population and the divine power.

The celibate asceticism of the monks was likewise enormously respected. But there were also extreme ascetics, outside the monasteries, who were admired even more, to the point of adulation. This puritan respect for rigorous living, which had a long pagan history, was based on the conviction that such men, by their earthly hardships, would succeed in doing what it was everyone's chief aim to do —escape eternal punishment. Their way of life was held to be justified by the contempt for the human flesh and condition displayed by St. John the Baptist and St. Paul; and Jesus himself, it was pointed out, had departed to a solitary place and gone up into a mountain to pray. In late Roman and Byzantine times such self-denial, based on a total distaste for humanity and flesh, assumed bizarre self-dis-

Left: The main doorway of the south front of Qala'at Sem'an, as seen today. The monastery was founded around the time of the eastern (Byzantine) emperor Zeno (474-491), surrounding the column atop which St. Simeon Stylites lived for many years. It owed its fame to the numerous pilgrims who came from many countries to venerate him and stayed in the monastery's guesthouses.

Below left: The ideal of the ascetic hermit withstanding all temptation. Like Christ in the wilderness, and St. Antony in the desert of Egypt, St. Simeon Stylites withdrew from society and was assailed by the forces of evil. On this silver gilt plaque (from a sixth-century Syrian reliquary casket now in the Louvre) Simeon is shown on top of his column, beset by a snake representing evil temptation. The public equated asceticism with spiritual strength and efficacy.

Then they arrived at the column
[of St. Simeon], they contemplated
the height of it, and the harsh,
uncompromising countryside, and wondered
that a man so delicately nurtured
could bear the cold of winter and
the summer's heat, the menace of the
rain and the blast of the wind....

Simon Metaphrastes

Far from the shoals of life here let us
find safe water....
This is the one care of the monkish life,
To find a harbour on that quiet shore
Where toil is done, and hardship is no more.

Theodore of Studium

ciplinary forms; thus, St. Jerome wrote eloquently of the hardships and hallucinations of such desolately solitary lives.

In an age when martyrdom of blood no longer existed, these austere holy hermits served as substitute martyrs and roused the ordinary Byzantine to wondering enthusiasm and fervent awe. Many a pilgrimage was undertaken to their lonely caverns and cliffs; the star attractions of this ascetic world were very often Syrians, wild wandering "men of fire" in tattered skins. Even though some churchmen, notably St Basil, preferred more moderate behavior, these self-mortifiers were widely felt to be the best intercessors of all.

Above: Pedestal of the column of St. Simeon Stylites at Qala'at Sem'an, which pilgrims from many parts of the Byzantine empire came to see. Syria, where the monastery stood, was a breeding ground for religious movements of numerous kinds, many of them unorthodox and fanatical.

Left: Ruins of another monastery, in Isauria (southwestern Asia Minor), constructed during the reign of the emperor Zeno (474-491), whose family originated from this mountainous region. The rough and desolate local terrain was easily associated in the mind of believers with the ascetic ideal.

THE NATURE OF CHRIST: THE GREAT DEBATE

There are many stories illustrating the passionate interest of the people of Constantinople in theology, which they spoke about at all times, however seemingly inappropriate. According to their own convictions, this fascination was logical enough. For since relationship with God seemed by far the most important thing in the world, then it was also all-important to get that relationship right—which could only be done by continually striving to understand and define the nature of the deity with all possible accuracy. As a result, attempts by the Church to achieve such definitions, and inventions of deviant theories which achieved wide acceptance but earned official rejection as "heresies," were among the most influential phenomena of the age, attracting the attention of millions.

The Byzantines had a good preparation for this sort of exercise, because of the traditional Greek capacity for clearly articulated philosophical thought. But to this they added a love of hair-splitting definitions and details that was entirely their own. These debates on

All these heresies are banned from the heavenly realms: the heresy which rejects the perfect humanity of Christ (his possession of a soul endowed with reason and intelligence)... as well as the heresy which rejects the divinity of Christ and holds it to be inferior to that of God the Father, or again the heresy which negates the divinity of the Holy Spirit.

Cosmas Indicopleustes. Christian Topography 6.27

Man or God? Christ's true nature became the subject of bitter controversy during the early Byzantine empire, and the divisive issue had to be resolved by a Church Council. This painting, from the sixth-century Rossano Codex, emphasizes the divine nature of Christ, who is shown being acclaimed and worshiped by the apostles.

the nature of Christ, and on all the problems and dogmas and questions of discipline involved in the question, were the main themes of the recurrent Church Synods and Councils that became the parliaments of Christendom, and provided the most significant available opportunities for free public speech. Such discussions often attained crucial political significance and engendered an atmosphere of crisis—exacerbated by the bitter resentments of the patriarchs of Alexandria and Antioch against their colleague in Constantinople, whose claim to preeminence, on the grounds that his city was the imperial capital, they disputed.

A bombshell was launched by Arius of Alexandria (d. 336), who concluded that Jesus could not be God or truly divine, since, being the Son, he derived his being from the Father, and was therefore both younger and inferior. His belief was ardently espoused by the German tribes and kingdoms, which liked its patriarchal character. Within the Roman and Byzantine empires, however, despite periods of success, his doctrines proved unacceptable. In 451, the Council of Chalcedon concentrated on the problem whether Jesus had two natures or one. They concluded that he had two, the divine and the human, and that these two natures were to be recognized in Christ even after his Incarnation, their difference being preserved despite the unity of person.

But although this proved satisfactory enough to Rome, the east, where there was a mystical tendency to accentuate the divinity of Christ and obscure his humanity, found it deeply repugnant and counterattacked by propounding the doctrine of a single nature *(mone physis),* in which the human substance was

completely absorbed by the divine. This Monophysitism became very strong in the oriental provinces, where it soon assumed nationalistic and even seditious overtones.

But the east was also the home of an entirely different doctrine as well, that of the Nestorians, who not only insisted on Christ's two natures but held them to be entirely separate, so that these "heretics" were accused of stressing his human nature at the expense of its divine counterpart. Nestorianism, like Monophysitism, attained a powerful following upon the eastern peripheries of the empire, and beyond them in Sassanian Persia. Nestorian remnants still survive in Iraq and Iran.

Such were the intractable problems that seemed of the utmost, overriding urgency to Byzantine court, society, and Church, and engaged many of the acutest brains of the age. A series of emperors, Zeno, Justinian I (whose

wife, Theodora, was a Monophysite), and then Heraclius tried to reconcile the sharply divergent views, which so gravely threatened imperial unity. Heraclius' solution was to propound a "Monothelite" doctrine declaring the natures of Jesus to be separate but commingled—why bother so much, he hoped people would feel, about the two natures *if they acted in unison?* But the compromise made no impression on the east, which remained as hostile as ever. Indeed, when the Arabs invaded Syria, Egypt, and Iraq, one of the chief reasons why the inhabitants of those countries offered only a feeble resistance was because such disputes about the nature of Christ had estranged them from Constantinople. It was only when these "heretical" lands had been lost to the Arabs for ever that such controversies began to die down.

The condemnation of Christ by Pontius Pilate, also from the Rossano Codex (Museo Arcivescovile, Rossano, Italy). Here Christ appears as a human figure, brought before an earthly judge and condemned to a form of execution considered in Roman times as particularly degrading. It was Arius of Alexandria, in the early fourth century, who rent the Christian world by suggesting that Jesus, as the son created by God, was less than autonomous and could not therefore be himself divine. The Rossano Codex was one of the great Byzantine Gospel Books, probably originating from Constantinople. It is one of the "Purple Codices," so called because of the color of the dye, which suggests that it was intended as an imperial gift.

DESTROYERS OF IMAGES

The disputes about the nature of Christ were followed by an even fiercer and more far-reaching convulsion, inspired by those who sought to destroy all sacred images: the Iconoclasts. Images (icons) of Jesus, the Virgin Mary, and the saints had received ever increasing popular veneration since the establishment of Christianity as the state religion. By the sixth century, panel paintings portraying them were abundantly displayed in churches, wayside shrines, and private houses, and the practice continued to grow. The Byzantine community, which attributed a deep spiritual meaning to art, experienced an intense upsurge of loyalty to these holy objects. It saw them as talismans endowed with miraculous properties and bearing direct, solemn, potent witness to the Mystery of the Faith.

But then, at the prompting of certain bishops

against such "Iconodules" (slaves to icons) with violence and executed a considerable number of them, earning in return the nickname of "Dung-Name" (Copronymus). Thenceforward the Iconoclastic movement

A simple cross *(right)* replaces the mosaic showing the human form: this bare outline of the cross was substituted, in the eighth or ninth century, for the figure mosaic which occupied this space in the Church of Saint Irene at Constantinople (built on the site of a temple of Aphrodite and reconstructed by Justinian I in the sixth century). Throughout the empire images were replaced by symbols during the Iconoclastic movement.

Iconoclasm, which prevailed as official policy from 726 to 787 and from 815 to 842 when it was finally rejected, created the gravest of all the religious dissensions that convulsed the Byzantine church and empire. This illustration from a Byzantine manuscript depicts a debate on the problem of the worship of Images, a practice favored by the Iconodules and forbidden by the Iconoclasts.

of Asia Minor, the emperor Leo III published an epoch-making edict forbidding the use of images in religious worship (726). Those who resisted suffered a persecution which became more severe in the reign of his son, Constantine V, whose oppressive measures were ratified soon afterward by a council attended by 338 bishops. This Iconoclasm, however, was strongly opposed by the monks, many of whom derived revenue from the painting of such pictures. But Constantine V turned

was to torment the empire for more than a century. There have been many theories about its origins. But its principal cause was theological, which is not surprising, since theology was held to be the most important of all branches of knowledge. Moses in the Old Testament had ordered the Jews not to bow down to graven images, and the eighth-century emperors and their advisers were convinced that the veneration of miracle-making had gone much too far.

*The man looking at the icon directs his mind
    to a higher contemplation.
No longer has he a confused reverence.
Imprinting the icon within himself, he fears
    him as if he were present.
Eyes stir up the depth of the spirit.
Art conveys through colors the Soul's prayers.*
                                        Agathias

*There shall be rejected, removed,
    and cursed out of the Christian Church
every likeness which is made out of
    any material whatever by the evil art
of painters.*   *Council of Constantine V*

There had been protests against such exaggerations before, especially in the eastern provinces. And now there appeared to be a very special reason to object. For the Byzantine population, though they had repelled the Arabs from Constantinople, were still suffering traumatically from their conquests; the empire was going through terrible times. This could only mean, to the religious minds of its peoples, that God was punishing them for some failure connected with their attitude toward Him. And the nature of this failure could now be discerned. The revered icons had proved powerless to save town after town from destruction and looting: so it seemed necessary to draw the conclusion that this trust in painted images must be a mistake and an impiety.

Such convictions were particularly strong in Asia Minor, where the suffering had been greatest, where the best soldiers had their origins, and where simple clear-cut puritanical beliefs were preferred to dubious Greek practices. Moreover, the same wave of feeling against images had appeared very recently among the Arabs as well, whose caliph Yazid II (720–724), allegedly at the prompting of a Jew from Tiberias in Palestine, had likewise destroyed all the images of his Christian subjects.

But Yazid's veto did not prove permanent, and it was from the Arab empire that a Greek led the movement against Byzantine imperial Iconoclasm. He was John of Damascus (ca. 675–749), who defended the images as silent sermons, books for the illiterate, symbols and mediators that illustrated the Mysteries of the Almighty: "If God revealed himself in human nature, why not also in visible images? We do not worship *them*, but *through* them." Monks throughout the empire echoed similar sentiments, and at Constantinople official policy began to go into reverse. After a period of conciliatory measures, the veneration of images was restored by the empress Irene at the Seventh Ecumenical Council (787).

But views continued to differ, and in the following century persecutions started again: such was the fear of informers that even husbands did not dare discuss the question with their wives. Finally, in 843, Iconoclasm was formally condemned by a further Council. The step was widely hailed as the suppression of the last of the major Christian heresies, and the "Sunday of Orthodoxy" on which the Council made its decision is still an important day in the Greek Church.

Art had not died under the Iconoclast empire. But now the Byzantines, finally rejecting oriental puritanism, returned to the full richness of their habitual practice, which permitted them to interpret the doctrine of the Incarnation in terms of artistic beauty.

Emperor Leo III (717–741), initiator of the Iconoclast movement in 726, shown on a gold coin (British Museum, London). His destruction of images aroused opposition among many churchmen.

Left: One of the magnificent icons at the monastery of St. Catherine, Sinai, which escaped destruction. The principal figure is that of St. Peter, and the painting was made in the sixth or seventh century.

By the tenth century, when this miniature was painted, the Iconoclastic movement had run its course, clearing the way for a fresh upsurge of the classical, humanistic style. This painting is from a manuscript of the *Theriaca* (Book of Beasts) of the Hellenistic poet Nicander, now in the Bibliothèque Nationale, Paris.

CHURCH OF THE HOLY WISDOM

earlier church on the site, constructed by Constantine I and later rebuilt by Theodosius I, had been destroyed in the Nika riots of 532, along with many other buildings in Constantinople. The rebuilding program gave Justinian a unique opportunity to enrich his city with brilliant works by the outstanding architects of the day. Three of the four churches built under Justinian I have survived, but none compares with Haghia Sophia in size or brilliance of conception. Modern-day art historians, as impressed with the building as was Procopius, rank it with the Parthenon and with St. Peter's in Rome as one of the most important buildings in European history.

The great, successive, creative periods of Byzantine artistic history had a long past behind them, but it was under Justinian I that the movement was definitively launched. The branch of the arts that led his achievement was architecture; and the most talented endeavors were inevitably lavished upon the churches, as centers of religious life—which was the center of life itself—and microcosms of heaven above.

The architectural masterpiece of the age was the Church of the Holy Wisdom (Haghia Sophia, Aya Sofya) at Constantinople, rebuilt after Constantine's original church had been burned down in 532. The rebuilding, completed in 535, was supervised by Anthemius of Tralles and Isidore of Miletus, clever men eager to take advantage of an unprecedented opportunity. Anthemius was an expert on the architectural application of geometry, which occupied a preeminent place in the studies of the day. For Byzantine aesthetics were highly mathematical and rhythmical, stressing harmonious symmetry and order, balanced eu-

It would tax even Homer's tongue,
the poet of thunder and lightning,
to hymn the marble pastures that the whole
world brought together to grace
God's temple walls, as far as the eye could see,
and the outspread floor beneath.

Paulus Silentiarius, on Haghia Sophia

rhythmic movement expressed in the control of mass and space, and careful study of optical proportion.

The most essential feature of Haghia Sophia's structure was the blend of two preexisting architectural formulas: the traditional, longitudinal basilica in which the nave had been divided from the aisles by rows of columns, and the cross-shaped and centralized church surmounted by a cupola or dome—a formula of which the origins are variously attributed to Italy, Syria and Persia; and to Armenia, where remarkable and varied examples are still to be seen. The domes were placed over a circle and later over a square, with the aid of squinches (vaulted niches) or, more recently, curved pendentives in the four angles.

Of such blends between the basilican and centralized types of buildings, Haghia Sophia is the climactic masterpiece. This is a huge aisled basilica with the roof resting on massive piers, surmounted in the center by a mighty dome. The original dome was quite shallow, but it

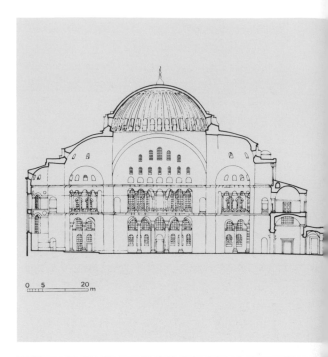

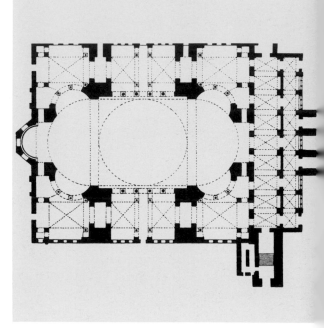

collapsed in 558 and was replaced by the steeper, ribbed dome which, defying all laws of statics and onslaughts of earthquakes, still survives today. The sidestress of its 107-foot diameter is met by transepts under half-domes abutted by niches. Huge yet not overbearing, subtly balanced upon the gentle flow of its gradient, this exalted design, "describing man's course, exalting him, and returning him to earth," translates the cruciform emblem of Christianity into a vision of the infinite. Architecture almost rises beyond its earthly limitations and becomes as immaterial and impalpable as the heavenly vault itself. Though final and unrepeatable in spatial and spiritual conception alike, Haghia Sophia

nevertheless served as a model for the future. For the Byzantines, and then the Slavs who learnt from them, found that the cross-domed formula, to which this church had given such perfect expression, ideally suited the requirements of their liturgy: the faithful participated from the aisles and galleries, while the churchmen officiated in the center.

The other essential and characteristically Byzantine feature of Haghia Sophia—much less easy to appreciate in its present condition—was the extraordinarily colorful nature of the interior, accentuated by every device of glowing mosaics and glittering metals and ivories, and purple hangings and flickering lights. To the Byzantines, light was the first of the elements, and light, though incorporeal, was expressed by the use of contrasted colors, conceived in rhythmical terms: the most favored colors were white (silver) and green, and above all purple and gold—which jointly symbolized the divine and imperial majesties. In Haghia Sophia the lights, colors, and spatial forms all emanated, according to a carefully worked out plan, from the central dome, and the people at the sides of the church saw from afar this glory streaming from the center, the seat of the Godhead. It must have been a moving experience to come in from the dark outside world and encounter this radiant spectacle.

Seen today from the exterior, the Church of the Holy Wisdom offers an altogether different aspect from the original design. Massive buttresses were built to support the walls after various earthquakes. The church was converted into a mosque after the Ottoman conquest (1453) and has been maintained as a museum since the time of Atatürk in the modern, secularized Turkey. The drawings at left present the floorplan of the church and a side elevation.

51

Below: View of the dome of the Church of the Holy Wisdom, from below. The model for innumerable others, constructed of special bricks from Rhodes weighing each only one-twelfth as much as an ordinary brick, it was built in the sixth century (559), though it is not the original, over-daring version which had collapsed during an earthquake soon after its completion, in 558. When the second dome, the present one, was constructed, its diameter was reduced and the piers reinforced by thick outside walls.

Right: The interior of the Church of the Holy Wisdom, the supreme masterpiece of Anthemius of Tralles and Isidore of Miletus, architects of Justinian I, who on the completion of the building, was said to have declared: "Glory be to God who has found me worthy of this work! I have outstripped you, O Solomon!" (A reference to the legendary temple of Solomon that had surpassed all other buildings.) The essence of the plan is a blend between two types of design: the traditional, longitudinal, aisled basilica, and the centralized form of structure. The pulpits, and great plaques with inscriptions from the Koran, were introduced when the building was a Turkish mosque. The resplendent, varied marble decoration can still be seen, though the brilliant mosaics are lost.

But who could fittingly describe the galleries
... or enumerate the many colonnades and
the colonnaded aisles by means of which the
church is surrounded? Or who could recount
the beauty of the columns and the stones
with which the church is adorned? One
might imagine that he had come upon a
meadow with its flowers in full bloom. For
he would surely marvel at the purple of
some, the green tint of others, and at those
on which the crimson glows and those from
which the white flashes, and again at those
which Nature, like some painter, varies
with the most contrasting colors. And
whenever anyone enters this church to pray,
he understands at once that it is not by any
human power or skill, but by the influence
of God, that this work has been so finely
turned. And so his mind is lifted up toward
God and exalted, feeling that He cannot be
far away, but must especially love to dwell
in this place which He has chosen.

Procopius, on Haghia Sophia

PAINTINGS, TEXTILES, AND METALWORK

Though less spectacular and often less impressive than Byzantine mosaics, the empire's other art media offer much to admire. This Coptic textile, a fifth-century work from Akhmim (Egypt), now in the Victoria and Albert Museum, London, portrays a flying angel in graceful form. Amid the various important regional workshops manufacturing Byzantine textiles, those of Egypt in particular produced works in the highly distinctive Coptic style.

Wall paintings, in so far as they have survived from this period, come from remoter churches and sites and do not therefore represent the finest art of their day. A partial exception is provided by Italy, where Christian fresco traditions had already existed in the catacombs, and still remained active. Elsewhere, occasional paintings appear in the Asiatic provinces, notably in the region of the eastern frontier where much earlier examples had already borne evidence to Syria's role as a great cultural meeting point between west and east. As for panel painting, it was Egypt that had shown the way, with a remarkable series of mummy portraits of Roman imperial date. Egypt also provided the first important icons, made in considerable quantities at the monastery of St. Catherine on Mount Sinai from the sixth century onward. Brilliant manuscript paintings, too, date from the same period, reflecting so great a variety of cultural influences that it is generally impossible to determine their place of origin; but where the coloring includes a lavish use of purple, it is a sign that imperial initiative was at work.

both countries left their mark on subsequent Byzantine textiles. At first all the silk had to be imported from the east, but in about 552 a Persian traveler (or perhaps a group of monks) returning from Khotan (Sinkiang) was said to have smuggled silkworms, eggs, and mulberry seeds into the empire. In the years around 700 some of the finest silk embroidery, rich in green and gold, can be ascribed to Constantinople itself, where the best materials were reserved for imperial use. When, shortly afterward, the Iconoclastic movement prevailed, the figured style had to be replaced by non-figurative motifs such as those favored in Moslem countries, from which textiles were exported to Constantinople and copied by its weavers.

Constantinople was also the main center of Byzantine metalwork. This included cups, dishes, chalices, plates, and Gospel covers, all abundantly studded with inlaid stones and glass in accordance with the polychrome fashions inherited from the later Roman empire. Moreover, in view of the immense devotion lavished on sacred relics, special care was dedi-

Right: Fifth-century silver cosmetics box, Louvre, depicting the raising of Lazarus from the dead. Even objects such as this, designed for an entirely secular purpose, display religious designs.

Rich hangings and textiles were a feature not only of Byzantine churches but also of the larger private residences and palaces; and in addition such objects were in great demand as exports to the west, and as gifts to its princes. Silk was especially favored for these purposes. The earliest centers of its manufacture, dating from the fifth century A.D., included Syria, where the process may have originated; although Persia and Egypt have been suggested as alternative sources, and it is true that

cated to jeweled reliquaries. These, in the eighth and ninth centuries, were sometimes inlaid with the vitreous glaze of enamel. During this period, dark colors were favored for this process—translucent emerald greens, deep blues and purples. Two main techniques of enameling were employed. The first, which appeared at Constantinople in about the fifth century, was *champlevé*, in which the enamel is set in depressions punched into the background, or, subsequently, carved out of it.

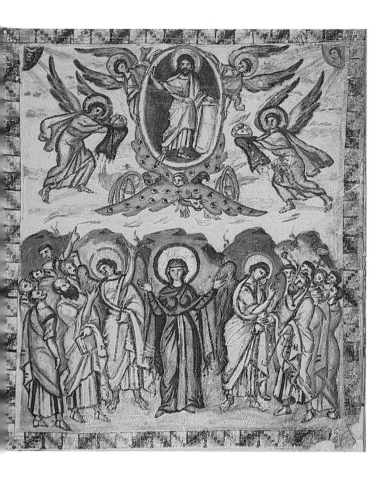

This miniature painting of Christ's ascension to heaven, from the Rabbula Gospels (from Zagba, eastern Syria, ca. 586–589), incorporates local Syrian artistic traditions and certain oriental influences, including vividness of color and dramatic gestures. The Virgin Mary, bottom, is flanked by St. Paul (left) and St. Peter.

Two examples of brilliant Byzantine metal working: A large silver plate from Cyprus *(above)*, 613–629, depicting in classicizing style the struggle between David and Goliath; 19¼ inches in diameter, the plate forms the centerpiece of a set of nine devoted to the story of David. This gold necklace *(below)* with crescent-shaped pendant, about A.D. 600, is inlaid with rock-crystal, emeralds, and paste gems.

The throne of Maximian, archbishop of Ravenna (545–553), the most magnificent complex of ivory carving of all time. Made up of a large number of ivory plaques in different styles and by different artists—probably coming from Constantinople—it is covered with plaques on both sides and on its back, including ten panels devoted to the life of Joseph as told in the Old Testament.

Next, very soon afterward, came the *cloisonné* technique, in which the enamel inlays are set in cells *(cloisons)* bordered by narrow gold or silver bands. Such works should not be classified, as they usually are, among the "minor arts," since they achieved the same excellence—and were dedicated to the same religious purpose—as masterpieces of larger dimensions.

THE ART
OF THE MOSAIC

The Church of San Vitale at Ravenna provides our finest examples of mosaics from the golden moment of Byzantine art, in the sixth century A.D., executed in superb styles that cannot have been inferior to those of Constantinople (where no great church mosaics of this period survive). The apse mosaic from San Vitale, ca. 546–547 *(top)*, portrays the Redeemer and angels between San Vitale at left and Bishop Ecclesius, founder of the church.

Among other fine mosaics of San Vitale, Ravenna, these two examples show Justinian *(left)* and the empress Theodora *(right)* surrounded by their courts—which were considered to mirror the court of heaven itself. The brilliantly executed figures, in their elaborate court dress, participating in a procession or ceremonious offering, tellingly display the blend of classical and oriental styles of which Byzantine art was composed; the fusion is not yet quite complete.

Artists and craftsmen at Alexandria had discovered that glass, of which there were large factories in the area, was a useful substitute for the small cubes of stone that had been used for many centuries to make mosaics. A less heavy and more luminous material, glass lent itself aptly to the sort of illumination that Byzantine architects desired, since its cubes could be set at an angle, and slightly roughened to catch and refract the light. The cube could also be coated with gold and silver dust, or other coloring materials. Seen through daylight tempered by the alabaster windows, or lit at night by lamps or candles, the mosaics on the walls or vaults of the churches looked different at every hour of the day or night.

Byzantine experts on aesthetics saw this art as a form of music in which blends of contrasted color stood for the harmonies. And the figures thus depicted not only provided a ceremonious, dramatic backdrop, but played their full parts in the liturgy. They were the Bible of the poor man and woman who could not read. But in addition, as time went on, they came increasingly to appeal to the initiate, offering multiple meanings symbolically relevant to the rituals enacted in the church over which they presided.

The mosaics to be seen in Haghia Sophia today are of dates subsequent to Justinian, but the brilliant development of the art, in his own age, can still be found at Ravenna, the capital

Six details from Byzantine mosaics (sixth to eighth century) showing the close attention paid to naturalistic detail. Donkey and eagle, from the Great Palace, Constantinople. Tiger, from Damascus. Cup, rivers of Paradise, and flowers of Paradise, from San Vitale.

of the Italian province he reconquered. Designed, probably, by a westerner, but modeled on the Church of Saints Sergius and Bacchus at Constantinople, Ravenna's San Vitale (526–547) has a lightly floating dome upheld by an octagon, and is the most complex structure of the period to have survived into our own time. Its mosaics illustrate the new, enlarged appreciation of this art as a means of architectural ornament, and show that it could be used for religious and patriotic instruction alike. The principal apse is filled by a picture of Christ enthroned upon the orb of heaven with his angels and saints, rendered in fresh and beautiful colors. On the panels at the side of the presbytery are the most famous of all Byzantine mosaics, portraying Justinian and his empress Theodora and their courtiers. These groups of compositions are, technically speaking, of such high quality that they may well have been the work of imperial artists from Constantinople itself. Their creations display clearly the two principal tendencies, of separate and different geographical and cultural origins, that were at work in Byzantine art. The treatment of Jesus is naturalistic, Hellenic and classical. The court scenes, however, are presented in a much more eastern manner, employing frontal poses and heavy impressive tints, and depicting crowns and robes that could have been at home in Sassanian Persia. The employment, side by side, of the two contrasting techniques in one and the same build-

ing shows that these two main streams of Byzantine culture had not yet blended completely. By the time of the accomplished figure mosaics at Thessalonica (Salonica), displaying St. Demetrius and the church donors (ca. 635) in the church bearing his name, this blend is achieved and the truly integrated, delicate, rather abstract Byzantine style has emerged. Later, under the Iconoclasts, such figured designs became impossible, and even the best decorative work was done beyond the frontiers, notably at Arab Damascus. When, however, the Iconoclastic movement had run its course, Byzantine artists once again began to carpet the walls and arches and domes of their churches with figure mosaics, marking by their narrative succession the annual cycle of sacred events.

The religious mosaic, like so much other Byzantine art, possessed a functional purpose: it was a medium whereby the relations between heaven and humankind could be effectively, concisely, and splendidly delineated. These pictures were all public confessions of faith in the grandeur of God, and declarations of pious acceptance of His will. Traces of the classical humanism were still apparent. But they were increasingly taking second place to a deep preoccupation with the transcendental and immutable, an absorption with the invisible world of which the material world is only a shadowy replica. Thus the mosaicists of the Byzantine empire, ever searching for new and more significant expressions of these ineffable truths, and devoting a heady blend of spiritual aspiration, aesthetic sensibility, and passionate feeling to their task, celebrated the glories of their faith in one of the greatest religious arts the world has ever seen.

Demetrius between the prefect Leontius and Bishop John, seventh-century mosaic from the Church of St. Demetrius at Thessalonica (Salonica), Greece, second city of the empire.

Overleaf: Justinian I and Theodora his wife, details of the mosaic (seen opposite) of the Church of San Vitale, Ravenna. Justinian, "addicted to long vigils and abstemious diet" (Gibbon), idolized the controversial Theodora, whose portrait inspired this anonymous comment by a Byzantine author: "The artist made a fair shot at her eyes. But that is all. The texture of her hair, her glowing golden skin—these are not there. To picture Theodora you need one skill and one alone—to paint the sun."

57

TOWARD THE BYZANTINE FUTURE

After the Sassanian Persians, the Arabs, and the Avars, the Bulgars became a threat to the Byzantine empire; they were beaten back by Basil II (976–1025), of the Macedonian dynasty, known as Bulgaroctonos (the Bulgar slayer), who stands at the center of the picture in this illuminated Psalter, surrounded by images of Jesus Christ, two archangels, and saints. Under Basil the fortunes and strength of the Byzantine empire once again rose to new heights.

Right: A sign of the limitation of the emperor's absolute power. This miniature from a Byzantine historical manuscript (now in the Biblioteca Nacional, Madrid) depicts a conflict between the noble courtiers and the emperor Basil I, seated far right. By refusing to eat or to move from the palace, the courtiers were protesting the imprisonment of Prince Leo, whom the emperor did not believe to be his own son. Even in a state without any effective representative institutions, protests could nevertheless be registered and had to be treated seriously by the emperor.

In the centuries to come, the Byzantine empire continued to display unique powers of pertinacity and survival, and long remained by far the most powerful state in the western world. The magnificent court of the emperors was adorned with mechanical devices to impress upon visitors the awe-inspiring sanctity of God's vice-gerent on earth. Their capital, continually adorned with new artistic masterpieces, and rivaled only by Baghdad as a center of commerce, reached the height of its splendor under Basil I (867–886) and his successors of the "Macedonian" dynasty.

Nations which formerly ruled over others were then enslaved in their turn. This was the case with the Assyrians who became subject to the Persians, just as the Persians and all their subjects became subject to the Macedonians, and the Macedonians to the Romans. And these events occur in an alternating fashion according to chance of time and Tyche. Nor is there anything constant in human affairs nor unchangingly eternal. Just as every individual man or animal suffers birth, growth, decay and destruction and death, thus is it also in human affairs, governments, and dynasties. They also are in constant flux and change, and never constant. They come into being, progress, and then, gradually decaying and changing into the opposite state, they come to an end and die.

Theodore Metochites (d. 1332), on the decline of the Byzantine empire

The ensuing reign of Leo VI (886–912), who completed a legal recodification begun by his predecessor, foreshadowed encroachments upon the central government by the aristocracy. Nevertheless, Basil II (976–1025) was as powerful as any emperor throughout the whole long Byzantine epoch—and as any ruler of his day in any country. During his reign, Vladimir of Kiev was converted to Orthodox Christianity and linked to the imperial house by marriage. Thereafter, despite the loss of the last Byzantine bases in Italy and most of Asia Minor (1071), and despite also the rise of important Bulgarian and Serbo-Macedonian rival states, the emperors of the Comnene dynasty (1081–1185) continued to rule the most important state for thousands of miles around.

The Fourth Crusade of the western Christians,

by turning aside from its mission directed against the Moslems in order to seize Constantinople instead (1204), temporarily brought the empire down. However, the Greeks recaptured the city in 1261, though the revived Byzantine state, under the menace of the Ottoman Turks who had succeeded to the Seljuk heritage, remained only a shadow of its former self until Mehmet II finally put an end to its independence in 1453. The year immediately preceding its fall witnessed the death of the most original of all Byzantine thinkers, Gemistus Plethon, who dreamt of a new,

polytheistic religion that would supersede Christianity and Islam alike.

It has been necessary, in the foregoing paragraphs, to stray beyond the chronological boundaries of this book in order to stress the astonishing duration and durability of the Byzantine empire. For no less than a thousand years, in good times and bad, amid tremendous and ever recurrent vicissitudes and shocks and dangers, its recuperative resources and vitality always enabled it to achieve revival and renewal. And so this nation and community proved a uniquely potent preserver of all that was meant by civilized society—including the ancient Greek classics. There was no truly Dark Age of Byzantium.

Nor, in spite of modern efforts to find them, were there any real Renaissances either: for the Byzantines never thought that the old past

had died and required a rebirth. This attitude had its disadvantages. It meant that original and creative ideas, and longings, in literature and science were few and far between; men like Gemistus Plethon were all too rare, since the majority of writers showed comparatively little capacity or desire to advance beyond what they had inherited from the past. Yet this defect was more than compensated for by the magnificent beauty of the Byzantine visual arts, remaining within the formal, largely religious framework that had been selected for them, and yet continuously and creatively

Top left: Detail of a painting on the façade of a church at Berenda, Bulgaria, thirteenth or fourteenth century. The appearance of the Cyrillic script accompanying a figure depicted in essentially Byzantine style illustrates the spread of the Orthodox religion to Slavonic lands.

evolving within that framework throughout the centuries. These arts exercised an enormous influence on the Germanic and Celtic west and Slavonic east alike. Thus it was the Byzantines who made the future development of European culture possible; without them, there would not have been any. So great and decisive and widespread was their impact that Byzantium must be seen no longer as a state or an empire, or as a cultural unit confined to any specific area or epoch, but as a whole way of life, a major phase of the civilization of the world.

The Seljuk Turks—shown on this Persian bowl—migrated from the eastern Asian steppes and in the eleventh century arrived in Asia Minor where they presented a grave and continuing threat to Constantinople for two hundred years.

Left: In its last centuries, as in the heyday of its splendor, the Byzantine empire remained strongly imbued with religious fervor. The pious devotion of this group of nuns, from a work painted around the year 1400 (formerly at Lincoln College, Oxford, and now in the Bodleian Library), typifies the most enduring trait of the civilization of Byzantium.

THE
EXPANSION
OF ISLAM

The mission of Mohammed—the birth of the Moslem faith—was the most decisive religious event of this whole age. Beginning in the Arabian desert soon after A.D. 600, inspired by local deities as well as by the monotheism of the Jews and Christians, and splendidly delineated by the Koran, Islam quickly gained very numerous converts. But it was more than just a religious phenomenon. Knowing no distinction between Church and State, this absolutist faith gave rise to a centrifugal political and military explosion of unprecedented impact. Within ten years Islam dominated the Near East, sweeping aside the Greco-Roman and Persian political structures that had ruled there for so many years. Within three generations, by the early eighth century, Islamic armies had fought their way to Pakistan and China in the east, and across Africa all the way to Spain.

*Fight those who do not
    believe in Allah, and the
Last Day, and do not forbid
    what God and his apostle
have forbidden, and do not
    follow the true religion
of those to whom scriptures
    were given, until they pay
tribute out of hand,
    being brought low.*

Koran, Sura 9.29 ff.

The lightning-swift conquests of the Arabs
brought powerful artistic and intellectual influences to a wide expanse of the Mediterranean world. The lively floor painting of a
mounted huntsman *(opposite page),* second
quarter of the eighth century, comes from
Syria (National Museum, Damascus). At the
opposite end of Europe, in Moslem Spain,
there arose strikingly beautiful mosques: this
mihrab (niche indicating the direction of Mecca), an eleventh-century work *(left),* is to be
seen in the Aljafería mosque at Saragossa,
Spain.

RISE AND FALL
OF SASSANIAN PERSIA

Persia, after a period of strength under the Sassanians, was exhausted by its wars with Byzantium and became a target for early Moslem depredation. The sard seal *(right)*, third to fifth century A.D., depicts a Sassanian king. Many such seals have been discovered, portraying a wide range of Sassanian personages, including kings, princes, princesses, noblemen, and priests. Museum of Fine Arts, Boston.

The only great power with which the Roman emperors during their first two centuries had to deal was that of the Parthians. These were a people of Iranian speech, originating from the area southeast of the Caspian Sea, who maintained a loose, federal control over the entire vast, cosmopolitan region that extended from Rome's eastern frontier to the borders of India. But in the 220s A.D. the Parthians were overthrown by the Sassanian Persians, who came from a district north of the Persian Gulf; and these Sassanians ruled for four hundred years. They retained the Parthian capital Ctesiphon on the Tigris (in what is now Iraq), but their principal religious center was the holy city of their ancestors at Istakhr near Persepolis. They took over a great deal from the Parthians, but were also far more nationalistic and powerful. For they were

Above: The southeast gate of Takht-i-Sulaiman in Iranian Azerbaijan, identified with the ancient Gazaka. According to recent archaeological surveys, Takht-i-Sulaiman, in the northwestern region of the Persian empire, had been a sacred place for many centuries, and possessed a dynastic and religious significance for the Sassanian rulers. *Center:* On this Sassanian intaglio, the fire god, son of Ahuramazda, is shown rising from an altar. Cabinet des Médailles, Bibliothèque Nationale, Paris. *Right:* Sassanian fire-altars at Naqsh-i-Rustem (near Sivand, S. Iran). The two altars, about five feet high, are carved out of the solid rock. The maintenance of the "eternal fire" was central to the ritual of the Sassanian religion, which consisted of the reformed version of Mazdaism introduced by Zoroaster.

Textile, probably fifth century A.D. The design shows an east Roman or Byzantine emperor with prisoners captured from the Sassanian Persians in one of the recurrent wars between the two states. Victoria and Albert Museum, London.

eager to emphasize their inheritance of ancient Persian imperial claims.

By establishing closer and more effective control over the non-Iranian nomads on their northeastern borders, the Sassanian Persians helped to save first the Roman and then the Byzantine empire from the impact of these ferocious hordes. But that had not been their intention, and in spite of intervals of long peace or watchful truce, the Sassanians were at other times formidable enemies, first to the Romans and then to the Byzantines. At such times, spectacular warfare would break out across the northern fringes of the Fertile Crescent (with the divided Christian kingdom of Armenia often the bone of contention) causing terrible damage to both the contestants alike.

The Sassanian king Kavadh I (488–531) restored internal order broken by nomadic White Hun incursions, and went on to fight two wars against the Byzantine empire. But these, like the prolonged wars of Khosrau I (531–578/9) against the same enemy, proved inconclusive. In the east, however, Khosrau extended his territory as far as what is now Afghanistan.

The powerful, intolerant Sassanian state Church practiced a Fire Cult and worshiped the sun-god Ahuramazda, according to the alleged precepts of Zoroaster, a legendary figure of the seventh century B.C. Kavadh I

temporarily turned away from the Zoroastrian church in favor of Mazdak, founder of an offshoot of the Manichaean faith which believed in two original principles of Good (Light) and Evil (Darkness). Disgusted by this step, however—and by the Mazdakites' communistic views about the ownership of property and women—the nobles and clergy replaced Kavadh by his son Khosrau I, who had Mazdak himself and many of his adherents put to death and reestablished the orthodoxy

of Zoroaster, which still survives in India and Iran, among the Parsees and Gabars.

Khosrau I, known as Anushirvan ("of the immortal spirit"), was regarded as the ablest and wisest of the Sassanian kings. He initiated a revolutionary process by which the old feudal, aristocratic structure was loosened and replaced by the *dekkans*, soldiers and courtiers who provided professional service directly dependent on the crown and enabled it to operate as a military despotism. Khosrau's renown as an enlightened ruler stood so high that, when the Byzantine emperor Justinian I closed the philosophy school at Athens, the last Neoplatonists turned to Ctesiphon as their refuge.

Recurrent tension between Persia and Byzantium did not stop commercial and cultural contacts. The Persians were eager to profit

from the superior technical skill of the Byzantines—and the fairytale, sophisticated Sassanian court at Ctesiphon, with its great barrel vaulted palace, the Taq-e-Kisra, reconstructed by Khosrau I, echoed the styles of Constantinople. Conversely, the Byzantines continued to trade, whenever possible, with the Sassanian empire. The designs of their artistic masterpieces incorporated many features derived from the highly prized Persian textiles; and Constantinople relied on the important Sassanian silk-weaving industry until, in the time of Justinian, it was able to create one of its own. The Persians had learned the fabrication of silk from the Chinese, with whom they traded extensively, and in return, the sophisticated techniques of Sassanian silverwork, displaying gilded reliefs of royal hunting scenes,

were copied by the early T'ang court of China. The Persians also had useful contacts with India, from which Sanskrit medical writings reached Ctesiphon in the course of the sixth century—as did the game of chess.

Whereas Khosrau I had been a great military commander, his luxurious grandson Khosrau II (590–628) did not possess the same capacity. Restored to the throne, after serious internal risings, by the Byzantine emperor Maurice, he felt impelled, when Maurice was murdered, to fight a war of revenge against the next claimants to the imperial title. In these campaigns he at first achieved stunning victories, capturing Antioch, Damascus, and Jerusalem (611–614)—from which he carried off the True Cross to Ctesiphon—and occupying Egypt.

Never had the Sassanians achieved such successes against Byzantium, and it seemed that under Khosrau II, now known as Parvez ("the Victorious"), Persia's ancient ambition of controlling the entire Near East had almost been attained. But then occurred a massive reversal of fortune. For after Heraclius had taken the field in 622, there followed a period of six years in which the Byzantines recovered all that they had lost, and Sassanian Iraq and northwestern Iran suffered devastating invasions. At Ctesiphon itself, revolution broke out, and Khosrau II was assassinated.

The wars had drastically weakened Byzantium, which rapidly lost huge provinces to the blows that the Arab caliph Omar I struck immediately afterward. But the Persians, their great gamble a failure, had been even more disastrously enfeebled. When they, too, became Omar's targets, the resistance organized by the last Sassanian monarch, Yazdegerd III, proved wholly inadequate. In 637 the fate of the empire was virtually decided at Kadisiya on a canal of the Euphrates, and Ctesiphon fell. Four years later a further defeat led to the gradual loss of western Iran, and in 651 Yazdegerd was murdered at Merv in the extreme northeastern region, which was likewise completely overrun. The independence of Sassanian Persia had come to an end. Under Arab rule, the country in due course came to play a significant and indeed dominant part, but it was not to become an independent nation again for another nine hundred years: and the ancient hostility between Iranians and Arabs is still with us.

Right: The monarch shown engaged in a hunt on this fifth-century Sassanian silver plate is probably Firuz (ca. 457–483), a persecutor of the Jews. Hunting was a characteristic activity of the Sassanian monarchy and an appropriate means of displaying the ruler's warlike prowess. Sassanian silversmiths employed a sophisticated technique embodying figure reliefs and (as in this example) partial gilding.

The Sassanian kings conducted a more powerful and centralized administration than their Parthian predecessors, and thus posed a correspondingly greater threat to the Romans and then the Byzantines. This portrait *(above)* of a fourth- or fifth-century Sassanian monarch shows the typical hair style, beard, and crown.

ARABIA

The Arabian peninsula, cradle of Moslem civilization, is a vast area extending between Africa and Asia, a region marked by great geographical diversity. Mecca, Mohammed's birthplace, is situated in mountainous western Arabia, in a narrow valley devoid of fertile farmland *(opposite page)*, so that the town depended entirely for its subsistence on trade and pilgrimages. From an early period Arabia was active in trade with the east in incense and spices. Between the third or second century B.C. and ca. A.D. 525 (when it fell under Abyssinian rule), much of the southwestern area was governed by the

Himyarite kings, with only brief interruption. The Himyarite rulers issued coins of gold, copper, and *(above)* silver, bearing their images and various symbols. Well before Mohammed, the Arabians had already worshiped Allah among other deities, and possessed a major shrine at Mecca, where the sacred stone *(right)* was kept. A black meteorite, said to have been given to Ismail (Ishmael) by the angel Gabriel, it is kept enclosed to this day inside the square shrine called the Kaaba.

The term "Arab" is variously and ambiguously used today, as a linguistic or cultural or ethnic term, or all three. In the sixth century A.D., however, it was generally employed to refer to the Semitic, Arabic-speaking inhabitants of the Arabian peninsula, living in small, fragmented, independent groups.

Arabia was, and is, subject to violent alternations between long droughts and periods of greater humidity. Moreover, its territory provided startling contrasts between fertile lands and arid deserts. Especially productive were parts of the kingdom of the Himyarites, in the Yemen (southwestern Arabia). This state also became extremely prosperous as a halfway house for the trade in gold and spices (particularly frankincense) with India, and as the starting point of the caravan route up into Mesopotamia and Syria.

However, a marked decline became apparent in the sixth century. Christians from the Ethiopian kingdom of Aksum invaded the Yemen and established a puppet ruler on its throne. He did not last long, and a native regime under the powerful and energetic Abraha took his place. But after Abraha's death in about 570 the Himyarites were too weak to continue repairing the great Ma'rib dam which had irrigated their soil, and its collapse reduced the country to barren desert. The sedentary tribes of the region reverted to nomadism, and thousands of emigrants evacuated the Yemen and moved to other parts of Arabia.

In the extreme north of the peninsula, along the present-day Saudi-Arabian frontiers with Jordan and Iraq, there were two states of considerable dimensions. One was the kingdom of Ghassan which in the sixth century became a client of Byzantium. To the east of Ghassan was the older kingdom of the Lakhmids, a satellite of the Sassanian Persians. Among its population, both Zoroastrian (Mazdaean) and Christian (Nestorian) sects played a large part. But there were also a great many Jews of the Diaspora in the Lakhmid kingdom, as there were in Ghassanid territory as well. However, both states came to an end around 600, when they were swept away in the recurrent troubles between Byzantium and Persia. At that juncture, the entire peninsula disintegrated into a mass of tiny, separate communities.

This situation gave the growing town of Mecca, not far from the Hejaz coast, its great chance. Strategically placed on the frankincense caravan route, midway between the Yemen and Syria, Mecca was able to attract

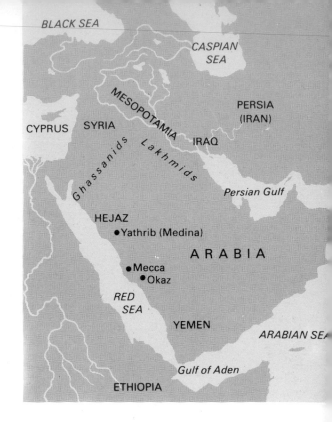

much of the wealth that passed along this road, and rapidly became the richest city in the peninsula. Its merchant oligarchy, led by the house of the Quraysh and in particular by what was known as its "inside" branch, began to invest large sums in profit-sharing companies. These new merchant princes of the Near East lived in a hectic atmosphere of money fever, frenzied free-for-all speculation, and abruptly seesawing fortunes, which provided a sharp contrast with the old-fashioned tribal, communal morality and mentality of the nomad Bedouins (*badawi*, desert dwellers) round about.

Mecca was also renowned, from ancient times, as the leading religious center of the region. This prestige was based on its ancient pilgrim sanctuary of the Kaaba, a cube-shaped structure thirty-five feet high containing a black stone; during the months of the sacred festivals connected with the Kaaba even the Bedouin refrained from harassing the caravan traffic. The Meccans worshiped three god-

desses in this shrine, but its principal deity was Allah, whom ascetic theologians, known as the Hanifa, came to interpret in an increasingly monotheistic sense. The most famous of these religious thinkers was a man of Mecca, Zaid ibn Amr, who died when Mohammed was a youth.

These monotheistic views, accompanied by the preaching of a strict moral law, did not originate, as has been romantically supposed, from the solitary meditations of the desert Bedouin, but from Judaism. For the collapse of the Ghassanid and Lakhmid kingdoms caused their large populations of Jews to migrate to the new trading center of Mecca. There were many Christians, too, in Mecca, and although they were less numerous than those in the north and south of the peninsula, they evidently possessed some influence in the city, since the design of the Kaaba itself, when the building was reconstructed in about 600, took its inspiration from a Christian church of Ethiopia—indeed, the new decorations even included paintings of Jesus.

That Arabia should have become the nucleus of one of the most outstanding political organizations and civilizations of this or any other epoch seems at first sight strange, since as the above photograph, and the map on the other page, immediately suggest, it was considerably off the beaten track. That is to say, it stood outside the spheres of the influence of the great empires of the day, Byzantine and Persian. But that was to prove its strength: impelled by a teacher of genius, it lopped off half of one of them, and destroyed the other.

This bronze lamp from Arabia, a work of the first century B.C. now in the British Museum, testifies to the wealth of the country during the Roman period, when the Romans tried unsuccessfully to seize the southwestern regions. The decoration is similar to that used in contemporary architecture. *Left:* The Kaaba shrine at Mecca, repository of the sacred stone, from a miniature, Topkapi Museum, Istanbul.

MOHAMMED

Mohammed (ca. 570–632) was a member of the Meccan family of Bani Hashim, which belonged to the ruling tribe of the Quraysh, though not to its principal and richest ("inside") branch. His father died before he was born, and his mother before he was six. At the age of twenty-five, he married a wealthy widow of forty, Khadija, who had employed him as a camel-driver in the caravan trade and later became his first convert. Mohammed's decisive religious experiences were felt in his fortieth year, when he became convinced that he was the recipient of divine revelations. Three years later, he began to preach at Mecca, fervently proclaiming the one God, the all-powerful Creator of the Universe, a God not only of justice but of merciful blessings to which every man and woman must respond in heartfelt gratitude.

Apart from a few relatives and friends, however, the Meccans were quite unreceptive, since Mohammed placed great stress on generosity and charity, an attitude they regarded as an attack on their commercial profits. This rejection prompted Mohammed to seek refuge elsewhere, and the solution appeared when the

The great prophet inspired a rich tradition of iconography. This fabric *(right)* is the supposed banner of Mohammed (in the Topkapi Museum, Istanbul), though, in fact, it is of much later date than his lifetime. The crossed swords symbolize the power of Islam, which after the prophet's death expanded in an unparalleled explosion across huge areas of Asia, Africa, and Europe.

The Islamic ban did not always prevent imaginary portrayals of Mohammed. The scenes below are from a medieval manu-

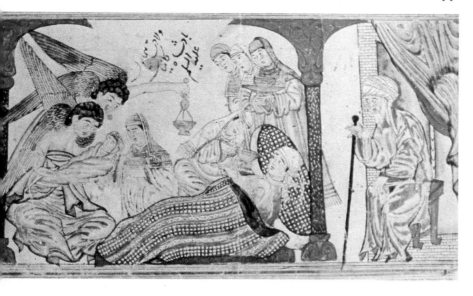

script of the *Universal History* by Rashid al-Din, the great Persian historian who died in 1318. In addition to depicting the birth of the prophet, they show Jesus Christ riding on a donkey beside Mohammed on a camel *(above right)*, since Jesus, like Abraham and Moses, was accepted by Mohammed as a forerunner whose message was superseded by the prophet's own. In this Turkish miniature painting *(right)* of the preaching of the new religion, Mohammed is shown with his face veiled. Spencer Collection, New York Public Library.

people of Yathrib invited him to leave Mecca and go to them instead. Their town was an agricultural center in an oasis of date palms and ricefields two hundred and fifty miles north of Mecca; from now onward, it became known as Medina (Madinat-an-Nabi, the city of the Prophet). Its leaders invited Mohammed to join them because their community was rent apart by disputes between the two principal Arab tribes among the population. It was felt that an outside arbitrator was needed; and Mohammed was chosen because his preaching was particularly insistent on the

70

imperative need to override such divisions. His arrival at Medina, attributed to 622, is celebrated as the Hegira (Emigration). This was the turning-point from which the supporters of Mohammed, the Muslims or Moslems, calculate their era. For it was now, according to tradition, that Islam took shape as a new type of organized community of Believers *(umma)*. This meant that Mohammed was no longer only the head of a religious movement, but a political leader as well.

He was strongly influenced by the monotheistic thought of the Jews, who were so numerous in Arabia; and he even hailed Abraham and Moses as his own forerunners. Nevertheless, the Arabian Jews refused, for the most part, to cooperate with him, and eventually, by playing skillfully on their disunities, he suppressed them by force (628). But with the Christians, too, his links were very strong, since it was from them that his enormous emphasis on the imminence of the Last Judgment was derived. However, close relations were made impossible by the Christian doctrine of the Incarnation of Jesus, whom

He had founded a considerable secular state. Yet, utterly Arab though he himself was, this state, startlingly enough, was no longer bound by the old Arabic tribal rules of kinship and bloodfeud—and not by the commercial money-worship of Mecca either. Instead it was bound by the completely different revolution-

In his fortieth year, Mohammed was visited by the angel Gabriel while praying and meditating on a mountain *(left)*: from a manuscript in the Topkapi Museum, Istanbul. The prophet is shown veiled and encased in flame. After his withdrawal from Mecca to Medina (the Hegira), the prophet finally succeeded in reconquering his home city, where he returned the black stone to the Kaaba shrine *(far left)*; in this miniature from a manuscript of the *Universal History* by Rashid al-Din (Edinburgh University Library), the prophet and his followers are shown enwrapping

Mohammed was prepared to see as a predecessor—in the line of Abraham and Moses—but no more: he believed that the message revealed by God to Jesus had been superseded by the revelations now disclosed to himself.

In spite of his withdrawal to Medina, Mohammed continued to declare that Mecca was still the central shrine of his movement. But friction continuously occurred with its rulers, who subjected Medina, and the followers of Mohammed, to harassment. In 630, however, he invaded Mecca and took it over, though still retaining Medina as his capital.

ary ties of the new Islamic religion—ties that overrode the old Arab distinctions and taboos, and were based instead on Mohammed's monotheistic faith, of which so many features were derived from the Jews and Christians.

He emerges as a figure of towering spiritual fervor and commanding moral ascendancy, overcoming immense problems by a formidable blend of statesmanlike persuasion and readiness to resort to force.

the stone, with the Kaaba behind them. It was later asserted by the Shi'ites that Mohammed chose his son-in-law Ali as a successor *(center picture)*, an allegation which led to the decisive split in the Islamic faith that still exists today. This painting is also from the Rashid al-Din manuscript. A scene frequently depicted in Islamic art is the prophet Mohammed's ascension to heaven, mounted on Buraq, a mare shown with human head. The version of the scene here *(above)*, with the archangel Gabriel at upper left, is from a Turkish manuscript in the Bibliothèque Nationale, Paris.

THE KORAN

In addition to fragmentary non-Islamic sources, we know of Mohammed from Moslem biographies *(sira)* of the eighth and ninth centuries (based on earlier versions now lost), and from reports of his sayings and actions *(hadith)* collected in the ninth and tenth, but above all from the record of his teaching in the Koran, of which the first-hand evidence dates from shortly before 700.

The early chapters of the Koran are passionate and rhapsodic; but the subsequent part of the work, dating from Mohammed's later and more established years, passes to a calmer handling of the social problems that engaged his attention. His vehicle is prose, sometimes rhymed. He had a brief but astonishing literary tradition to draw upon, since in the course of the sixth century Arabic poetry had suddenly and elaborately developed its classical form over a wide region of northern and central Arabia. Moreover, at Okaz, not far from Mecca, a market was regularly held, at which poetry of many kinds was recited, and could be heard by Mohammed. Inspired by these austere yet richly brilliant models, he himself played on the deep-toned instrument of the expressive Arabic language with powerful boldness and wide emotional range: so that the Koran has always been looked upon as a model of style and eloquence.

The first of its hundred and fourteen chapters, the Opening, is a short prayer to God. The rest of the work is in the form of an address from God himself, speaking in his own person, and at times giving orders introduced by the imperative "Say!" These messages, Moslems believe, are the literal words of God, the essence of every communication He had previously sent to humanity—words which Mohammed had been chosen to transmit during a long series of trances, each chapter being a single revelation communicated to him by the archangel Gabriel at some time or other during the final twenty years of his life, and subsequently recorded without human interpolation.

And so the Koran provides a framework for the conduct of human affairs—not only in seventh-century Arabia, it was stressed, but everywhere from all eternity, and in every field of life. For Islam claims to supply a complete and exhaustive code for the whole of life, rejecting western distinctions between Church and State, between religion and politics, as illusory.

God, according to Mohammed, created each and every human being as his own deputy and

Mohammed and his teachings in the Koran were responsible for a complete change in philosophy and a new way of life for the Arabs. But his message was also spread by more secular means; the *ud* or lute was gradually reserved for the playing of exclusively Islamic music, and this meant that even the representation of the instrument *(top right)* took on religious associations. This miniature painting *(above)* is a later example of the use of illustrated manuscripts to spread a knowledge of the Islamic way of life.

This letter *(above)* is said to have been written by Mohammed in his own hand and to contain his seal. The addressee is the Lakhmid king of Hira (in northern Arabia)—a reminder that apart from writing the Koran, Mohammed became a political figure and virtually head of state.

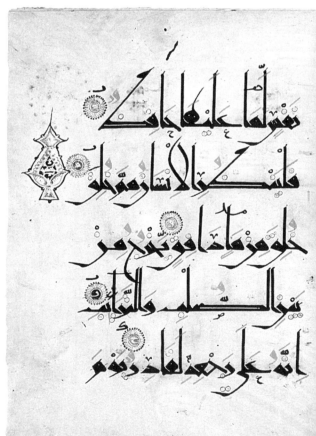

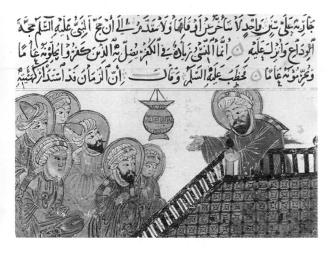

Praise the name of thy Lord the Most High,
Who hath created and balanced all things,
Who hath fixed their destinies and
  guideth them,
Who bringeth forth the pasture,
And reduceth it to dusky stubble,
We will teach thee to recite the Koran, nor
  aught shalt thou forget,
Save what God pleaseth; for he knoweth alike
  things manifest and hidden;
And we will make easy to thee
  our easy ways....

Koran, Sura 87.1 ff.

representative *(khalifa)*, so that they need no priests as interpreters—in the mosque, anyone could take the place of the Imam, who is only the "one placed before." God has also ensured that all men and women are provided with all the bounties and potentialities they need. But to make the best use of these gifts they require His guidance, and that is what the Koran, backed by a corpus of traditional social and legal usages *(sunna)*, provides.

The power of Islam lies in its total simplicity. It is faith reduced to its starkest elements, subjecting the speculative, contentious Judeo-Christian world to the swift and effective shock of a rigid, positive, all assertive dogma. It is a dogma that abolishes each and every distinction between one human being and another. All alike owe total, unquestioning obedience to the will of the One transcendent yet near and mightily active God, as interpreted by Mohammed. Among the Five Pillars, the Moslem's religious duties, this obedience is the first: "there is no God but God, and Mohammed is his Prophet." The other duties are of a practical nature: recitation of the five daily prayers, fasting in the month of Ramadan, payment of the tax for the poor, and if possible, a pilgrimage to Mecca *(hajj)* at least once in a lifetime. These were disciplines imposed in order to correct and dispel the social and spiritual anarchy that pervaded Arabian life.

The Koran devotes an especially large amount of attention to women. Moslems were permitted four lawful wives, and this was an improvement in the status of women, not a deterioration, since until Mohammed's time, in the Arab world, polygamy had been unrestricted. He himself kept his wives in segregation. But he did so because of their special status as wives of the Prophet, and denied that this personal practice need form a precedent —though it was copied.

Yet the Koran, true to the circumstances of its place and time, pronounced as follows: "Men are superior to women on account of the qualities with which God hath gifted the one above the other, and on account of the outlay they make from their substance for them. Virtuous women are obedient, careful, during the husband's absence, because God hath of them been careful. But chide those for whose refractoriness ye have cause to fear; remove them into beds apart, and scourge them: but if they are obedient to you, then seek not occasion against them: for aye, verily, God is High, Great!"

An ornate binding of the Koran dating from the ninth or tenth century; place of origin unknown.

Top left. Mohammed preaching at a pilgrimage; this manuscript illustration is from an Iranian copy of the *Chronology of Ancient Peoples* by Al-Biruni.

Left: Koran from Iraq or Iran, eleventh century. Shown are verses 1–9 of Sura 86, beginning: "In the name of Allah, the Compassionate, the Merciful. By the heaven, and by the nightly visitant! Would that you knew what the nightly visitant is! It is the star of piercing brightness. For every soul there is a guardian watching over it....." The lettering is of the eastern variety of Kufic. Collection of Prince Sadruddin Aga Khan, Geneva.

73

O believers! a Fast is prescribed to you as it was prescribed to those before you, that ye may fear God, for certain days....
As to the month Ramadan in which the Koran was sent down to be man's guidance, and an explanation of that guidance, and of that illumination, as soon as any one of you observeth the moon, let him set about the fast; but he who is sick, or upon a journey, shall fast a like number of other days. God wisheth you ease, but wisheth not your discomfort, and that you fulfill the number of days, and that you glorify God for his guidance, and that you be thankful.

Koran, Sura 2.79—81

Persian miniature of Moslems on horseback celebrating the end of the month of fasting, Ramadan, observance of which is one of the "five pillars" of Islamic faith. The fast was created by Mohammed at Medina (ca. 623) where he had been ridiculed by Jewish rabbis for his ignorance of their faith. Ramadan replaced their single Day of Atonement and the direction of prayer was changed from Jerusalem to Mecca. Bibliothèque Nationale, Paris.

THE CONQUEST OF THE EAST

After the death of the Prophet, the rulers of Islam for many centuries to come were the Caliphs, to whom it was held that his religious and political leadership had been deputed. The earliest of the line were chosen from among his oldest and most faithful followers. The first, Abu Bakr (632–634), father of one of Mohammed's wives Aisha, was only elected to the office after prolonged argument. He was a spiritual, kindly man of unfaltering resolve and unruffled calm: and these qualities saved Islam, because his immediate task, which he successfully accomplished, was to deal with a threatened break-up of the precariously achieved unity of Arabia. The further expeditions he planned outside the peninsula did not materialize, but the reign of his successor Omar I (634–644), an ardent and impulsive yet sagacious man, witnessed conquests of gigantic size.

Gradual emigrations from Arabia had been taking place for centuries, under economic

Right: The courtyard of the Great Mosque built by Ibn Tulun in Cairo after Egypt, in the ninth century, had become independent of the Abbasids under his dynasty; Cairo was embellished with important public buildings. This is one of the earliest examples of the pointed arch, some centuries before its exploitation in the west by architects inaugurating the Gothic style.

The aqueduct leading to the Ummayad palace of Khirbat al-Mafjah, near Jericho (Israel). It was built around the time of Hisham (724–743), when the caliphs were stabilizing the territories their predecessors had overrun; this area had formerly belonged to the Byzantine empire. Water was of fundamental importance throughout the East, as exemplified by this Nilometer *(right)* on Rhoda Island, Cairo. The annual rise of the Nile was proclaimed throughout Egypt—the records for the period between A.D. 622 and 1522 are nearly complete.

great mosque. Equally important colonies were established in Iraq, at Kufa and Basra. As for Persia, its conquest ultimately changed the entire character of the Arab empire and movement, because that non-Semitic, Iranian country, despite its unique future contributions to Islamic civilization, could never really be brought into line.

And indeed, once these decisive wars had been fought and won, complete assimilation of the conquered countries was not sought by the Arabs. "If God had so desired," declared the Koran, "he would have made all humanity a single people." It is true that polytheists and idol-worshippers were given the choice between Islam and the sword. But the forcible conversion of Christians and Jews was never

pressure. But this was a centrifugal explosion of a wholly unprecedented order. For Khalid al-Walid conquered the whole of Syria and Palestine from the Byzantines, and Amr ibn al-As took Egypt; while Omar's other generals simultaneously obliterated the empire of the Sassanian Persians, annexing Iraq and Iran after victory at Kadisiya (637).

Syria, although its Arab settlers were at first a very small minority, was soon to become the capital of the new empire. Egypt, though it was at first wholly alien and always retained its own individuality, became gradually Arabized. The process was assisted by the foundation of a military colony or encampment at Al-Fustat (Cairo), together with a

Cyprus and inflicted a heavy defeat on the Byzantine fleet (655). The eastern borders, too, were advanced as far as Herat in Afghanistan. However, the heavy losses and experiences incurred in these operations led to revolts, and Othman, at the age of eighty, was assassinated by men from Egypt and Iraq. The risings created a grim precedent and weakened the prestige of the monarchy as a bond of imperial unification.

The consequences were immediately seen in the reign of Mohammed's cousin and son-in-law Ali, who was elected Caliph in Othman's place (656–661). Although loyal and pious and magnanimous, Ali lacked statesmanship and youthful vigor; and the circumstances of his accession caused the empire's First Civil War. For Ali's accession was not recognized by Moawiya, the governor of Syria, who was related to Othman and vowed to exact retribution for his death. After a preliminary battle —which went in Ali's favor—the two armies

Below left: Mosaic from the bathroom of the Great Hall of the palace of Khirbat al-Mafjah, showing how much the Moslem artists of this region owed to their non-Islamic predecessors. This and other mosaics in the palace are derived from the formal, geometric patterns of mosaics in the Christian churches of Syria.

Coptic (Egyptian) painting of Christ. The Arab caliphs, though favoring Islam, did not interfere with the internal affairs of the Coptic church—in contrast to some of the previous Byzantine rulers who had tried to impose their own, Orthodox version of Christianity. The Coptic language, however, which had flourished before the Moslem invasion, was quickly replaced by Arabic.

countenanced. All they were required to do was to pay a land tax and a poll tax to their Arab rulers, and provide them with contributions in kind to support their garrisons, and then they could keep and cultivate their lands in peace.

After Omar had been murdered at Medina, the Caliphate passed to Othman of the Ummaya, a branch of the Quraysh (644–656). The first member of the old Meccan aristocracy to hold this office, Othman was indolent and nepotistic, but his commanders remained active. They probed the Byzantine frontiers in Asia Minor, and for the first time the Arab empire possessed navies. Manned on a voluntary basis by Syrians and Egyptians, they occupied

stood face to face at Siffin in northern Syria (657); but then they agreed to submit their dispute to arbitration. As a result, Ali seems to have been deposed. But meanwhile the puritanical group of the Kharijites (*khawarij*, seceders) intervened. These fanatics, who refused to recognize any dynastic (or racial) privilege, and were destined to disturb the Islamic world for a century to come, declared that the arbitration was an act of treason to the only possible arbitrator —who was God himself. Then they attempted to put both Moawiya and Ali to death; but it was only Ali they succeeded in striking down, making him the martyr of the Shi'ite movement, of which more will be said later.

FROM ARABIA TO EUROPE

Right: The minaret of the Great Mosque at Kairouan, Tunisia, from which the call to prayer is given five times a day according to Moslem practice. Kairouan was founded in 670 as an advance camp for the Arab invaders of north Africa.

The mosque at Cordoba in Spain *(above)*, at the western limits of the Arab empire, of which the construction began in 785.

Top: Ummayad painting depicting six monarchs defeated in the advance of Islam; the first four are identified in Greek and Arabic as the Byzantine emperor, the king of the Sassanian Persians, King Roderic of the Visigoths in Spain, and the king of Aksum (Ethiopia).

Moawiya I (661–680), founder of the Ummayad dynasty, had already been proclaimed Caliph before Ali's death. His reign witnessed a huge renewal of Arab expansionist enterprise. First, the armies of Egypt under the legendary hero Okba ibn Nafi began the invasion of the Maghreb (northwest Africa). Seizing Tunisia, the granary of the west, they founded a garrison city at Kairouan (670), a convenient military base situated between the great coastal city of Carthage, which had not yet been captured, and the numerous indigenous Berbers, who held out in the Atlas mountains of the south. Then, in 680–681, Okba undertook his epic March to the Sea —the Atlantic Ocean.

At the same time Moawiya was directing other armies against the Byzantine empire's Asian frontier as well, and for four years he subjected Constantinople itself to annual sieges, though they proved a costly failure. In the far east of his territories, however, he was much more successful, and garrison cities were founded in Afghanistan and Baluchistan serving as bases for further expeditions to the territories round about.

Moawiya was one of the most gifted statesmen and organizers the Arabs have produced. Relying on the powerful army in Syria, where he had previously won a great reputation as governor, he married a woman belonging to the strongest of the Syrian tribes and established his capital at Damascus, which commanded many routes and a good supply of water. So Arabia's political primacy, already threatened by Ali when he moved his capital to Kufa in Iraq, was finally lost. But Moawiya's choice of Syria as the nucleus of his empire was unpopular among the Iraqis. Nor did the traditionalists —or adherents of Ali —feel pleased when Moawiya set aside the previous tradition of an elective Caliphate by making his followers take an oath of allegiance to his son Yazid I (680–683), so that his own aristocratic family, the Ummayads, was converted into a hereditary dynasty.

It was just after Yazid's accession that Ali's son Hussein was killed at Karbala, giving the Shi'ite movement a new emotional impetus. Then Abd al-Malik (685–705) had to fight a series of dangerous and disintegrative civil wars. But finally he was victorious, and the unity of the empire and authority of the Caliphate were brilliantly restored. Next, with the aid of an administrator of genius, Al-Hajjaj, Abd al-Malik set about the task of

reconstructing the crumbling state organism into a centralized monarchy. Then, freed from his internal problems, he resumed the advance in north Africa, where his army and fleet captured Carthage (697–698), so that the whole country was in Moslem hands. The entire balance of power in the Mediterranean had now been shifted; and having already destroyed one of the two great states in the region, that of the Persians, the Arabs had also, not for the first time, gravely impaired the power of the other, the Byzantine empire. Abd al-Malik's son Al-Walid I (705–715), although himself an indolent man, enjoyed an

even more spectacular reign, during which Ummayad conquests reached their furthest extent. In Asia Minor, Arab armies broke across the Byzantine frontiers with impunity. Beyond the eastern borders of their empire, the great commander Kutaiba ibn Muslim crossed the River Oxus and overran gigantic territories: Bokhara, Samarkand, and Tashkent were captured, and in 712 his armies even advanced as far as Kashgar on the frontier of China. In the very same year, too, another general, Mohammed ibn al-Kasim, a cousin of Al-Hajjaj, started out from Basra in southern Iraq and marched all the way to Pakistan,

Bottom left: The Great Mosque at the Ummayad capital of Damascus. When the Moslems occupied the city in 635, they converted part of the Christian basilica of St. John to their own use. However, in 706 Al Walid I demolished the church and built this new mosque. It was originally covered with panels of marble and mosaics; but most were destroyed by fire in 1893.

The spread of Islam: in dark brown, the Arabia of Mohammed, and in the lighter shade, the sphere of Islamic rule in A.D. 750 before the fall of the Ummayads.

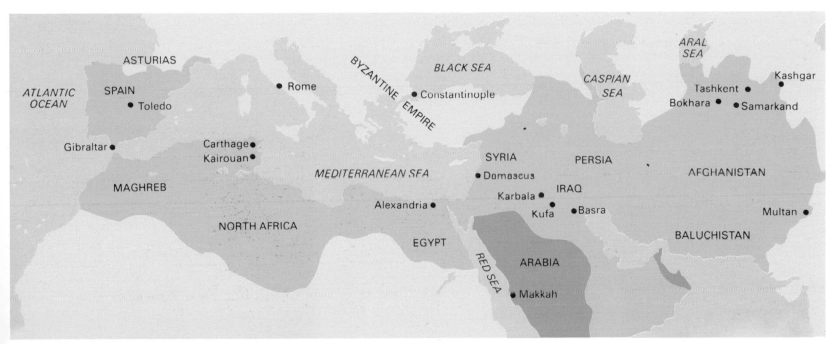

where he fought a victorious campaign against the local monarch and took Multan. Meanwhile, on the coast of north Africa, the governor Musa ibn Nusair set up his freed slave Tarik as local governor of Tangier. Thereupon Tarik, with a small army mostly consisting of Berber soldiers, crossed over into Spain, landing near Gibraltar, which still bears his name (Jebel Tarik). The Visigothic rulers of the country attempted to bar his way, but their defeat at Guadalete on the River Barbate (Wadi Bakka) in 711 spelt the end of effective resistance. Their capital, Toledo, opened its gates to Tarik, and in the following year Musa himself arrived and completed the conquest of the country, except Asturias in the north where a small Visigothic state continued to hold out.

The Mausoleum of Ismail (d. 907)—of the Samanid house, the first Persian dynasty to rule in Islam—at Bokhara, in what is now the Uzbek Republic of the Soviet Union. Previously occupied by the western Turks, Bokhara had fallen to the Ummayads in 676, followed gradually by the rest of Transoxiana, but broke away from the Abbasid dominions in the ninth century.

79

THE UMMAYAD EMPIRE

The ever increasing power concentrated in the Caliphs' court at Damascus compelled them to assume more and more the character and appearance of kings. Only a centralized monarchy could govern an expanding world empire, and in order to achieve such a system they made use of administrative and economic arrangements they already found installed, thus maintaining a much more elaborate system of government than any Arabs had ever thought of before. For, once they had become an imperial nation, they were obliged to set up a stable and workable state—a concept of which the tribal society of the Arabs, knowing no citizens but only kinsmen united by blood-ties, had no understanding; indeed, their language even lacked a word to describe such an idea.

Nevertheless, the Ummayad regime remained firmly in the hands of the Arabs—or rather, of their warrior aristocracy, a hereditary,

environments they had invaded, contributing their religion and language, but taking all else from the peoples they had conquered.

In particular, their annexations brought great supplies of gold and other valuables, which made many leading Arabs very rich indeed. They invested their fortunes in land and built up a huge new area of free trade. These commercial activities were greatly supported and encouraged by an Arab gold coinage, of fine purity. Developed by Abd al-Malik—allegedly because Byzantine pieces with the figure of Christ were unacceptable—this Islamic currency came to rival or even exceed the Byzantine coinage as a massive international medium of exchange.

The ruins of many castles of the Ummayads have been discovered in Syria, but it is their great mosques, modeled on the Prophet's Mosque at Medina, which are the most notable monuments of their civilization. The

Qusayr Amra, a hunting lodge built in the reign of Al-Walid I (705–715) in the middle of the desert some forty miles from Amman (Jordan). Ruins of no less than thirty palaces of the Ummayad caliphs have been found in Syria. The establishment of such lavish residencies (in countries outside Arabia) was a far cry from the tribal societies of the Arabs less than two centuries earlier.

Above right: The depiction of this female figure by a Syrian artist illustrates the last efflorescence of the old Hellenistic style common to many of the Qusayr Amra reliefs, of which this is one.

segregated social elite, which could only be entered by birth. Its members formed a supreme military caste: all were liable to military service, and all received stipends from the state, since Arabs traditionally lived off loot and did not pay taxes. These dominant noblemen, unregenerate, articulate, self-confident, adjusted readily to all the varying societies and

Dome of the Rock at Jerusalem was built by Abd al-Malik as a sort of rival Kaaba, incorporating the rock where Abraham was said to have offered his son Isaac for sacrifice and where Mohammed was believed to have ascended to heaven. A centralized structure ringed by two octagonal ambulatories, the building is surmounted by a graceful wooden

dome on a high drum, adapted from Syrian designs, and decorated by formal mosaics in which Byzantine and Persian motifs are elegantly combined. But the Ummayads' principal contribution to architecture was the longitudinal, congregational mosque, seen at its greatest in Al-Walid's building at Damascus. It was erected on the site of a Byzantine church of John the Baptist; and in the mosque, too, the superb mosaics were the work of Byzantine craftsmen. The depiction

Verily we have revealed to thee as we revealed
to Noah and the Prophets after him, and as
we revealed to Abraham, and Ismail, and
Isaac, and Jacob, and the tribes, and Jesus,
and Job, and Jonah, and Aaron, and
Solomon; and to David gave we Psalms.
O men! now hath an apostle come to you with
truth from your Lord. Believe then, it will
be better for you. But if ye believe not, then,
all that is in the Heavens and the Earth is
God's; and God is Knowing, Wise!

Koran, Sura 4.160 ff.

The regime of the Ummayads was far more tolerant of minorities than most governments in the west, and the Arabs were not a proselytizing race. Nevertheless, the foreign men and women who became converts to Islam were numerous, since this was obviously the best way to share in the profits of empire. And in due course these converts, the *mawali*, were to assume a dominant position in the Islamic world. In dealing with the *mawali*, Ummayad policy was not sufficiently imaginative. True, officially speaking, Islam made all its converts equal. But in reality things did not work out like that. The Arabs were too sure of their own superior status to give other people full equality, so that even after the non-Arabs had been converted, they still remained socially and economically inferior. And the Ummayads did not dare entrust important administrative functions into their hands. In consequence, they gradually became alienated. Many turned to dissident activities—and to the Shi'ite theology which encouraged such rebellious practices.

Yet the major significance of the Ummayad state remained. It had wholly replaced the empire of the Sassanian Persians, and had, in addition, substituted its rule for that of the

Mosaic *(left)* from the palace of the Ummayad caliph Hisham (724—743) near Jericho. The artists who made these mosaics were probably Byzantine Greeks. The Ummayad rulers, far from destroying the long-established economy, culture, and art of the lands they had conquered, merely adapted these to suit their own particular needs and ideas.

Overleaf: The octagonal Dome of the Rock, Jerusalem, completed in A.D. 691/2. It was built under the aegis of Abd al-Malik at a time when civil strife prevailed in the southern part of the empire and the pilgrimage to Mecca was often impossible; believers could instead make two circuits of this mosque in Jerusalem. The Rock is believed to be not only the site of Solomon's first Temple, but also the scene of the Night Journey of Mohammed (Koran, Sura 17). The magnificence of the building itself was at least partly designed to overshadow the Christian Church of the Holy Sepulcher, which Abd al-Malik feared would draw too much of the attention of his co-religionists away from Islam.

of figures was forbidden by Islamic rules; but these mosaics show that even without them the art could achieve a rich and distinctive beauty all its own. The square towers at the corners of the buildings, imitating the towers of Christian churches, are forerunners of Islamic minarets, of which the oldest surviving example is at Kairouan in Tunisia.

Byzantines—and others in the West—over enormous areas. Moreover, it had not replaced their regimes by a desert, but by a civilization possessing many positive and original qualities, and borne on the wings of a mighty new religion.

Another example of the interior decorations of the palace of Qusayr Amra, but this time in a quite different style from that shown on the opposite page. This fresco was skillfully painted to achieve a three-dimensional effect.

THE SHI'AS

The biggest rift in the Ummayad harmony was the work of the Shi'as. In the first place, the assassination of their hero, the caliph Ali, in 661 had given the dead man a new and enormous posthumous importance. The Shi'a—meaning "party," the party of Ali—claimed and claim that he ought to have become Caliph much earlier, indeed immediately after the death of Mohammed, who in the last year of his life had appointed him, they believe, as his trustee and successor. In consequence his three forerunners in the Caliphate, championed by the Orthodox (Sunni), must, according to Ali's followers, be regarded as usurpers, and he himself as the first legitimate ruler after the Prophet himself. The Shi'ites also rejected the Sunni view that the Caliphate was elective, pronouncing it instead to be an office conferred by God—upon Ali. His supposed grave at Najaf, near Kufa, is still visited today by thousands of pilgrims who venerate him as a half-divine saint and curse his supplanters.

Nineteen years after his death, his second son, Hussein, tried to assert the claims of his family once again, but was hacked to pieces with

Top right: A *mihrab*, or ornamental niche, inside the Great Mosque of the Abbasid caliph Al-Mansur at Baghdad, indicating the direction of Mecca toward which the faithful turn in prayer. Al-Mansur overcame a menacing revolt by the Shi'ites. The stucco decoration (*top left*) is from the caliphs' palace of Khirbat al-Mafjah, in a style borrowed, like that of so much of early Islamic art, from the Byzantine Greeks. The fort of Ukhaidir (*above*), built in the desert near Karbala, may have belonged to Ibn Musa, a powerful court official who was exiled by the caliph Al-Mahdi and became governor of Kufa in 778. The nude female bather (*right*) from the palace of Qusayr Amra shows how the representation of figures, though banned from public and religious buildings, was widely tolerated in private apartments, including those of the caliphs themselves.

seventy-two of his supporters at Karbala in the same region. The Shi'ites saw Hussein's death as a second martyrdom, which they could never forgive and perpetually sought to avenge. One of its immediate consequences was political: the non-Arab converts to Islam, the *mawali*—especially in Iraq and Persia—flocked to the party of Ali and Hussein, seeing this Shi'a cause as a means to further their own drive to secure equality with the Arabs. In the later years of the seventh century, they found a leader of genius in Mukhtar, who became one of the principal pioneers of the authoritarian Shi'ite theology of the future, but was killed in 687.

*When his Lord made trial of Abraham by
commands which he fulfilled, He said,
"I am about to make thee an Imam to
mankind": he said, "Of my offspring also":
"My covenant," said God, "embraceth not
the evil doers."
And remember when we appointed the Holy
House as man's resort and safe retreat, and
said, "Take ye the station of Abraham for
a place of prayer": And we commanded
Abraham and Ismail, "Purify my house for
those who shall go in procession round it,
and those who shall abide there for devotion,
and those who shall bow down and prostrate
themselves."*

Koran, Sura 2.118–119

Subsequently the movement entered a phase of social revolutionary violence, and all sorts of ancient eastern beliefs were mobilized in the struggle against the Caliphate, including a variety of mystic and millenarian ideas. In particular, the Shi'ites came to believe that there is a sinless, infallible Imam in every successive epoch, and that each of them is Mohammed's successor to whom God has entrusted the sole guidance of his servants; some believers even went so far as to assert that Ali and the Imams were actual incarnations of the Godhead.

The Ismaili branch of Shi'a, led by the Aga Khan, recognizes seven of these Imams in the course of history, but the main body of the Shi'ites acknowledges twelve, starting with Ali, continuing with his descendants and ending with Mohammed al-Muntazar al-Mahdi (the Expected and Rightly Guided One), who disappeared in about 873/4 and is preserved unseen against his Second Coming; he is the "hidden Imam" still awaited by the faithful and destined to restore justice and righteousness to the world. These "Twelvers" have been the official church of Persia since the sixteenth century, and possess strong followings

in other countries too, particularly Iraq. The death of Hussein at Karbala is still mourned every year on its anniversary, when a powerful drama is staged to reenact the event, and the faithful flog themselves in a rite of atonement. Christianity has often been rent by grave divisions between Catholic, Orthodox, and Protestant; this has effectively prevented it from becoming a world power, and even now steps toward unification are only faltering. But Islam has been in the same position since the deaths of Ali and Hussein. It is true that in the early days the Sunni and Orthodox were dominant, but the rift between Sunni and Shi'a has persisted, and is at its height today.

Far left: Statue of an Ummayad caliph from the palace of Khirbat al-Mafjah, ca. 744. Perhaps the builder of the palace, and subject of the statue, was the eccentric Yazid III. In this period the centrifugal forces threatening the unity of the Arab world, including the threats posed by the Shi'ites and Kharijites, increased in number and intensity.

Center: The entrance gate at Qasr al-Hair al-Sharki in the Syrian desert. Through holes in the floor of the gallery projecting over the entrance could be poured boiling oil—an innovation transmitted to the West by eleventh-century Crusaders.

This statue of an enthroned Ummayad ruler at the Syrian palace of Qasr al-Hair al-Gharbi, southwest of Palmyra, probably portrays Hisham, in whose reign (724–743) the palace was built. Hisham overcame many difficulties, including a Shi'a rebellion in Iraq, and placed the government of the empire on a sounder basis.

THE ABBASIDS

The Ummayad tide began to turn back when the armies of Suleiman (715–717) suffered an even more disastrous repulse from the walls of Constantinople than their similar failure half a century earlier. Hisham (724–743), too, suffered a setback at the hands of the Byzantines; and then the forces of his general Abd al-Rahman al-Ghafiki, who had advanced from Spain into France, were defeated by Charles Martel at the battle of Poitiers (732)—a rebuff which marked the limit of the northern expansion of the Arabs, although they did not leave France immediately. Then followed the reign of the last of the Ummayad Caliphs, Marwan II. He was a man of ability and resolution, but came too late to save his disintegrating regime and was overthrown. The coup was led by a secret, subversive organization which had been in existence for forty

dynasty, which was to rule for five hundred years. The leader of the rising that set him in power, Abu Muslim, was a Persian slave, and the numerous non-Arab *mawali*, including Shi'ites, who flocked to his ranks and became pillars of his Caliphate included many people of that race.

The energetic and ruthless Al-Mansur (754–775) consolidated the power of the new royal house. As a sign that a new era had begun, Al-Mansur established a new imperial capital at the Iraqi market town of Baghdad on the Tigris (762), beside a canal which linked it to the Euphrates. Created originally as a garrison headquarters, Baghdad was soon to become a uniquely cosmopolitan and civilized center, urbane, refined, and luxurious, comparable even to Constantinople. This definitive establishment of the capital in Iraq, homeland of

The objects depicted on this and the opposite page show a few of the remarkable artistic achievements of the Arab world under the rule of the Abbasids. Among the examples of stonework are *(above)* the Tarik-khana Mosque in Damgan, Persia, 750–786, and *(above right)* the arcades of the later Abbasid palace in Baghdad, "the City of Peace," Iraq. Textile manufacture was well developed in this period, as shown by this fragment *(right)* of linen and silk. The inscription begins: "In the name of God, the Compassionate, the Merciful. Thanks be to God the ruler of the world," a reflection of the pervasive influence of religion in all aspects of life and art.

years under the descendants of Mohammed's uncle Abbas. One of these men, Abu'l-Abbas, was now proclaimed Caliph (750), and the Ummayad house at Damascus had fallen.

The accession of Abu'l-Abbas took place in an atmosphere of sanguinary terror and treachery. But these events inaugurated the Abbasid

the ancient sacred autocracies of Babylon and Assyria, accentuated the Abbasid tendency to monarchical despotism. These rulers were no longer the approachable sheiks of the past, but divinely authorized despots flanked by ministerial staffs and supported by a salaried bureaucracy and regular armed forces.

Bronze ewer from a grave in upper Egypt, an example of the luxurious ware, greatly influenced by the Sassanian forms and styles, which was used at the tables of the Arab aristocracy. The ewer is said to have belonged to the last Ummayad caliph Marwan II (744—750) when he was making his last stand against his Abbasid pursuers. Museum of Islamic Art, Cairo.

Above: Ivory Persian chessman, eighth or ninth century, showing an armed rider of the Arab armies. Chess had apparently been learnt from India by the Sassanian Persians in the sixth century, and later became known to the Arabs, who in turn transmitted the game, directly or indirectly, to various parts of Europe.

However, relying as they did upon the *mawali* for their support, the Abbasids made a deliberate endeavor to found their policy no longer on the interests of the Arabs alone, but instead on the universalist principles of Islamic piety, based on faith and not on race. Having come to power on the crest of a religious movement, they stressed their spiritual authority: for, once ethnic Arab supremacy had become blurred, religious unity and conformity was the only conceivable foundation for the regime. So now the Shi'ites, however much they had done to raise the new dynasty to power, found themselves dropped. For the Abbasids decided that only the pure (Sunni) orthodoxy was stable enough to knit the empire together.

This was the time when Islamic law *(sharia)* took on its systematic form. Founded on the Koran and on the traditions and on *ijma* or Universal Consent (the belief that the practice of the Islamic world is what the majority

Right: Miniature from the *Makamat* of Al-Hariri, a historical work of the twelfth century depicting everyday life in the eastern towns. This scene shows the public library in Hulwan, near Baghdad; the books are on the shelves in the background.

Above: Abbasid coins of the eighth and ninth centuries. On the left is a silver dirhem (from "drachma") issued at Nishapur—one of the more than sixty mints extending as far as Balkh in northeastern Khorasan (N.E. Persia). Such coins have been found as far away as Viking Scandinavia. On the right is a gold dinar of Al-Mutawakkil (847–860), the reverse showing a dromedary, a nostalgic recollection of the remote desert origins of the Arab Bedouin. Indeed, the first conquering armies of the Arabs had consisted of tribesmen mounted on these beasts, as shown in this miniature *(right)*.

believe or want it to be), the Sharia was not only a legal code but a total, unifying way of life—Mohammed's religious and social doctrines cast into practical shape. Among the four schools of law that became particularly prominent, the earliest, favored by the Abbasids, was the Iraqi school established by Abu Hanifa (d. 767). Lawyers and theologians attained a new importance in the community. And literary personages, too, became prominent. The first great Arabic poet among the Persians was the blind Bashshar ibn Burd (d. 784). In the eighth and ninth centuries, splendid Persian Korans were made at Basra and Kufa. The pursuit of knowledge was encouraged by the use of paper, manufactured at Baghdad from 793. Physicians of the court—many of them Nestorian Christians—translated Greek scientific works into Arabic.

These were all activities which bore witness to the emergence of a powerful, cultured middle class in the Abbasid empire. Among them, a great quantity of traders, of many races, played an important part. Thousands of Arab coins have been found as far afield as Sweden; and goods came from China along the caravan route to Baghdad, and then down the Tigris and Euphrates to the seaport of Basra. Strong connections were also formed with India, from which the use of "Arabic" numerals was learned, either through the translation of a Sanskrit treatise ordered by Caliph Al-Mansur

in 773, or perhaps by way of Islamic Spain. Decimal and cipher systems, too, were imports from Indian sources.

Under Harun al-Rashid (786–809), the most renowned of the Abbasids, the empire reached the height of its power and prosperity, and Al-Mamun (813–833) notably gave particular encouragement to science and philosophy.

Yet during those very reigns, and in the century to come, the peripheral territories—north Africa, Sicily, eastern Iran—although remaining Islamic, broke away from the Abbasids (as Spain had already), until by the end of the millennium their rule had shrunk to a small area around Baghdad: and Arab unity has never yet been established again.

These three Persian plates display the wide range of styles developed under the Abbasid caliphs. From left to right: Samanid pottery from Khorasan, tenth century; a silver gilt dish inscribed in Pahlevi, seventh to eigthth century; and glazed pottery from Nishapur, ninth century. The plate on the left illustrates the incorporation of Moslem philosophy into artistic works—the inscription reads: "Whosoever shall testify his faith, will be raised up high, and whatever occupies his mind, he gets accustomed to. Blessed be the possessor."

Left: A trading boat on the Euphrates: Arab manuscript of the school of Baghdad (thirteenth century). The Abbasids had enormously developed near and middle eastern commerce, and contacts with the Far East were extensive. Baghdad remained the capital of a (greatly reduced) Abbasid state until 1258, when it was captured and sacked by the Mongol Hulagu, grandson of Genghis Khan. Bibliothèque Nationale, Paris.

ISLAMIC SPAIN

Coin *(right)* of the Spanish Ummayad ruler Abd al-Rahman II (822–852), under whom the wealthy Cordoba court cultivated Arabic literature and exquisite refinement. *Left:* Coin of his predecessor Al-Hakem I (796–822). The succession of the young king had been disputed, and a rebellion at Toledo, which was repressed with a savagery that caused the death of many of the city's Visigothic and other inhabitants, obliged him to recruit many professional soldiers (often Slavs or Berbers), imposing severe taxes in order to pay for them.

Opposite page: The first Great Mosque of Cordoba, built by Abd al-Rahman I (756–788), founder of the independent Ummayad dynasty of Spain, on the site of a Roman temple and Visigothic church. In accordance with an idea suggested by Roman aqueducts, the two levels of horseshoe arches were erected to raise the height of the roof. The vaulting, perhaps of Persian origin, is supported on 665 marble columns—some plundered from Roman temples, others gifts from the Byzantine emperor Leo IV, who also sent his own workmen and sixteen tons of mosaic cubes.

The first generations of the Moslems in Spain led lives full of troubles. Within a space of thirty years, the suspicious Caliphs sent out more than twenty-three governors on the four-month journey from Baghdad. One reason for the Caliphate's anxious attitude was that the Berbers from north Africa, who had won the Arabs their Spanish victory, were afterward perpetually restive. Finally, they rose up in a great rebellion, which started in Africa and spread across the Straits of Gibraltar. It was this, more than anything else, that made it impossible for the Arabs to continue expansion in Gaul after the Franks had defeated them near Poitiers (732).

As for Spain, its southern regions were eventually pacified: yet the new ruling house of the Abbasids at Baghdad found it too hard to control the rapidly splintering groups of Arab chieftains in the country. It was at this stage that Abd al-Rahman I al-Dakhil ("the Immigrant"), the huge, red-haired son of an Ummayad prince and a Berber slave girl, first escaped from the Near East to north Africa, after the Abbasids had murdered his relatives, and then, with the help of his family's local clients, crossed over to Spain and established an Emirate on his own account, independent of the Caliphs and their north African deputies. Thus was the gradual disintegration of the hitherto united Arabic empire begun. By a blend of conciliation and ruthlessness, Abd al-Rahman I dealt with the grave problems that beset him on all sides. He set up his capital at the market city and river port of Cordoba, center of a rich agricultural hinterland. There he laid the foundations of the Great Mosque (786) which, after massive expansions in the following century, became the most spectacular Islamic building in the world, mesmerizing the eye with its seemingly limitless forest of twelve aisles of columns, rhythmically repeated in every direction.

In the course of his reign Abd al-Rahman I formed a professional army of forty thousand men, mainly Berbers and ex-slaves from Slavonic lands under Syrian and Berber officers. It was fortunate for him, however, that after Moslem rebels had invited Charlemagne to intervene in the country, the retiring Frankish army was ambushed by Gascons (Basques) and destroyed at a place traditionally located at Roncesvalles (778), immortalized in the *Song of Roland* (in which the Moslems, instead, are presented as the enemy).

The reign of Abd al-Rahman's grandson Al-Hakem I (796–822) witnessed increasing signs of the remarkable intellectual activity for which Moslem Spain was later to become famous. Plagued by rebellions, however, he had recourse to vigorous oppressions, which were so effective that Abd al-Rahman II (822–852) was able to reign for the most part in tranquillity—only broken by a Norwegian Viking raid on Seville (844). Then, under the authoritarian Abd al-Rahman III (912–961), Spain was the most prosperous, populous, orderly, and civilized country in western Europe.

It was the policy of the rulers to allow independent town councils to continue to function. They also improved slave conditions, and created peasant landholdings. Fertility was much increased by irrigation—and the country made huge economic advances. At the outset, a large region was placed under a Christian Visigothic count, and for the first century of Islamic rule the Catholic church of the Visigoths continued without very much hindrance. Christian converts to Islam were not particularly numerous, but there were many Mozarabs or "Arabizers," Christians who wished to resemble the Arabs and adopted most Arab customs. Although they were treated as inferior to Moslems, and not allowed to rise above them (or employ them as servants), this blend of the two cultures produced an extraordinarily rich cross-fertilization—as was to be seen in the centuries that followed.

THE ISLAMIC EXPLOSION

Carved ivory box made for Almoqueira, prince of Cordoba, in about 967. During the ninth and tenth centuries the brilliant Emirate of Cordoba—described as a Caliphate after 929—made the Hispanic peninsula one of the great cultural centers of the world. Musée du Louvre, Paris.

Right: The Great Mosque at Samarra, Iraq. Begun in 847 by the Abbasid caliph Al-Mutawakkil and constructed of burnt brick, it is the largest mosque in the Moslem world. The circular minaret with its external spiral ramp was inspired by the temples of the ancient Babylonians. In 836 Caliph Al-Mutasim was compelled by the disorderliness of his Turkish bodyguard to leave Baghdad, founding his new capital seventy miles away at Samarra. Half a century later, however, the capital was moved back to Baghdad, and Samarra declined and became uninhabited.

Within the brief span of three generations, the lightning advance of the Arabs had brought them and their religion all the way from Arabia to Europe.

These astonishing triumphs were gained by relatively small bodies of Arab tribesmen, mounted on camels and horses, fighting their best battles on the edges of the deserts where they felt at home. At first, expansion abroad seemed just a convenient substitute for the traditional petty raiding, which was no longer allowed. For such reasons Mohammed himself, at the time of his death, had been planning to march north into Syria. But when his successors began to carry out the plan, vast new horizons soon became apparent. The Byzantine provinces, and the Persian empire in its entirety, succumbed with surprising speed, because their former rulers had alienated their subject populations by crushing taxation, and had exhausted themselves by their wars against each other. And so the unknown Arabs abruptly terminated a millennium of Greco-Roman and Persian rule over territories of enormous size.

These Arabs won their victories all the more conclusively because they were inspired by a religious loyalty and fervor their enemies could not match. The rightness and necessity of a Holy War *(jihad)*—a term still often referred to by Moslem politicians today—was never far from their minds. The Koran is not explicit on the subject. Yet it suggests that the establishment of justice upon earth is one of the basic purposes for which God has sent his guidance and his Prophets. And it was an obvious deduction that this justice would only take effect when and where the Brotherhood of Islam was able to triumph. It is true that Mohammed stressed God's compassion and mercy—and that the Holy War does not figure formally among the Five Pillars. Nevertheless, the *jihad* was seen as a duty to be carried out by heart, tongue, hand, and sword: and those who fought in such a cause were assured of happiness in the world to come.

Fortified by this inspiration, the Arabs had turned the map of the Near East and the Mediterranean inside out, and it would remain that way for evermore.

The union between Arabism and Islam which enabled them to accomplish that feat seems a strange one, because these twin loyalties were based on different and indeed opposite premises—tribal and universal respectively. Yet the two concepts contrived to complement

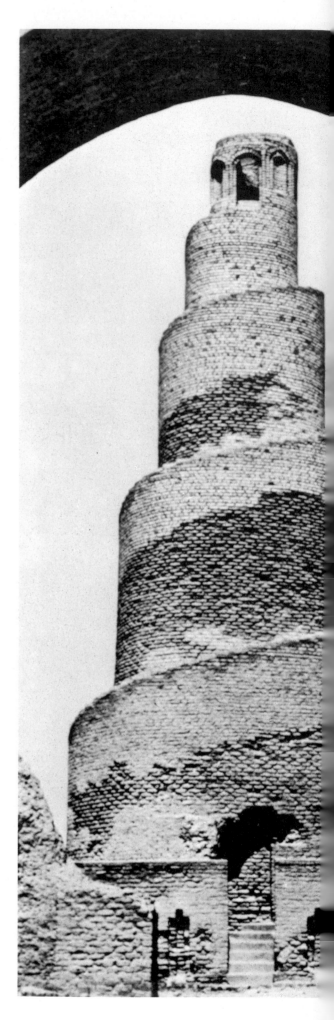

and support one another: which was the secret of the Arabs' phenomenal success. True, in addition to their problems with subjects of other races, they themselves were not entirely united within their own ranks; tribal conflicts persisted within the enormous realm. Yet such internal frictions remained secondary to the general picture, which displayed Moslem Arabs confronting and overwhelming the world.

And so they established the conditions in which their new Islamic civilization could be extended over territories of huge dimensions, including those where alien, urbanized cultures had flourished for century after century since ancient times. And, except in Spain and (now) Israel alone, the religion they introduced into the various lands they conquered still remains dominant in those countries today.

And fight for the cause of God against those who fight against you: but commit not the injustice of attacking them first: God loveth not such injustice:
And kill them wherever ye shall find them, and eject them from whatever place they have ejected you; for civil discord is worse than carnage: yet attack them not at the sacred Mosque, unless they attack you therein: but if they attack you, slay them. Such the reward of the infidels.
But if they desist, then verily God is Gracious, Merciful.
Fight therefore against them until there be no more civil discord, and the only worship be that of God: but if they desist, then let there be no hostility, save against the wicked.

Koran, Sura 2.186—189

The first expansion of the Moslems took them into the Near East where they shattered the might of the Sassanian Persians and took wide territories from the Byzantine empire, both these powers being severely weakened by their recent war. From these new lands come the two intricately fashioned objects below: a vial made from glass, which would have served to hold perfume, and a golden basin with bezoar. The Islamic *jihad* (Holy War) by no means had the same destructive influence on the conquered nations as is normally associated with war.

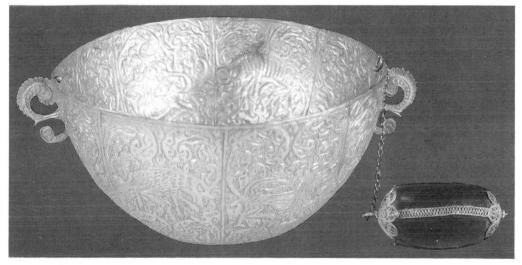

93

THE GERMAN KINGDOMS

Medieval Europe, with its Christian traditions, was born from the wreckage of the Roman empire. The waves of Germanic tribes that overran the western empire in the fifth century were soon settling and founding new states. Few of them, however, proved durable. Italy, for example, was to remain unstable for centuries to come. The Ostrogoths, who entered Italy soon after the removal of its last Roman emperor (A.D. 476), fell in turn to Byzantine and Lombard armies; but the papacy, all the while, was emerging as a secular power of considerable substance. The Visigoths in Spain were eventually forced to surrender the greater part of their territory to Moslem invaders. The most tenacious Germanic power proved to be the kingdom of the Franks. The Merovingian and Carolingian dynasties extended their domain over present-day France and much of Germany, stemmed the Islamic tide at Poitiers, and under Charlemagne, conquered the Lombards in northern Italy. Though Charlemagne's realm could not survive him intact, the institutions he fostered—his new western imperial regime, monasticism, feudalism, ecclesiastical schools, a strengthened papacy—were to exert a decisive influence upon the shape of European society.

Our Lord Jesus Christ
 has set you up as the ruler
of the Christian people,
 in power more excellent than the Pope
or Emperor of Constantinople,
 in wisdom more distinguished, in
the dignity of your rule
 more sublime. On you alone depends
the whole safety
 of the churches of Christ.

Alcuin to Charlemagne

The mosaic in the church of Sant'Apollinare Nuovo *(opposite),* built by the Ostrogothic king Theodoric in the early sixth century at his capital in Ravenna, shows the king's palace — symbol of the new power of the Germanic peoples who now came to dominate Europe following the fall of Rome. The most durable of their states was eventually established to the north, under the Franks, whose king Charlemagne (crowned emperor in Rome in 800) is believed to be the subject of this equestrian statue, from the cathedral treasury at Metz, Lorraine, now in the Louvre at Paris.

THE OSTROGOTHS IN ITALY

The first German ruler of Italy was the tribal chieftain Odoacer, commander of a mixed German army in the country. Removing the last Roman emperor at Ravenna in A.D. 476, he was hailed by his troops as king, taking over, for their benefit, one third of the land, mainly in the plains of the north and northeast. But he in turn was overthrown by the Ostrogoths.

These "bright Goths" were the eastern branch of the Gothic peoples. From Scandinavia, the country of their origin, they had found their way to the Ukraine, where they formed a huge, underdeveloped state. But then they started moving once again—and the eastern Roman (Byzantine) emperor Zeno (474–491) managed to divert them against the frontiers of the western empire instead of his own. Piling their families and possessions into wagons and driving their herds before them, some two hundred thousand of these people poured into Italy across the Julian Alps. Their leader was Theodoric, whose reign (493–526)

The Ostrogoths did not succeed in achieving a synthesis between their culture and that of the Romans: their jewelry, for instance, remained thoroughly Germanic. These two silver brooches, partially gilded and with niello adornments, from the Schmuckmuseum, Pforzheim, Germany, were made in about A.D. 500, soon after the beginning of the Ostrogothic regime in Italy. They were originally surmounted by five knobs, those in the middle taking the form of fantastic animal heads, which also appear at the lower extremities of the brooches.

The woman's gold make-up jar and silver spoon of early sixth-century date (left) were discovered at Desana in Lombardy. The jar was covered with forty-two amethysts of which only four remain. Museo Civico, Turin.

lasted for half the total duration of the Italian kingdom that they founded at this time. Theodoric massacred his fellow Germans in Odoacer's army and gave his own Ostrogoths their lands in addition to other territories in more southern parts of the peninsula. Yet after those initial convulsions his reign was so peaceful that, in retrospect, it came to be regarded as a golden age, and Theodoric was looked back upon as a monarch of humane,

magnanimous sensibility. For whereas the Ostrogoths constituted the army, he left the old civilian administration of the emperors intact, retaining its capital at Ravenna, and he worked for coexistence with the Romans. Since he and his Germans were Arian Christians—believing in the subordination of the Son to the Father—and were thus separated by a great religious gulf from the Catholic Roman population, internal peace was by no

Though it lay a few miles inland, in fairly swampy terrain, Ravenna had its port on the coast, known as Classis, shown in this mosaic from Sant'Apollinare Nuovo. The mosaic indicates that the port (originally established by Augustus) was well fortified, with guard-towers and formidable walls. Three ships are depicted, with curved prows and massive steering oars; one has its square sail spread.

The art of Italy following the downfall of the western Roman empire continued for some time to be strongly influenced by Byzantine styles, with infusions of varying strength from near eastern and Germanic sources. This detail from a diptych in the Kunsthistorisches Museum, Vienna, shows the sixth-century Ostrogothic queen Amalsuntha, daughter of Theodoric, regent for her son Athalaric, and wife of Theodahat.

Theodoric came to power in Italy following his defeat of Odoacer the Herulian in 493. His kingdom also included Sicily, Provence, and most of Switzerland, Austria, and Yugoslavia. His successors, in the following century, were suppressed

by Belisarius and Narses, the generals of Justinian I. This bronze coin of the Ostrogothic kingdom (Staatliche Museen, East Berlin) formed part of a currency bearing witness to the relative stability of Ostrogothic Italy in an otherwise violent age.

Further examples of Germanic jewelry from this period. The gilt bronze belt buckle with garnets and glass in multicolored cloisonné, a fifth-century work from Herpes (Charente, France; now in the British Museum, London), may have been the work of an Italian artisan working under the Ostrogoths. The middle piece is an Ostrogothic gold pendant, likewise with garnet and glass inlays, from a hoard found at Cesena, in the Romagna, south of Ravenna (Metropolitan Museum of Art, New York). The bronze buckle *(far right)* is also from a tomb in the Romagna (Germanisches Nationalmuseum, Nuremberg). The goldsmiths' styles in the various states of western Europe influenced each other in complex fashions, but often the inspiration still came from Italy.

The progress of Christianity has been marked by two glorious and decisive victories: over the learned and luxurious citizens of the Roman empire; and over the warlike barbarians of Scythia and Germany, who subverted the empire and embraced the religion of the Romans....

The life of Theodoric represents the rare and meritorious example of a barbarian who sheathed his sword in the pride of victory and the vigor of his age.

Edward Gibbon *(chapters 37, 39)*

means easy to achieve. But Theodoric displayed restraint and tolerance, directing his Ostrogothic counts to limit themselves to the problems of their own compatriots, and leave the Romans alone.

It could have been a promising balance; the Germans provided the vigor and public spirit and the Romans the skill and civilization. Yet that is not quite how Theodoric saw it. "An able Goth," he is believed to have said, "wants to be like a Roman: only a poor Roman would want to be like a Goth." And so, despite the

shock that this would be likely to cause, he imposed Roman law on the Ostrogoths—who thus, alone among the German peoples of western Europe, lost their own. Nevertheless, Ostrogoths and Romans were scarcely permitted to mix; and Theodoric perpetuated the Roman veto on intermarriage.

He extended his kingdom up to the Danube and throughout most of what is now Yugoslavia. He also put into practice a far-sighted aim of seeking permanent agreements with some of the other German states of Europe, under his own hegemony. Thus he helped to save the Visigoths from complete destruction

Byzantine ruler Justinian I determined to put a stop to the Ostrogothic defection. The war which resulted from this decision lasted for more than eighteen years, because the imperial commanders, Belisarius and Narses, found themselves inadequately supplied with reinforcements, since so many Byzantine troops were needed in the east. Besides, for much of the time the Ostrogoths had a talented, generous, and humane leader of their own, King Totila (541–552). Nevertheless, they finally succumbed to the Byzantine armies and were wiped out of national existence. They had collapsed because the Ostrogothic archer-infan-

Theodoric died with his kingdom still intact, and was buried in a specially built mausoleum at his capital, Ravenna *(below)*. The building represents an unusual hybrid, in which the exact artistic influences and antecedents remain a subject of dispute. Perhaps it is best considered simply as an original creation, de-

by the Franks, whom he did not allow to occupy the Mediterranean ports of France—though this prohibition could not be enforced for very long. In addition, although this also proved transient, he arranged a system of marriage alliances with several German dynasties. Thus Theodoric acted as an independent and powerful monarch. Yet, officially speaking, he was still a subject of the east Roman (Byzantine) empire: his titular overlord was the emperor Anastasius I, who defined and recognized his position, and alternately flattered and bullied him.

Once Theodoric was dead, however, the great

trymen were not quite a match for the Byzantine cavalry; but above all because Theodoric's plan to knit his German and Roman subjects together—separated as they were by religion and so much else—had never really achieved its aim: so that the Byzantines readily found an Italian fifth column. The country suffered incalculable damage in the course of these long wars.

signed, appropriately, for the founder of a new sort of state. The porphyry sarcophagus of Theodoric inside the mausoleum *(left)* was later broken open and his body desecrated by supporters of official Byzantine Catholicism, out of hatred for the Arian branch of Christianity to which he, like so many other Germanic leaders, had belonged. It had been Theodoric, however, who had established the Ostrogothic kingdom on a sound footing as a virtually independent state, despite the tenuous suzerainty of the Byzantine emperor, though his successors were not able to resist Justinian's reconquest.

A CULTURE IN TRANSITION

It was significant of the Ostrogoths' failure to set their stamp on Italy that the literary glories of their regime were purely Roman. They were provided by two Roman noblemen, Boethius and Cassiodorus, who did a great deal to keep alive the historical and scholarly traditions of the past and to give the dawning Middle Ages strong literary links with Roman antiquity. Benedict of Nursia also played a vital role at this time, as the most important molder of medieval monastic life. The Benedictine monasteries were to be instrumental in preserving much of classical learning throughout the Middle Ages.

Boethius, as Roman consul under the Ostrogothic regime in the year 510, detail from an ivory diptych, Museo Civico Cristiano, Brescia. *Center:* Miniature painting of Boethius' library, from a manuscript at Trinity Hall, Cambridge. *Far right:* The scribe Ezra, early eighth century, shown to illustrate the great tradition of passing on the learning of the past: Biblioteca Laurenziana, Florence.

BOETHIUS

The erudite Boethius (ca. A.D. 480–524) rose to the rank of consul—for the consuls of ancient Rome still survived under the Ostrogoths. Their king Theodoric, whose interest in learning was keen, made him head of

alternating with verse, the work investigates the comforts a philosopher can derive from his intellectual beliefs. Brave, moving, and impressively calm, the writer gave solace to countless thousands in the centuries that followed. Although he was probably a Christian, he does not discuss the consolation to be found in the Christian faith, concentrating entirely on pagan philosophical doctrine. He records that, although God

CASSIODORUS

Boethius' successor as head of the Ostrogothic civil service was another former consul, Cassiodorus (ca. 490–583), who, although perhaps of Syrian origin, likewise belonged to the Roman aristocracy. After the death of Theodoric he was promoted still further, but retired in 537 and dedicated himself to learning and religion. Following a stay at Constantinople, where he gained considerable influence, Cassiodorus returned to Italy—by this time in Byzantine hands—and established on his Calabrian family estates a hillside hermitage, Castellum, and the monastery of Vivarium (*vivaio,* fishpond). At Vivarium intellectual activity was stressed to a degree that the monastic life had never previously known. Above all, the monks copied Greek and Latin manuscripts day and night, so that the monastery, although it only existed for a century and a half, played a great part in the preservation of ancient books for the benefit of countless subsequent generations.

Cassiodorus' *Institutes of Divine and Secular Literature,* designed to educate his monks, was a book that received continuous Christian attention throughout the Middle Ages. He also wrote a summary of Roman history *(Chronica).* Its achievement was to provide a compendium of all the worldly sciences, so that Cassiodorus joined Boethius as a transmitter of classical civilization to pos-

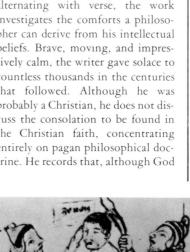

Above: Lady Philosophy appears to Boethius in his prison cell, from an eleventh or twelfth-century manuscript, Biblioteca Nacional, Madrid. *Above right:* The Muses of the four great arts, Staatsbibliothek, Bamberg, Germany. Finally, the Sects of Philosophy: Trinity Hall, Cambridge.

the civil service and showed him marked favor. However, Boethius later fell into extreme official disfavor, accused of conspiring against the king in favor of the Byzantine emperor (Justin I). Thrown into prison in 522 at the fortress-town of Pavia (Ticinum), he was executed two years later.

In prison, under sentence of death, Boethius wrote his renowned *Consolation of Philosophy.* Cast in the form of a dialogue between himself and Philosophy, conducted in Latin prose

governs the world, right does not always prevail. And yet his philosophical meditations leave him with hope.

Boethius also wrote many other philosophical works, in addition to treatises on music, geometry, and arithmetic. Adept in logic, an expert Latinizer of Greek technical terms, he preserved and handed down vast portions of the classical heritage.

The earliest known portrait of St. Benedict of Nursia, in the catacomb of Hermetes at Rome, sixth century. *Far right:* The restored monastery of Monte Cassino, after the second World War. *Below:* Christ in Majesty, miniature painting from the Codex Amiatinus, Biblioteca Laurenziana, Florence. *Below right:* In this miniature from a manuscript at Monte Cassino, St. Benedict is shown with an abbot of the monastery, which was the most important of his foundations.

terity at a time when most of Italy was about to be submerged by destruction. An equally important work was his *History of the Goths*, which has survived in the *Getica* of the German historian Jordanes;

although this is only an abridgment of the original work, it still contains a mass of important information. Cassiodorus' Gothic history set itself the noble aim of reconciling the Goths and Romans, though a good many points were stretched in favor of the Ostrogothic regime, which still existed at the time of the first edition.

BENEDICT

Benedict of Nursia in central Italy (ca. 480–ca. 547), living at the same time as Boethius and Cassiodorus, also played a vital role at this time, as the most important molder of medieval monastic life. He was educated in Rome and stayed on there during most of the upheavals at the end of Ostrogothic rule. Then, however, followed a period of ascetic rural solitude, after which he moved south to establish his outstanding foundation at Monte Cassino (529?), where he spent the rest of his life, while his sister became the superior of a nunnery nearby.

Benedict built upon the monasticism which had arisen in Egypt in the third century A.D., and had subsequently been brought to the west by Athanasius, bishop of Alexandria, about A.D. 341, and elaborated by John Cassian in southern France in his *Institutes* and *Collations* (dialogues of the Desert Fathers). Benedict guided his monks and nuns by a *Rule* he had written for them. Its contents can be reconstructed from a surviving document that seems to include it (and also includes one of his sources, the anonymous *Rule of the Master*). Benedict's Rule evidently comprised directions on all the principal aspects of monastic life: so that it has been described as the greatest single document of the entire Middle Ages. Its author divided the working day of his monks and nuns into three carefully balanced parts, of roughly equal dur-

ation; first, a routine of regular prayer and praise built round seven daily services; secondly, work, normally manual work in the house or fields or garden; and thirdly, four hours devoted to the reading of the scriptures and sacred writings. What was required of these dedicated persons, above all, was that they should subdue their unruly passions and give up their own wills, both to God and to the community. They must embrace the vocation of priesthood and take three perpetual vows, of obedience, chastity, and poverty. In-

dividual possessions they had none. Yet they were to be adequately fed, and were allowed some time to relax. For this, despite its severities, was a relatively temperate, uneccentric, tolerable Rule, designed not for spiritual supermen and superwomen, but for ordinary Christians. It was a Rule that aimed at universality and general application, always the objectives of the Catholic church; in a world of flux, Benedict offered a stable foundation. Very Roman in his moderation and restraint, he was Roman,

once again, in his insistence on discipline. Correcting the more emotional, record-breaking excitements provided by eastern ascetics and holy vagabonds, he applied the Latin genius for law and order to the monastic institutions under his control. Benedict's *Rule* had only been intended for Monte Cassino and a few other Italian foundations of his own, and he entertained no thought of a general Order. But so vigorous and effective had monasticism become in his hands that his regulations soon began to spread through-

out western Europe—with the active support of the papacy, which found them an invaluable prop to the Church. As a result, within two hundred and fifty years of his death, the *Rule* was accepted and followed by a huge number of new foundations, and had driven all rivals from the field. For three or four hundred years to come, his influence was so overwhelmingly strong that the entire period has been characterized as the Benedictine Age.

GREGORY THE GREAT

Despite objections from Constantinople, the bishopric of Rome, or papacy, had long since begun to assert its primacy. This claim rested on the belief that the papacy had been founded by St. Peter, and the city's position as capital of the Roman empire confirmed its prominence. Later, though Rome ceased to be an imperial capital, these claims became still more insistent, at a time when the Popes were the only figures in Italy strong enough to negotiate with German invaders such as Alaric I and Attila. The papacy's adherents stressed the validity of the pontifical in addition to the imperial power. Moreover, the Popes owned a great deal of land; and the revenues they derived from it were supplemented by huge donations from the faithful, as well as by the proceeds of an influx of pilgrims even more numerous than those streaming to Jerusalem itself. Amid the famines and plagues of the Ostrogothic-Byzantine wars, more and more people appealed to the papacy to fill the administrative vacuum and relieve their sufferings. And the papacy responded.

Times were still terrible in Italy when

Gregory I the Great (590–604), formerly prefect of the city and then a monk, was elevated to the Holy See. New waves of German invaders, the Lombards, were approaching from the north, and the collapsing administration of Byzantine Ravenna seemed almost helpless against them. Gregory the Great, confronted by this peril at the very gates of Rome, proved a good deal more resilient. Comparing the city to a ship battered by the tempest and on the point of foundering, he accepted, in the spirit of a patriotic Roman, full responsibility for the lives and welfare of his fellow Italians. Then, by tough and effective diplomacy, he succeeded in halting the Lombard advance and restoring a measure of security. Although this independence of action was still, ostensibly, qualified by subordination to the Byzantine throne, it meant, in effect, that Rome and the papacy were beginning to go their own way. Gregory reorganized the large papal lands into the "patrimony of St. Peter"—the forerunner of the papal state which, as we shall see, was established in the following century. With these resources behind him, he then proceeded to a far-reaching system of poor relief for the many destitute and displaced persons of the region. As regards church affairs, he was subsequently credited with the renowned plainsong or "Gregorian chant": it may have been invented a century later, but its attribution to him is a measure of the fame he attained.

But he also looked far beyond the churches of the metropolis or affairs relating to his immediate possessions. Detecting the great advantages which the papacy could derive from Benedictine monasticism, Gregory made the monasteries, by a masterstroke, a sort of permanent reserve army at the disposal of the Pope himself. He also adopted a vigorous policy of extending and expanding the Catholic church in foreign lands. The Arian heresy, so greatly favored by Germans, was subjected to his constant attacks. Moreover, he sent the Benedictine monk Augustine to begin the conversion of England to Christianity—and not only to Christianity but to Catholicism—under his own personal direction. This was an important step toward tight control and centralization, a step which was later to be repeated in many other parts of the western world.

Gregory was described as a bald man with light brown eyes, long slender arched eyebrows, thick red lips, an aquiline nose, and a swarthy complexion that was often flushed in later life. As befitted the great secular post

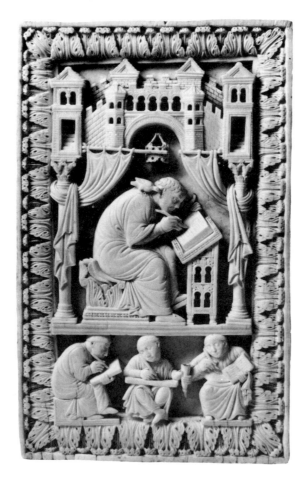

Initial letter Q from a manuscript of one of the works of Gregory I the Great, Pope from 590 to 604 (Bibliothèque Publique, Dijon). A monk is shown laboring in the fields with a scythe. Gregory did much to cultivate and expand Benedictine monasticism, based on the *Rule* of St. Benedict which specified that monks should undertake five hours of manual activity every day.

Right: Pope Gregory I is shown at his desk on this ninth- or tenth-century ivory, perhaps from Trier, West Germany. The dove perched on his shoulder was said to have uttered divine guidance into his ears as he wrote his *Commentaries*. In the background of his study is seen a skyline of towers, gables, and battlements. The scene below is a monastic writing room in which three monks are at work, one of them holding an inkwell. Kunsthistorisches Museum, Vienna.

of city prefect he had held before occupying the Holy See, he was a portent of administrative activity. His letters, of which more than eight hundred have survived, are full of orders and reprimands. He was also the first Pope to keep a competent filing system; it is due as much to him as to anyone else that in many languages the word for "cleric" (*clerc. clerk. klerk*) is interchangeable with "scribe." Yet, despite his official background and Roman efficiency, he was no "bridge" between the ancient and medieval worlds like Boethius and Cassiodorus. For Gregory knew no Greek— and loathed classical culture. On the other hand, as a Pope who had also been a monk, he was acutely sensitive to the needs of popular devotion—and perfectly prepared to encourage its superstitious inclinations, as can be seen from his *Dialogues* on the lives and miracles of Italian saints.

But this responsiveness to the public also enabled him to bring unrivaled psychological insight to bear on the themes he presented to them in his more serious theological writings. Outstanding among these works was his book on *Pastoral Care*—showing a characteristic preference for good conduct over correct dogma—which became as necessary a guide for medieval bishops as Benedict's *Rule* was a guide for monks. But this was only one of many ways in which Gregory's enormous activity, and in particular his elevated conception of the papal office, single him out as one of the principal founders of the western Middle Ages. Under Gregory, the medieval

He was a man of venerable life...
even from his boyhood. he had
the understanding of an old
man.

Pope Gregory I the Great.
Life of St. Benedict

papacy was already coming into existence, and his feats ensured that it would become not only the dominant secular power of Italy, but one of the great formative influences in European history: the major force which (however little Gregory fancied the classics) more than any other institution transmitted to the future the ideas and principles of ancient Rome.

This illustration of St. Luke is from the so-called Gospel of St Augustine. which may be the volume that Pope Gregory I dispatched to England in order to honor the conversion to Christianity of King Ethelbert of Kent. Library of Corpus Christi College, Cambridge. St. Augustine had been sent out to England in 596, and in 610 was consecrated archbishop at Canterbury.

These lead *ampullae* or flasks, sixth or seventh century, contained the oil for the lamps burning around the graves of famous martyrs, whose names were often inscribed on the flasks. Representations of the Crucifixion were still very unusual at this date. From the Treasury of the Cathedral of Monza, Italy, which was founded by the Lombard queen Theodelinda in about 595. An inscription in the cathedral records that in the time of Pope Gregory I the Great a priest named John brought seventy of these flasks (of which sixteen survive) to Rome, from where they were probably sent by Gregory to the queen.

Another gift from Gregory to the Lombard king Agilulf and his wife Theodelinda, in 613, was this cover of a Gospel *(bottom)*. The daughter of a Bavarian duke, Theodelinda influenced her husband to leave Arian Christianity in favor of Catholicism.

THE LOMBARDS
AND THE STRUGGLE
FOR ITALY

The "Iron Crown" of Lombardy, made of gold inlaid with jewels, takes its name from the thin plate of iron that lines the diadem and that is said to have been hammered from one of the nails used at the Crucifixion (the crown, from Monza, is also referred to in Italy as the "sacred nail"). Though often claimed to be older, the crown was made in the tenth century and altered later. From 1311 on, it was used at the coronation of Holy Roman Emperors, and Napoleon placed it on his own head.

Ornamental gilded bronze plaques for shields *(above)* from Ischal-Alz (near Traunstein in Upper Bavaria). These animals, two eagles and a leaping wolf, may have been designed by German craftsmen for a member of the Lombard nobility. Prähistorische Staatssammlung, Munich.

The Germanic Lombards seem to have been pastoral dwellers in north Germany until late in the fourth century A.D., when they began to move down to the upper Elbe and Moravia. Then in about 487–488 they occupied war-ravaged Austria north of the Danube, and shortly afterward they met Christian (Arian) missionaries for the first time.

In the later 530s the Byzantines began inciting them against other German peoples. But then the covetous eyes of the Lombards fell on Italy, and in 568 a horde of them crossed into that country, accompanied by their wives and children, and by warriors of other tribal groups. "The Lombards had their hair parted on either side of their foreheads," said their historian Paul the Deacon, "hanging down their face as far as the mouth." They were skillful archers who used cavalry more than other Germans. But they were also, in other respects, the most savage of all the tribesmen who moved into the Roman empire during the period of the wanderings of the peoples. Under the leadership of their king Alboin, the Lombards' invasion of northern Italy was virtually unopposed; within a year and a half they had conquered all the principal cities north of the Po except Pavia, but that too fell in 572. It was in this northern region, as the modern name of Lombardy testifies, that they mainly settled—though even there only as a minority. But at the same time they also pushed further south and established autonomous duchies based in Spoleto and Benevento. This meant that the Byzantine province of Ravenna (of which the population was already alienated by heavy taxation) found itself surrounded, menaced, and virtually isolated by Lombards on both sides. As a result, relentless hostility from Constantinople characterized the two centuries of Lombard rule on Italian soil. For the Byzantines now had ample cause to regret that they themselves, by their earlier demolition of the much weaker Ostrogothic state, had created the Italian vacuum into which the Lombards had then so decisively moved.

The invasion by the Lombards was a decisive landmark in the history of Italy. For they destroyed the country's political unity, which had lasted for so many centuries. And Italy did not become unified again for thirteen hundred years.

Nor was the new Lombard state a very effective unit in itself. Its monarchy, being more or less elective, possessed no guarantee of continuity and was highly insecure. Moreover, even outside self-governing Spoleto and Benevento, Lombard territory was divided into thirty or forty duchies and counties of which the leaders often acted very much on their own. Before long, therefore, the kingdom already seemed to be breaking up. After an interregnum, however, its recovery was begun

The Lombards, who invaded Italy from the north in the sixth century, left an enduring legacy—part of which was the destruction, for many centuries to come, of Italian unity. They also created, or sponsored the creation of, artistic masterpieces, for example in the church of Santa Maria in Valle (the Tempietto) at Cividale, Friuli, northeastern Italy. Seat of a Lombard duke and patriarch, Cividale was enriched with some of the finest art of the

Lombard epoch. The church was apparently built during the reign of the last king of the Lombards, Desiderius, captured by Charlemagne in 774. This view of the nave *(left)*, which is approximately 20 feet square, shows several examples of the ornate decorative carving in Byzantine style (see also the detail of a relief, p. 108). The seventh-century Lombard cross *(above)*, found in France, is one of a number of remarkable gold crosses illustrating the talent of the Lombards, and the Germanic peoples in general, for this type of ornamental metalwork.

105

by Authari (584–590), who warded off a Frankish invasion. Moreover, he, and then his successor Agilulf (590–615) after him, married a Catholic princess named Theodelinda from the Frankish protectorate of Bavaria, hoping by this means to disrupt a potentially dangerous Franco-Byzantine alliance. Then Agilulf extended the Lombard dominions until Byzantine territory in Italy was virtually limited to a few strips of shoreland; and even Rome itself was only narrowly saved from him, by the exertions of Pope Gregory the Great.

After a century's pause, Liutprand (712–744), the most impressive king the Lombards ever had, resumed their triumphant military advance and made his power felt in their own autonomous duchies as well. A fine gold coinage, in competition with the Byzantine currency, reflected increasing commercial activity, especially along the line of the Po which was the chief Lombard route of contact with the outside world. Liutprand also encroached still further on Byzantium's Italian province, until finally the ferocious Aistulf (749–756) obliterated it altogether, annexing Ravenna itself in 751. By this time, only a number of coastal cities remained free of the Lombards. After their original invasion, Byzantium had retained Genoa, Amalfi, Naples, and above all Venice and its islands: and now these centers were left to pursue their lucrative activities in virtual independence.

A wise man ought no more to take it ill when he clashes with fortune than a brave man ought to be upset by the sound of battle. For both of them their very distress is an opportunity, for the one to gain glory and the other to strengthen his wisdom. This is why virtue gets its name, because it is firm in strength and unconquered by adversity. You are engaged in a bitter but spirited struggle against fortune of every kind, to avoid falling victim to her when she is adverse or being corrupted by her when she is favorable. Hold to the middle way with unshakable strength.

Boethius. Consolation of Philosophy, *IV. 7*

Aistulf also annexed a lot of papal territory. But his triumph in this direction was short-lived. From 654 onward there had been a long series of Greek and Syrian Popes, who have left artistic masterpieces in the paintings of the Church of Santa Maria Antiqua at Rome. But after this long series of pro-Byzantine easterners the Holy See was now occupied once again by a Roman, Stephen II. Stephen was so alarmed by this Lombard menace, which manifestly threatened Rome itself, that he appealed, not to Byzantium which would not and could not help, but to the Frankish (Carolingian) king Pepin III the Short (751–768). Pepin responded, and in the course of two expeditions forced Aistulf to give most of his conquests back to Stephen II, who thus laid the foundation of the temporal States of

Certain works of art can be associated with the Lombards while they were still migrating through Europe, on their way toward Italy: for example this elaborate brooch found in Rebrin, Czechoslovakia. Executed in cloisonné technique, with pendant gems, it dates from ca. A.D. 400. Kunsthistorisches Museum, Vienna.

A major artistic contribution of the Lombard epoch is the series of stone reliefs on the altar of San Martino in Cividale, commissioned by Duke Ratchis (744–749) in memory of his father Duke Pemmo, and now in the Museo Cristiano at Cividale Cathedral. The three scenes from this altar shown here are *(left to right):* the Visitation of the Virgin, from one side of the altar; Christ in His Majesty, from the altar front, surrounded by angels; and *(far right)* the three kings of the East, worshiping the newborn Christ, from one of the sides of the altar. Although the iconography is derived from the Byzantine world, no trace of Byzantine or oriental influence can be detected in the style, which carries the abstraction of the human figure to the highest possible pitch: bodies are treated as mere ornaments, little more than symbols, and no attempt is made to render three-dimensional space.

the Church which in revived but diminished form still exist in the Vatican today.

Then Pepin the Short's son Charlemagne, in response to a further papal appeal, forced the Lombard king Desiderius to surrender and put an end to the existence of his state (774), taking to himself the title of King of the Lombards as well as of the Franks. His conquests signified that most of Italy was henceforward doomed—for centuries to come—to be ruled by sovereigns who lived north of the Alps. Moreover, the event also exercised a remarkable and permanent effect on the papacy. For it meant that the Popes were finally able to consider themselves free of Byzantine control, and to move over into the western orbit in which they have remained ever since. Moreover, their emancipation from Byzantium meant that they could with greater plausibility than ever (despite the protests of the Orthodox east) claim for themselves a rival, universal power. Their claims were also supported by a forged document, the *Donations of Constantine* (ca. 775), which granted the papacy temporal jurisdiction over the whole west—allegedly on the instructions of Constantine the Great more than four hundred years previously—and thus provided a theoretical basis for Rome's growing universalist assertions. In practical terms, however, the papacy was losing its freedom of action to the Franks, as Pope Leo III showed when he crowned Charlemagne as "emperor" in 800.

Above: Gold medallion pendant with cloisonné enamel, of the seventh century, said to have been found at Comacchio near Ravenna (now in the Walters Art Gallery, Baltimore). Gold and enamel work of this delicate quality may be attributed to Byzantine craftsmen working for the Lombard rulers of Italy.

The jeweled cross, sole remnant of the crown of the Lombard king Agilulf (590–615), is in the Cathedral Treasury, Monza. The crown itself, on which his name was inscribed, was stolen in Paris in 1804 and melted down. The cross originally hung down from the center of the crown, and thus it seems likely that such crowns (which are also found among the Visigoths) were not worn but rather possessed a votive or funerary character.

THE LOMBARD AGE

By the seventh century Lombard Pavia was emerging as something like a capital city, which was an unusual and advantageous feature in the German monarchies of the time. Roman traditions were kept up within its walls, and a law school trained notaries for the royal court. The most important achievement of these jurists was the production of the first written legal code of the Lombards, the Edict of King Rothari (643), which was the best German codification of the age. Although written in Latin, and borrowing something from Roman law, it was not intended for the Roman population of the kingdom—who were allowed to live according to their own regulations—but was designed only for the king's Lombard subjects and was therefore German in character. But it was German with a difference, since what Rothari, like other

The highest development of Lombard art, with strong influence from Byzantine sources, is exemplified in the ample modeling and hieratic postures (not to mention the Byzantine robes) of these figures *(right)* from a stucco frieze in the church of Santa Maria in Valle, Cividale (Friuli), eighth century. See also the view of the church on page 105.

This relief, on the front of a gilt bronze helmet, shows the Lombard king Agilulf (590–615) enthroned. The helmet was found at Valdinievole, near Lucca, Italy. The designs show a new version of Germanic stylization.

Lombard kings, had in mind was to divert emphasis from the old clan and family allegiances, and all the bloodfeuds and vendettas that went with them, and stress loyalty to the nation and, above all, to his own person instead.

This policy was able to advance another step after the kingdom turned gradually from the Arian brand of Christianity to Catholicism (by 700). For the Catholic church weakened the family structure of the Lombards still further, by encouraging families to hand property over—and inducing the younger generation to become monks.

Liutprand (712–744) made an additional move toward internal consolidation, and the enhancement of his own royal power, when he applied his laws to Romans as well as Lombards. In accordance with a growing social conscience of the times, Liutprand's measures incorporated many Roman and Christian principles. For he was a zealous Catholic, and a munificent founder of monasteries.

Then they beheld Charlemagne, the man of iron, in his iron helmet, his arms covered with iron casing, his iron breast and his broad shoulders protected by an iron armor; his left hand bore raised up the iron lance, while the right was ever ready to grip the victorious steel....His horse as well was iron in color, iron in its courage.... Oh, the iron. Alas for the iron! This was the desperate cry of the inhabitants [of Pavia]. Iron shook the firmness of their walls, and the courage of the youth was undone before the iron of the elders.

Notker Balbulus (the Stammerer).
Charlemagne *(on his conquest of the Lombard kingdom)*

The most famous monastery in Lombard territory, however, was one which had been authorized by one of his predecessors, Agilulf, when he permitted the Irish missionary-monk Columbanus to found Bobbio near Piacenza, beside the pilgrim route to Rome; it became a famous center of learning. Only traces of the original church have survived, but there are important ecclesiastical remains of the Lombard age elsewhere. Eighth-century stucco figures in the Church of Santa Maria in Valle, at the ducal seat of Cividale (Friuli), may have been made either by Lombards or by Greek exiles; at any rate they are of the finest Byzantine style.

So are outstanding paintings, perhaps slightly earlier, at the regional capital of Castelseprio (Santa Maria Foris Portas), of which the Constantinopolitan models have now been identified. These are works that exercised influence on the art not only of Italy but of Transalpine lands as well. Indeed, they can be regarded as manifestations of an "Italo-Alpine" art, exercising influence, for example, on paintings in the Church of St. John at Müstair in the Grisons (Switzerland), where a double se-

of interlacing and animal motifs. Thus the art of Italy in Lombard times shows a bewildering variety, an exciting and not always fully integrated blend of the various influences that were at work.

Yet this very mixture typifies the Lombards' weakness. Unlike the Franks and Angles in France and England respectively, they only succeeded in giving their names to a small part of Italy; and the interracial, intercultural synthesis promised by the laws of Liutprand,

Byzantine style is immediately apparent in this Lombard wall painting, probably of eighth-century date, showing the Flight into Egypt. It is in the church of Santa Maria Foris Portas at Castelseprio in north Italy, which was a provincial capital of the Lombard kingdom but employed Greek artists; or perhaps they were Lombards trained by Greeks and employing Byzantine models. Castelseprio exercised strong influence on painters north of the Alps.

This elaborate marble baldachin (altar enclosure) in the Church of Santa Maria Maggiore at Bergamo, northern Italy, is a composite assemblage of different sections made between the eighth and twelfth centuries. The human figure at top, beneath the eagle, is in a non-naturalistic style indicating native Lombard craftsmanship.

quence of frescoes dates back almost to the foundation of the church by Charlemagne in about 800. Similarly, a group of bilingual manuscripts from Lombard territory is echoed in Bavaria. Yet, whereas these are cosmopolitan works, the polychrome jewelry of the Lombards, like that of the Ostrogoths, is instead characteristically German in its blend

and intended for a much wider area, never materialized. Nevertheless, it is unfair to condemn them as mere semi-nomads huddling together, their minds still in the forests of Germany; for the strange, composite society that they promoted left its stamp on the political fortunes, and legal and other institutions, of later Italy.

VISIGOTHIC SPAIN

The great group of German tribes known as the Goths, who moved southeastward through Europe in the second century A.D., had split up into an eastern and western branch, the Ostrogoths and Visigoths. Two centuries later the Visigoths ("valiant" Goths) came to live in Rumania. Under Alaric I they plundered Rome (410), but were then allowed to settle in Aquitaine (southwestern France). From there, Euric extended their territory over the southern half of France and declared himself independent (474–475). But his son, Alaric II, was defeated by Clovis'

tinued to build up a powerful and united kingdom, and replaced Arian Christianity by Catholicism as its official religion. Reccaswinth (649–672), whose magnificent crown jewels have survived, claimed kingship by God's grace and designation.

Visigothic rulers often tried, with varying success, to make their monarchy hereditary instead of elective, in the hope of lessening the frequency of murderous dethronements. Their main hope lay in the army, made up of infantrymen who wielded long two-edged swords and bows and spears, and each owed

The Visigoths, who settled in Spain in the fifth century, were unique among the Germanic peoples for the degree of cultural integration they achieved with the Romans. This eagle-brooch, however, shows a Visigothic art almost completely free of Roman influence. The gold and glass figure, made in the fifth century, is now in the Germanisches National-museum, Nuremberg.

Above right: Visigothic church of San Juan Bautista de Baños in Baños de Cerrato, Palencia, Spain, mid-seventh century. The churches built by the Visigoths during the period preceding the Arab invasion were among the most advanced of their time in western Europe, grafting novel ideas onto the classical architectural heritage.

Merovingian Franks at Vouillé near Poitiers (507). Thereafter he retained only a small corner of France, and withdrew with most of his followers to Spain, of which the greater part came under his control. The principal new homeland of the Visigothic immigrants was the region of Segovia in Old Castile, but Agila (549–554) also established himself at Mérida on the River Guadiana. Cordoba and the south had to be ceded to Justinian, but in compensation the Visigoth Leovigild asserted control over the northwest (584–585). Establishing his court at Toledo, Leovigild assumed the diadem and the purple, in imitation of Byzantine emperors, and struck the first independent national coinage in any former Roman province. Reccared (586–601) con-

direct, personal loyalty to the king. Toward the end of the seventh century, however, the Visigothic rulers found it increasingly hard to obtain enough soldiers. For the landed aristocracy was more and more divided among itself, and a new class of small-holders became hostile to the government. Civil wars and rebellions flared continuously, while the kings vacillated between savage repression and unwise clemency. As a result, the country became an easy prey to the Moslem Arabs when they crossed over from north Africa in 711. The Visigoth Roderic hastened southward, but at Guadalete he was defeated, betrayed, and killed.

The most arresting feature of Visigothic Spain was the interpenetration of the two cultures,

German and Roman. The Visigoths, it is true, remained a tightly knit warrior caste, only forming about one-fortieth of the population of the country; and the Romans, as usual, showed a tendency to hold these intruders at arms' length. Nevertheless, even before they arrived in Spain at all, the Visigoths had been the most Romanized of contemporary Germans, readily adopting Roman clothes and customs; and once they were on Spanish soil, the two communities, despite the persistence of tensions, achieved a closer symbiosis than in any other German kingdom.

This trend was especially successful among the privileged groups of landowning nobles, Visigothic and Roman. Indeed, the court of Leovigild not only adopted Byzantine fashions but removed the ban on intermarriage which dated back to Roman times. Then, in the seventh century, much of Recceswinth's long and peaceful reign was devoted to similar steps toward unification. Here the jurists played a significant part. For in an age when the ablest men saw the Law as the one incomparable inheritance from ancient times and the foundation of all government, successive Visi-

Written in silver ink on purple vellum, the Codex Argenteus, the Bible translated into Gothic by Ulfilas (Wulfila) the apostle to the Goths, is probably from the sixth century. Ulfilas converted the Goths to the Arian branch of Christianity, and thereby drove a wedge between the Germanic peoples and the churches of Rome and Constantinople.

The Visigothic church of San Pedro de la Nave, Zamora, northwestern Spain *(left)*, was probably begun in about 700, but the ornate capitals on the columns were not added until two hundred years later, when the region had come back into Christian hands, forming part of the territories of northern Spain ruled by the successors of the Asturian monarchs who had escaped incorporation into the Islamic realm.

gothic legal codes greatly helped to bind the two races together. The process of codification had already begun in the fifth century, and culminated in the *Liber Judiciorum* of Recceswinth. Roman or Hispano-Roman in its shape and most of its substance, this nevertheless incorporated certain Germanic ideas and customs, in addition to new laws promulgated by Recceswinth himself; and it was intended as a legal code for all his subjects, of both races.

The other notably outstanding Visigothic phenomenon was the Catholic church, which became official in the country after Reccared's conversion from Arianism in 587. Christianity in Spain had long been vigorous and fervent, and the new Catholic establishment (which has its memorial in unusually fine seventh-century churches) displayed the lasting Spanish ingredients of single-minded, uncompromising, intolerant, militant piety, paradoxically blending loyalty to the Popes with reluctance to accept papal orders. The relations between the Visigothic state and church were close and intimate. The bishops tended to identify themselves with the social and economic problems of the poor, whom they often protected, with royal support, against the nobility.

The characteristic manifestations of Spanish Catholicism were its Councils, which attained greater political significance than in any other German state of the time. A succession of these assemblies were held at Toledo between 589 and 694, earning the period the designation of the Century of Councils. Molding the Spanish church into a dynamic power under royal leadership, these Councils gave shape to the monarchs' ecclesiastical and secular decisions alike, playing a large part, for example, in the legal codifications; the king provided the agenda, and the Church the organization. While the Moslem conquerors, in the early eighth century, occupied by far the greater part of Spain, those members of the Visigothic royal house who remained alive fled with their supporters to the extreme north of the country, where they set up a small Christian state in the mountains of Asturias, separated from the Arabs by a wide no-man's-land.

The official whom they elected as their ruler, the semi-legendary Pelayo or Pelagius (ca. 718–737), finally repelled a raiding party of Arabs near the cave of Covadonga, and thereafter they left him alone, the more willingly because their soldiers did not like severe winters. Soon afterward Berber rebellions in Spain and north Africa caused the withdrawal of some of the northern frontier garrisons, whereupon Alfonso I (739–757) was able to annex Galicia and parts of northern Portugal and Old Castile.

Alfonso II the Chaste (791–842) established his capital at a strategically sited new city at Oviedo, and declared his ecclesiastical independence of the Visigoth church, now in captivity under the Arabs. It was said, however, that his nobles would not allow him to make an alliance with Charlemagne, but preferred a policy of insular self-dependence instead.

This was a beleaguered little princedom, practically cut off from the rest of Christian Europe. Its monarchs were not much more than cattle owners and guerrilla chieftains, with no regular administration or army. Yet the Visigothic society they inherited was gradually taking on a new shape under the influence of immigrations from the south; and the mixed civilization that evolved displayed original features, including elements of representative government. The Asturian rulers considered themselves Visigoths. Nevertheless it was the Latin tongue, infused with scarcely more than two hundred Gothic words, that became the Spanish language. It was from this diminutive state, eventually, that the Christian reconquest of Spain was gradually undertaken, and completed with the fall of Granada in 1492.

CLOVIS AND THE FRANKS

The Merovingian Franks, who became the first major power of western Europe following the collapse of the western Roman empire, developed a hybrid art style. An impressive example of Frankish metalworking skill: gilt helmet *(right)* of a resplendent, ceremonial type ("Spangenhelm") from Morken (near Bonn), ca. 600. It was found in the rich tomb of a Frankish (Merovingian) noble, which came to light in 1955. In the dead man's mouth was a gold coin of the Byzantine emperor Tiberius II Constantinus (578–582). Rheinisches Landesmuseum, Bonn.

This seventh-century gravestone from Niederdollendorf in the Rhineland (south of Cologne) depicts the deceased comb-

ing his hair (a sign of vitality) as he is menaced by double-headed serpents. The comb, sword, and the flask at his feet suggest pagan grave goods, but the other side of the stone bears a figure of Christ on the cross. Rheinisches Landesmuseum, Bonn.

The Merovingian bronze plaque *(above right)*, seventh century, shows a horseman, at a time before the stirrup had been adapted from eastern sources. Metropolitan Museum, New York.

Right: Cloisonné reliquary casket decorated with garnets, pastes, and an imitation Roman cameo; of the eighth century. The casket shows some resemblances to Lombard models, but was apparently the product of a provincial workshop on the borders of Alamannic and Burgundian territory, perhaps at St. Maurice d'Agaune (Valais, southwestern Switzerland), where it forms part of the Treasure of the Abbey.

The Franks, a word that means "bold" or "fierce," were remnants of older peoples who had rearranged themselves into three groups. One of these, the Salians, became federates of the Romans, whom their chieftain Childeric I (d. 482) helped against Visigothic rivals. His son Clovis (482–511), after succeeding to the leadership at the age of fifteen, vastly extended his power, by war, ruthless intrigue, and assassination.

Clovis and his Franks, like other Germans, were Arian Christians, and his first victim was the Catholic Syagrius, the last representative of Roman rule in northern France, whom he defeated at Soissons (486) and put to death. But Clovis' own most civilized subjects, the Gallo-Romans, were also Catholics, as was his wife Clotilde (although the state from which she came, Burgundy in southeast France, remained Arian). Clovis vowed that he too would become a Catholic if he was victorious

over the hostile Germanic confederation of the Alamanni, who lived round the upper valley of the Rhine. In 496–497 he duly defeated them and embraced Catholicism, followed by hundreds of other Frankish notables.

Some paganism lingered on, as tombstones show, and Clovis probably saw Jesus as a blend between a tribal chieftain and a war-god. Nevertheless, he had officially become a Catholic, and this decision meant that, unlike any other monarch in the west, he had placed himself firmly on what was destined to be the win-

This model of a village in Germany, as it was in the seventh or eighth century, illustrates the way of life of the Merovingian Franks. Originally, like other German tribes, a migratory people, they were unified under Clovis and brought within the Christian world. The outstanding civilizer of Germany, on Christian lines, was St. Boniface (Wynfrith of Crediton). His missions were greatly encouraged by the Carolingian Franks Charles Martel and Pepin III the Short, who saw in these activities an admirable opportunity to organize the hitherto recalcitrant Germans under a single authority.

The Merovingians favored the use of lightweight, portable objects such as this bronze ornament or finial, believed to be a sixth-century work *(below left)*. Its figures recall those that had appeared on Christian sarcophagi of the later Roman empire. Metropolitan Museum, New York.

Frankish gravestone *(above)*, Rheinisches Landesmuseum, Bonn. The gold seal ring *(below)* belonged to the Merovingian chieftain Childeric I (d. 482), father of Clovis. From a cast in the Ashmolean Museum, Oxford.

ning side, thus gaining something of the prestige of a second Constantine and establishing an alliance between the French monarchy and the Catholic church that was to last for over thirteen hundred years.

For, looking around him, Clovis concluded that the Arians had much less to offer. Their presbyters were less knowledgeable and useful than the Catholic bishops, and he had no desire for alliances with other Arian princes; he only wanted to fight and defeat them. So, after denouncing the Burgundians and Visigoths as heretics, he went into battle against them, with the full approval of the Holy See. His crowning victory was over the Visigothic king Alaric II at Vouillé near Poitiers (507), after which he took over most of Alaric's possessions in France—he would have taken them all if Theodoric, the Ostrogothic king of Italy, had not intervened to stop him. In the same year, by multiple murder, Clovis combined the three branches of the Frankish people under his own united rule.

The man who had achieved these results was a bloodthirsty, fraudulent gangster, the most grasping and energetic of the German rulers of his day (and a lover of practical jokes). His strength lay in his formidable infantrymen, equipped with throwing-hatchets, barbed javelins, and long two-edged swords (replaced by shorter one-edged swords in about 600). He was also fortunate in his geographical situation, which enabled him to create a new center of power in northwest Europe, because

he was in a position to maintain contact with the vast manpower resources of his German homeland.

He and his successors also owed much of their authority to the sacred character attributed to their monarchy; their wearing of long hair symbolized the primitive magic of their blood. Yet they had no real capital, but traveled continuously from place to place (with ruinous consequences for their hosts). Nor were they yet kings of France, or of any other territories either—they were rulers of a people which, although it had now become a historic force, was far from being a nation or a nationality. The abstract idea of a state did not exist; the people and things controlled by the monarch were his personal property, to be divided up like a private inheritance, often in circumstances of sanguinary fratricidal vendetta. Yet Clovis had started this ramshackle state on its long upward path.

MEROVINGIAN JEWELRY

The Merovingian monarchs presented a sumptuous image to the world. The reliefs on the tombs of their great men and women, for example at Jouarre east of Paris (ca. 662, 685), sometimes surpass even the finest Italian art. But, above all, it is the goldwork and jewelry that was deposited in such graves that shows the royal desire for conspicuous display, notably at Tournai (King Childeric I), Cologne (ca. 535), and St. Denis (Queen Arnegunde). Arnegunde, wife of King Lothar (Chlotar) I who ruled the Franks from 558 to 561, is believed to have died around the year 570. Her corpse was found wearing a gold ring, shoe buckles, and garter fastenings, all decorated with animal motifs, as well as a great deal of other jewelry—gold brooches set with garnets, gold hairpins, earrings, belt buckle, and a gold ring that bore her name. Some of the articles in this profuse display were obviously gifts (such as a man's belt buckle) rather than part of her normal attire. Thus her grave—along with those at Tournai and Cologne—provides ample testimony to the high development of Merovingian metalworking and the diversity of stylistic effect of which it was capable.

Merovingian jewelry is a remarkable blend of many influences, German, Gallo-Roman, Italian, Byzantine, Syrian, Egyptian (Coptic), and Armenian. The *cloisonné* technique (of metal cells) found favor at first, but was replaced in later Merovingian times by the related *cabochon* method (with colored stones patterned against a gold background). A favorite motif, as elsewhere, was the interlace, learned from Burgundy and Aquitaine, whose craftsmen had gained this knowledge from the eastern Roman provinces by way of the Rhone.

But it was upon designs incorporating animals, in various degrees of stylization, that the German, and particularly Merovingian, metalworkers concentrated their creative genius. These creations owe a debt to Gallo-Roman models. Yet they ultimately go back to the wonderful animal art of the European and Asian steppes, conspicuously illustrated by Scythian and Sarmatian work of the previous millennium. Recent discoveries at Obervorschutz in North Hesse suggest that it was by way of the German frontier that such motifs found their way to the Merovingian Franks.

In sharp contrast to classical ancient Roman tastes, the Merovingian designs formed under these influences showed little interest in anatomic naturalism, but instead became enormously simplified, stylized, and distorted; the animals' bodies are broken up and reassembled in the freest possible manner. A second phase, which began in the later sixth century A.D., displayed a ribbon technique in which the forms are elongated and intertwined in smooth, continuous, symmetrical patterns. It is possible to "read" such patterns superficially—that is, to piece together the jigsaw of disjointed animal limbs, and see where they fit together. But the inner meanings the artist intended to convey by these images remain elusive. It seems probable, however, that they were thought of as capable of working magic and exorcising evil spirits, like the art, for example, of the Maoris of New Zealand. By the same token, the precious and semi-precious stones used by Merovingian artists were chosen as much for their magical as their purely decorative qualities; each stone had its own peculiar powers.

The incredibly varied, rich, and imaginative animal style of the medieval Germanic peoples must be regarded as their principal contribution to the art of the world, which continued to exploit its possibilities for many hundreds of years. In this process, the Merovingians played a vital part, transforming their borrowings into a series of bold, complex themes that are the product of unexcelled technical virtuosity. This Merovingian metalwork and jewelry was eye-catching in the highest degree. It had to be, because in an epoch when jewels were portable wealth, they formed a yardstick of the owner's rank and status. Very often, they were the property of the kings themselves who presented them to their nobles as conspicuous gifts for services rendered.

The same spectacular qualities appeared in a remarkable series of Merovingian illuminated manuscripts—the earliest of such richly decorated medieval books to have come down to us. Developing their most characteristic styles in the early eighth century—under the same varied influences that were at work on the jewelry—they display gay coloring and dashing, brilliant draftsmanship, curiously different from the precise perfection of their counterparts across the water, in England and Ireland.

MEROVINGIAN
SOCIETY

While the Merovingians extended their territorial conquests, during the sixth century, eastward into Germany and throughout most of France, the organization of their society remained for the most part loose and chaotic. But their art, reflecting this society, was a dynamic one, in which military themes played a major role, as in the two large objects seen on these pages. The pressed gold disk *(below)*, a seventh-century work from Pliezhausen near Tübingen (Württembergisches Landesmuseum, Stuttgart), shows a mounted warrior (apparently guided by a patron deity) and a fallen opponent. Another galloping horseman *(page opposite)* is depicted on a Merovingian brooch, also from the seventh century, provenance unknown.

After a generation of civil wars, the Merovingian king Lothar (Chlotar) II executed Sigebert II and Brunhilda in 613 and reunited the whole Frankish kingdom. The coin *(opposite page)* is a gold piece *(solidus)* with his portrait and "Chlotarius Rex" on the obverse, and a cross surmounting a globe on the reverse. British Museum, London.

When Clovis was dead, his dominions were split up between his sons, who (insofar as they had headquarters) ruled separately at the northern towns of Metz, Orleans, Paris, and Soissons, but each owned a portion of the southern part of the country as well. This complicated division was ominous for the future—the first of eight occasions in the course of the next century and a half when such a split occurred.

Nevertheless, during the first two generations after Clovis' death, his house maintained its frantic outburst of aggressive energy. The penetration of Thuringia (531) meant that Merovingian territory had reached its furthest extent toward the east. Then, nearer home, the conquest of Burgundy (534) and Provence (537) signified that the whole of France (except Celtic Brittany) was now in the hands of the Franks. The acquisition of Provence was particularly important because it gave the Merovingian rulers access to the Mediterranean and enabled them to draw upon the wealth of heavily Romanized southern Gaul. They did not settle there in any numbers, and were little more than an army of occupation. But they commanded the support of the Gallo-Roman nobility—who had suffered no great material or cultural damage—and themselves quickly began to use the Latin speech, which in due course spread to the evangelized peasantry, and by 800 prevailed throughout the whole of Gaul in the form of French. The Salic Law *(Lex Salica)*, which partially reflected usages going back to the sixth century, displays a Frankish society in which no woman could inherit land while there lived a possible heir (a regulation which prevented many women of future European dynasties from ascending the throne). But in many other respects the distinction between Franks and Gallo-Romans was gradually becoming blurred.

The rewards the nobles gained from their Merovingian monarchs took the form of land. Land was what they were determined to have: for land, and land only, meant power. The fertile, climatically favorable valleys and open countryside were their coveted targets, though toward the end of the Merovingian period attempts were also being made to open up higher and more difficult ground. Mirroring the dual structure of the country, the aristocracy comprised two groups. Some belonged to old Gallo-Roman families, and the others were Frankish favorites of the monarch. From the latter he appointed Counts *(comites)* for defense, administration, and the judgment of disputes. The Counts combined civil and military power, and abused both.

The chaos of Merovingian government was the opportunity of the Catholic episcopate. Bishops fulfilled a conspicuous role because of their birth, their superior knowledge, and the ecclesiastical estates that formed their wealth. Generally appointed for life, they enjoyed personal inviolability, and felt safer than most of the nobles. Much disgraceful behavior was attributed to these churchmen. Nevertheless, they were highly esteemed, because a share of papal prestige had rubbed off on them; and besides, they were the links that held Franks and Gallo-Romans together. Until the early years of the seventh century, the ecclesiastics were kept under a certain amount of control by the kings. After that, they ceased to obey so dutifully.

But the major significance of the Church at this time lay in its monasteries and nunneries. Gaul had initially led the west in the establishment of influential monastic institutions, and the drive was maintained. By 585 some two hundred such centers existed on Frankish ter-

Frankish manuscript illuminations of the eighth century created a fantastic repertoire of forms that have no parallel in European art. The example below is the title page from the Frankish sacramentary of Gelasius (ca. 750–770), written near Paris, perhaps at Chelles. The design shows a cross with the Lamb of God at center and the Greek letters alpha and omega hanging from the arms; they are being pecked at by birds of paradise (birds and fishes being favorite motifs of these artists). Biblioteca Apostolica, Vatican.

The streets were laid with carpets, the houses bedecked
with bright-hued banners, and the churches adorned with gleaming white draperies.
As the royal party made its way in festive procession through
the streets of the city, the king asked the bishop: "Kindly Father,
is this then the kingdom of God, which you had promised me?" The bishop answered,
"This is not the kingdom of God, but only the first step on the path leading to it."

Gregory of Tours, relating the baptism of King Clovis at Reims

ritory, mainly south of the River Loire. Then the great Irish missionary Columbanus (543–615) arrived on the scene, and under his impetus many new institutions appeared; his foundation at Luxeuil in Burgundy (590) became the monastic metropolis of western Europe, and the nucleus of massive colonizing and missionary activity. By 700 there were four hundred monasteries, scattered throughout territory extending as far as the Meuse and Upper Rhine.

They were little islands of relatively well-edu-cated men, power points of the agricultural economy, headed by abbots who were accustomed to problems of government and set themselves to resist the anarchy of the age. Many of these monastic leaders received royal patronage; in particular, the fortunes of the Merovingian monarchy were deeply involved in the abbey of St. Denis outside Paris. Founded soon after 600, it was the recipient of lavish favors from the kings—who had residences nearby—and became the scene of a great annual international fair.

THE KINGS
AND THEIR HERITAGE

Gregory, Bishop of Tours (ca. 539–594), in his *History of the Franks*, gives us a picture of the Merovingian courts that paraded this wealth—an account laced with wry humor and horrific anecdotes. Many of these stories centered on two appalling queens, Brunhilda and Fredegund, who kept the kingdom violently divided (as it so often was) for nearly forty years.

Lothar (Chlotar) II (613–629), the great-grandson of Clovis, was able to reestablish unity, though in order to do so he was forced to make concessions to the great landowners. His cunning, energetic son Dagobert I (629–639), patron of St. Denis—and of the arts which reached their zenith in his court work-shops—kept thirty-nine mistresses and wives in his mansion at Clichy. Nevertheless, he also reunited the Frankish lands once again, and as his foreign neighbors became only too well aware, proved the strongest Merovingian king for a century. He was only about thirty-six when he died of old age. Very early deaths, likewise by natural causes, continued to be the lot of his successors—who were mostly nonentities.

This coin, a silver *denarius* of Charle-magne, portrays the emperor in a nostal-gically Roman guise. British Museum, London. More Germanic traits of the Merovingians' art appear in the buckle *(above)* from Germany, about sixth cen-tury, and the primitive-looking grave-stone *(right)*, seventh or eighth century, from France. Musées Départementaux de la Loire Atlantique, Nantes.

We have had letters sent to us from church dignitaries
*   which show a painful weakness in composition.*
On reading these letters and considering their lack of skill,
*   we began to feel afraid lest the writers' knowledge and understanding*
of the Holy Scriptures might also prove to be much less than it ought to be.

Charlemagne

It appears clear from the writings of Gregory of Tours that although the Franks lived in France, they did not noticeably belong to it; their presence seemed fortuitous, casual, and incongruous. Government seemed scarcely to concern them, and they did not manage, or trouble, to organize a salaried staff; such administrative jobs as had to be done were put in the hands of the king's own servants and retainers, who usually showed little concern for the welfare of the general population.

At first sight, the monarchs' display of fine jewels seems surprising, since their financial situation was precarious. Taxes came in, it is true, from the old Gallo-Roman towns, but they amounted to little more than a trickle, since in the absence of a civil service the old Roman arrangements for their collection had broken down. A remarkable degree of decentralization, not to say disorganization, is revealed by the Merovingian gold and then silver coinage, which was issued at no less than a thousand mints, mostly outside royal control. Moreover, trade with the east was largely controlled, not by the Franks themselves, but by Syrian merchants, until Syria was conquered by the Arabs—when this commerce fell into the hands of the Jews. And in any case, the balance of trade was unfavorable, since despite the needs for large imports (especially spices which were a dietetic necessity), the Franks had little but slaves and swords to export in exchange.

Nevertheless, the Merovingian monarchs saw their job as a means of making money, and money they made. In the first place, they raised funds from their nobles, to whom (especially from the early seventh century onward) they offered the considerable advantage of "immunity"—freedom from royal control—in return for cash. Secondly, they managed to extort enormous subsidies from the Byzantine emperors, who paid up willingly in return for military help against their enemies. This was one reason why the Merovingian kings fought their wars; but another was in order to annex new territory for themselves. Frequent territorial annexations were the best way of all for the monarch to enrich himself—and to reward, as was urgently necessary, his most important subjects and backers.

The Merovingian kingdom displayed an extraordinary blend of vices and strengths. Despite the glaring defects of monarchs, nobles, and churchmen alike—faults combining the most typical flaws of late Roman decrepitude and German barbarism—some of the old classical heritage had been preserved; the house had lost its roof, it has been said, but the foundations and walls stood firm. Indeed, the Merovingian dynasty lasted longer than most of the royal houses that history has recorded. Their rulers, before the time of decline, achieved grandeur, which was reflected in fine artistic achievements; and their kingdom was very large and amply endowed by nature. The Merovingians had begun the task of welding their various peoples—German, Gallo-Roman, and Celtic—together; and in due course, after many vicissitudes, the resulting blend would create the French nation.

Overleaf: In his attempt to revive and renew classical art, Charlemagne commissioned scholars and artists to create new manuscripts in the schools set up throughout the kingdom. From the Bible manuscript made (after his death) at Tours in 845–846 comes this miniature of Moses presenting the Ten Commandments (Bibliothèque Nationale, Paris). The recipients of the Law appear in the guise of Charlemagne himself, at center, and the members of his court, to judge from the contemporary clothing and crown and the facial appearance of the monarch (resembling the statue of Charlemagne from the Louvre seen on page 95 and the coin below left).

Below: This Merovingian low relief of seventh-century date was either a tombstone or a panel from a scene in the choir of a church. It was found at Gondorf in the Moselle region. The two doves on either side of the figure's head suggest that he may be intended to represent Christ.

121

THE CAROLINGIANS

The later, weak Merovingian monarchs of the seventh and early eighth centuries were unable to prevent power from falling into the hands of their magnates, including particularly the Mayors of the Palace who controlled the itinerant courts. Moreover, the different administrative regions of the kingdom, though geographically and linguistically heterogeneous, were each developing distinctive ambitions of their own and beginning to act independently of one another under the leadership of their separate Mayors.

These territories were Neustria, Austrasia, and Burgundy. Neustria, the old Merovingian center of power, comprised most of northwestern France with its natural capital at Paris. Austrasia lay farther to the east, on both sides of the lower Rhine; its principal center was Metz. The German aristocracy of Austrasia hated the Gallo-Roman nobles of Neustria; and the Mayoralties of the two regions quarreled bitterly over a strip of border territory round Reims. After long periods of tension, the Austrasian Mayor Pepin II (Pepin of Herstal) defeated his Neustrian counterpart at Tertry near Péronne (687). Thereafter he was only prepared to recognize the titular Merovingian monarch on the condition that he, Pepin, was empowered to appoint the Mayors both of Neustria and Burgundy.

There were a number of reasons why the Austrasians had gained this decisive success. For one thing, the lands they farmed were larger and richer. Moreover, the number of the inhabitants of these territories had greatly risen owing to the recent introduction of the heavy plow, so that the Mayors of Austrasia had more numerous and prosperous vassals than their rivals. Besides, these vassals and their tenants were drawn from the largely untapped population of the German homeland, which was a long way away from the Merovingian king and his court, so that they felt greater loyalty to the Mayor than to the monarch. That is to say, the Austrasian victory meant a decisive shift in the gravity of Europe. The axis of the continent had moved toward the great river plains of the north and northeast, where the Romans had scarcely left a tradition. It was here, in the future, that surplus food would create urbanization and all its skills and trades, and here too, therefore, that the embryonic civilization of western Europe would have one of its principal centers.

Pepin II's legendary bastard son Charles Martel ("the Hammer"), after whom the Carolingian dynasty is named, was a tough, gross per-

sonage who fought hard wars all along his eastern frontiers, starting a new expansive onrush that was to last for eighty years, and earned him the title of the second founder of the Frankish state. In western France, he defeated the invasion of the Moslem Arabs from Spain at the battle of Poitiers (732). This victory, although it did not yet succeed in excluding them from the country altogether, marked the limit of their expansion and the

beginning of their retreat. Charles Martel dealt roughly with church property, in order to reward his supporters; and yet, at the same time, he contrived to enjoy closer relations with the papacy and its missionaries than his predecessors had ever been able to maintain. His son Pepin III the Short (751–768), dwarfish yet strong enough to throw a bull, forcibly disembarrassed himself of his internal rivals, concentrated all three Mayoralties of the Palace into his own hands, and then urged Pope Zacharias to sanction the deposition of the last, feeble Merovingian monarch, so that he himself, instead, could formally take his place on the throne. Zacharias agreed, and after this unprecedented act of papal interven-

124

tion or acquiescence, Pepin was duly anointed king at Soissons (751/752). Then he was anointed again at St. Denis, this time by the Pope himself (who was Zacharias' successor, Stephen III). His two sons were anointed with him; the elder was Charles, subsequently known as Charlemagne. These ceremonies which, despite traditional features, were essentially novel as far as the Franks were concerned, effectively bestowed on the new Carolingian monarchy a sacred and inviolable character, inseparable from the Church. But the benefits were reciprocal. For after Pepin's anointments, the Pope obtained from him, in the Declaration of Quercy (754), a promise to restore to the papacy the Italian lands the Lombards had annexed from it. Pepin's promise, duly fulfilled in 755–756, was significant for the future. For it meant that he had created a temporal papal state in Italy; and he had made Frankish interests dominant in that country.

He also strengthened his kingdom in other directions as well. His capture of Narbonne from the Arabs accelerated their expulsion from the country, which his father had already initiated. The reduction of dissident Aquitaine, in the course of eight years of campaigning (752–759), meant the annexation of another prosperous, civilized territory of France itself. Raiders from Germany were firmly resisted along the Rhine. And further steps were taken to bring and keep Bavaria within the Frankish sphere of influence. Meanwhile, at home, Pepin inaugurated a comprehensive series of administrative, ecclesiastical, and legal reforms, designed partly to impose his own authority and partly to enforce his clergy's obedience to Rome. He also put a stop to the monetary anarchy that had prevailed throughout the kingdom; henceforward all pieces minted within the Frankish realm were stamped with his own name or initial.

This gilt chalice inscribed with the name Tassilo, Duke of Bavaria (ca. 777–788), was made for him by an Englishman or a craftsman trained in an English or Anglo-Carolingian school. The duke presented it to the abbey he founded at Kremsmunster, Austria, where it is still to be seen. The knot-work framing the ovals is a Lombard motif, recalling that the duke's wife Liutperg was the daughter of Desiderius, last king of the Lombards

Far left. This Byzantine silk textile bearing the design of a four-horse chariot was found in the tomb of Charlemagne at Aachen (Aix-la-Chapelle). Musée de Cluny, Paris.

Below: The crystal of Charlemagne's great-grandson, the emperor Lothar II (855–869), from Metz, probably made as an embellishment for an imperial throne or chair. Its eight scenes, starting at the top and proceeding clockwise, tell with a wealth of vivid gesture the Biblical story of Susanna, whom the Elders accused falsely; when Daniel convicted them of perjury, they were stoned to death and Susanna went free.

FEUDAL SOCIETY

The most important contribution of this epoch to the art of war was the stirrup, acquired by the west from China by way of the nomads who dominated the Asian steppes. It was probably the Frankish leader Charles Martel who first grasped the revolutionary military possibilities of this piece of equipment. Previous cavalrymen had been little more than armored bowmen, but the stirrup, by welding the rider together with his horse into a single, coordinated fighting unit, enormously increased the effectiveness of his attack.

When the advantages of this unfamiliar kind of warfare became apparent in northern France and Burgundy, the growth of a specialized aristocracy of mounted warriors, the forerunners of "feudal knights," inevitably followed; the old concept that every free man made a useful soldier now seemed obsolete and irrelevant. A different economic structure, too, had to be erected. For to become a fighter of the new species cost a good deal of money, and this set the national leaders a problem. The Merovingian monarchy had been content to receive cash from its noblemen in exchange for immunity from royal control. A Carolingian ruler still needed their money—but wanted them to spend it on themselves, so that they should become horsemen of the novel type in his service.

In other words, he wanted them as his vassals. Vassalage, the swearing of allegiance to a leader, had roots that went back into the dim past. It may have been Charles Martel who made it a matter of systematic and formal contract, involving definite mutual obligations on both sides. His vassals were bound to fight for him, and in return he would give them cattle or revenue or military office or, above all, land. It was in order to find sufficient land for this purpose that he seized so many properties of the Church.

Moreover, the same process occurred lower down the social ladder. Just as the magnates became vassals of the Mayor of the Palace or the king, so too, in their turn, free men of

lesser status were encouraged to become the vassals of a magnate, who kept them in his household or gave them farms on his manorial estate. This was a development of the ancient Roman institution of clients who supported and depended on their patrons; and in particular it had evolved from the practice of the later Roman empire, when people sought the security of the manors and gave personal service in exchange. It was in response to the Carolingians' need for up-to-date military forces that these traditions gradually developed into a thoroughgoing "feudal" system.

Under this system, in its most typical form,

allegiance to a leader (vassalage) was fused with the granting of a property (benefice). As arrangements of such a kind evolved, the Frankish world was organized in great groups of domains descended from the large estates of the later Roman empire but henceforward dedicated to the novel, revolutionary military needs of the Carolingian realm. The idea of state service had virtually disappeared; now there were only relationships between lord and vassal. The lesser partner was deprived of much of his independence. Yet this, in recent centuries, had not been worth a great deal, and he gained protection instead, which in so precarious a society came before everything else. Besides, in a community that was almost wholly agricultural, it was good for him to know that a bad harvest need not cause his ruin.

Below these élite or relatively élite groups that formed parts of the embryonic feudal society, there existed, as always, multitudes of peasants, working pieces of land under the direction of their masters. Technically free men, they were often virtually serfs, tied to their holdings and the lord's will or whim. However, in the course of the seventh and eighth centuries the large serf estates were partly replaced by small freeholdings, with the encouragement of the Church. By now, all the principal, interlocking elements of a lasting agricultural revolution were in place: the heavy plow, open fields, modern harness; also the triennial rotation of crops—which did more than anything else to transform the economy of western Europe.

Private armies were a product of the developing feudal system according to which tenants served as soldiers (partly as cavalry, which now formed an increasingly important arm) in exchange for housing and protection. This ivory, sixth or seventh century, shows a mounted prince or nobleman with seven followers, one mounted and the others on foot. Now at the Landesmuseum, Trier, Germany, the ivory may have come from the famous abbey of St. Maximin in that Frankish city (which was later devastated by the Vikings).

Left: A central feature in the feudal process, the arming of a new knight, is the subject of this pen-and-ink sketch in Matthew Paris' *Historia de Offa Rege* (ca. 1250), perhaps by the author himself. It shows King Offa of Angel (a continental Anglian ruler of the fourth century, ancestor of the English monarch Offa of Mercia) receiving his arms from his father King Wermund, no doubt with many anachronistic details. British Museum, London.

FRISIA AND GERMANY

When the hardy seagoing north Germanic peoples migrated in the fifth century, they used vessels such as the Nydam ship, this large rowing boat of the fourth or early fifth century A.D., found in a peatbog in the Anglian territory of south Jutland. Each oak plank was the full length of the boat and overlapped the one below; the edges were firmly fixed with iron rivets. Despite its length of more than seventy feet, the ship had no keel—merely a broad bottom plank—and no provision for a mast. It could therefore be blown sideways, and several days of continuous rowing were needed to take it across the North Sea. Designed to hold as many men as possible, it was evidently a warship. Schleswig-Holsteinisches Landesmuseum für Vor- und Frühgeschichte, Schleswig.

Right: Wooden figure of a bearded Scandinavian god, found in a peatbog at Broddenbjerg, near Viborg, in northern Jutland, Denmark, dating from before the year 500. This is early evidence for the pagan Nordic religion—known to us from much later literary sources—in which there were numerous gods, varying considerably in power and status, each governing particular human needs or actions. National Museum, Copenhagen.

A particularly important part in the economic life of the age was played by the Frisians, a German people whose shores and islands spread eastward from the mouth of the Rhine. During the fifth century the insufficiency of farmland on this marshy coast caused some Frisians, mixed with other tribesmen, to join the Anglo-Saxon migrations to England. But those who remained spread eastward as far as the Weser, and before long, southwestward as well, into their hinterland on the Rhine, which became known as Frisia Magna.

In order to protect themselves against floods, these people constructed their dwellings on "terps," artificial hillocks: "God made the sea," it was said, "but the Frisians made the coast." The inhabitants of their defensible farms and small villages, many of which have been identified by excavations, not only engaged in arable farming but bred cattle and wove textiles. Their export outlet and commercial center was Dorestad (Wyk te Duurstede), a port (and later a mint) near Utrecht on the Waal mouth of the Rhine. The ships constructed by the Frisians possessed a larger cargo capacity, and greater seaworthiness, than had ever been attained before; and this made them, in the sixth and seventh centuries, the most important maritime power in the North Sea, trading by river and sea alike with all their neighbors, and exporting "Flanders cloth" and many slaves.

These expansive activities of the Frisians, however, brought them into collision with the Carolingian Franks, who gradually wore

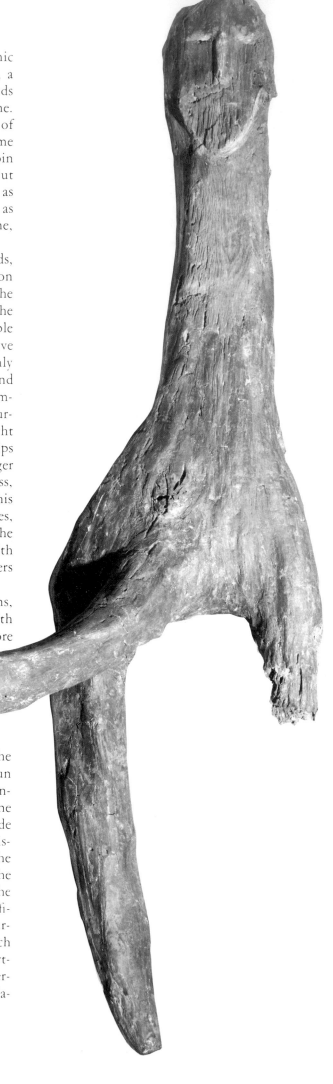

them down until Charlemagne (although he chose their cloth as a gift for the caliph Harun al-Rashid) obliterated the entire state, converting its inhabitants to Christianity. One reason why the Carolingian kingdom made war on the Frisians was to protect the Christian missions in their territory. For the Northumbrian St. Willibrord (658–739), the "apostle of the Frisians" and founder of the see of Utrecht, had encountered perilous difficulties at their hands. With Frankish encouragement, however, he settled at Echternach (Luxembourg, 697); and this served as a starting-off point for missionary activity in Germany beyond the Rhine, where the population had greatly increased in recent years.

"The apostle of Germany," who took advantage of this opportunity, was another Englishman, Wynfrith of Crediton, known as St. Boniface (ca. 672/3–754). His first visit to Frisia did not last long, because he too met with an unfriendly reception. But three years later Pope Gregory II instructed him to evangelize hitherto unconverted lands of Germany. After visiting many regions (including Utrecht, to which he returned for three years to preach under Willibrord), Boniface was consecrated bishop and given an even more far-reaching commission (722). In carrying this out, he had the strong support of Charles Martel, who saw these religious campaigns as a chance to extend Frankish power, and consequently went farther than any of his predecessors in supporting them. With this encouragement, Boniface embarked on an enormously energetic program, addressing huge congregations in their native languages, and organizing the Christians of Bavaria into the first national church east of the Rhine.

Next, Boniface was entrusted by Pope Zacharias with the reform and overhaul of the entire Church of the Frankish kingdom (741); and with the help of Pepin III the Short he undertook this huge task, dividing the eastern zone of the national territory into four bishoprics. He also founded, at this time, the greatest of his monasteries, at Fulda in Hesse (744), which became a model Benedictine missionary center and an outstanding factory for the copying of learned texts. Finally, after settling for a time at Mainz, which he raised to be the principal German bishopric, he made yet another journey to Frisia, where he and his companions were murdered.

Boniface was as vigorous in controversy as in action. His organizing genius was piously devoted to the service of the papacy, to whose friendly relations with his Carolingian patrons he thereby greatly contributed, though without any of their conscious political motives. He achieved great success in imposing his own formidable blend of northern dynamism and Latin order upon wild German territory; and this was a land where the recipe caused no cultural duality or conflict, since its populations had never had very much culture before. The new monasteries stood like fortified blockhouses on the frontiers of the faith, manned by monks and missionaries who preached, taught, built, farmed, healed the sick, and worked in metals. By launching the whole process, Boniface exercised as much influence on the history of Europe as any other Englishman who has ever lived.

 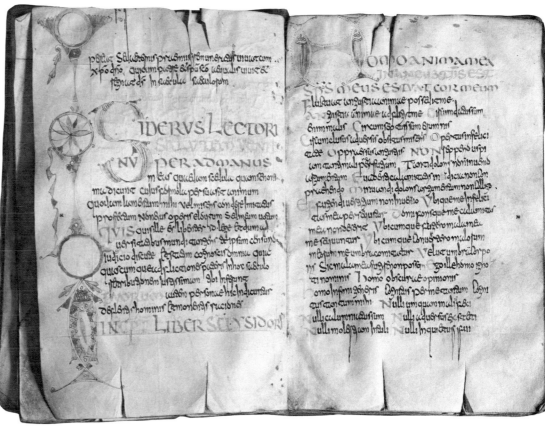

The so-called Pagyndrusis Codex, believed to have been the property of St. Boniface (d. 754). In the course of his organization of the East Frankish Church, Boniface founded the abbey of Fulda in 742, as a center of German monastic culture; this Codex remains part of its treasure. Under Abbot Rutger, the church at Fulda was rebuilt and enlarged (802–819) with the aim of creating a northern replica of St. Peter's Basilica at Rome—in spite of a petition to Charlemagne by the monks to stop "the enormous and superfluous buildings and all those other useless works by which the brethren are unnecessarily wearied and the serfs ruined." According to a legend, the book was cut by a sword when pagans tried to murder St. Boniface.

THE CONQUESTS AND CORONATION OF CHARLEMAGNE

After the death of Pepin III the Short, his elder son Charles (Charlemagne) became first the joint and then the sole king of the Franks (771). He was then able to proceed to the further territorial expansions for which his predecessors had prepared the way. To the north, the Frisians were finally conquered, and the Saxons of northwestern Germany (round the Weser) were savagely repressed in campaigns lasting more than three decades (772–804). They were also converted to Christianity by force—so that these were the earliest major European wars of religion. To the east, Bavarians and Slavs, and others, also felt Charlemagne's heavy hand, and his annexations extended as far as the Elbe and the borders of the Byzantine empire.

To the southwest, he established a Spanish "March," as recounted, with poetic license, in

The cover of Charlemagne's casket, in the cathedral at Aachen (Aix-la-Chapelle), Germany, shows the siege of Pamplona in northern Spain, the country in which the ambush of his armies at Roncesvalles became, in much changed form, the theme of the epic *Song of Roland*.

the *Song of Roland*. But most significant for the future were the wars he fought against the Lombards in Italy. Crossing the Alps at the instigation of a series of alarmed Popes—whom the Byzantines were too preoccupied to assist—he besieged the last monarch in Pavia, and after nine months compelled him to surrender (774). Thereupon Charlemagne himself assumed the title of King of the Lombards in his place.

He had made himself preeminent in western and central Europe, and its Church looked to him rather than to Constantinople for protection—and relied contentedly on his fervently antipagan, anti-Arian, and pro-Catholic policies. Four years' bloodthirsty confusion in

papal politics (795–799) placed Rome even further in his power, and Pope Leo III had to depend on him to save his own office, and indeed his life. On Christmas day of the year 800, Leo set a crown on Charlemagne's head, and he was publicly acclaimed as emperor. This meant that, from now on, the Popes depended upon Frankish protection. As for Charlemagne, his supreme prestige in the west had received spectacular recognition: for the papacy itself was under his control.

What exactly his new title of "emperor" signified was much more open to question. Only one imperial title was known in Europe and the Mediterranean world, and that was the rulership of the Byzantine empire: which was still known as "Roman." In Italy, there had no longer been an emperor since 476, but in the east the reigns of successive "Roman" Byzantine rulers had continued without a break. If, therefore, Charlemagne was going to become an emperor on his own account, it could only be in the same series; for there was no other. What, then, would be Constantinople's attitude to his proclamation? At the time it took place, the Byzantine monarch was an empress, Irene, and it was alleged that Charlemagne had plans to marry her. But this is not certain, and in any case she died. Thereafter, Frankish relations with Irene's vigorous successor, the emperor Nicephorus I (802–811), rapidly deteriorated—not only on account of Charlemagne's title, but because of their competing and conflicting claims to Venice and the Dalmatian coast. Finally, after prolonged negotiation, it was agreed that Charlemagne would acknowledge Byzantium's suzerainty over Venetia (to the disappointment of the Pope, who had hoped to be allowed to take the region over) in exchange for recognition of his imperial title—a grudging recognition, since the Byzantines chose to interpret Charlemagne's role as relating only to the Franks, defining "the Romans" as their own emperor's sphere.

The coronation brought no change in Charlemagne's policy, unless, perhaps, it intensified his already strong sense of his own religious authority. Yet the event had far-reaching implications, all the same. It had widened the split between east and west; and it meant that the Franks were now irremediably involved with the fortunes of the papacy. In future, pious Frankish rulers, and other German emperors after them, would proclaim as their main function the promotion of Christian unity by whatever means.

The throne of Charlemagne, in the cathedral at Aachen. Departing from the old Frankish custom according to which the kings and their retinues moved frequently from place to place—living off each of their successive hosts in turn—Charlemagne established his capital at Aachen, which was strategically placed for the supervision of the western and eastern parts of his dominions alike.

In the Talisman of Charlemagne (above), a fragment of wood, believed to have been part of the True Cross, is framed in two sapphire cabochons. These frames with their precious stones display the influence of Byzantine workmanship.

THE EMPIRE
OF CHARLEMAGNE

Right: This copy of a ninth-century mosaic symbolizes the new political and religious situation created in Europe by Pope Leo III's coronation of Charlemagne as emperor in the year 800; St. Peter is shown giving the pallium (stole of spiritual authority) to Pope Leo, and the standard (representing politico-military power) to Charlemagne. The mosaics were originally in the Triclinio or dining room of the Lateran palace, Rome, and the copies now adorn a reconstructed apse of the hall in the Piazza di Porta San Giovanni.

The Palatine Chapel, Charlemagne's royal chapel at Aachen, northwest Germany, where he most frequently resided. Although its ultimate inspiration is a building at Constantinople, it also resembles the church of San Vitale at Ravenna in its design. These echoes are noteworthy since Charlemagne's new imperial title implied a claim to rival the Byzantine empire in the west.

The most important surviving work of Carolingian architecture after Aachen is the Gatehouse (Torhalle) at Lorsch *(right).* It was one of the buildings of the abbey founded in 763 and rebuilt on an adjacent site from 774 onward, and is said to have resembled the original gatehouse at the Vatican Basilica of St. Peter's. A number of features of its architecture illustrate the classical revivalism of the period, which went back ultimately to Roman models.

Abandoning the practice of continual royal progresses through the land, Charlemagne, when not engaged in wars of conquest, established his favorite residence at Aachen (Aix-la-Chapelle), in the middle of his family estates—halfway between the Frankish homeland and the conquered territories of north Germany. There he turned to the task of reorganizing the administration of his empire. Its principal regional authorities were counts and bishops. They received the emperor's instructions either from his own letters sent to their twice-yearly assemblies, or from verbal directions issued by Charlemagne's *missi dominici.* These were royal officials who traveled continually on circuit throughout the empire. Operating in pairs—often one of them was a lay noble, and the other a churchman—they decreed, judged, and reported back home. Another of Charlemagne's measures was a general reform of the coinage, based on the pound of two hundred and forty pence (which remained current, in England, until only a dozen years ago). Yet despite all these efforts, the economic system of the empire remained too flimsy and fragmented to support the vast dominions it encompassed.

Insistent on strict, literal conformity with the letter of the divine law (though he disliked undisciplined, charismatic religion), Charlemagne instituted educational reforms, to which he attached great weight, since he considered it an imperative condition of national survival that government and Church should

FRISIA
SAXONY
• Aachen
NEUSTRIA
BRITTANY
• Tours
ALAMANNIA   BAVARIA
BURGUNDY   CARINTHIA
AQUITANIA
GASCONY
SEPTIMANIA
SPANISH MARK

Merovingian past, and with all the Germanic, Celtic, Scandinavian, and eastern ingredients which it had utilized. What Charlemagne was really trying to do was to create a mixed culture to which Frankish and Roman and Christian elements all had their contribution to make.

He built on work that others had done before him, but his own contribution too was enormous; for until his last years at least, his physical and mental energy was heroic. After his death, however, his empire fell apart immediately. For it lacked any sort of ethnic unity or durable binding force: it was only a brief episode of unwieldy, rough-and-ready amalgamation, which could not fail to break down once its creator was dead. Yet his personality lived on after him. Popular but formidable, a man who combined spacious vision and

work together to provide a well-trained clergy for the empire's old and new territories alike. With this massive task of urgently needed instruction in mind, he was entirely ready to import foreign talent. At this period, the brilliant culture of Northumbria was an obvious source, and Alcuin of York (ca. 732–804), the most learned man of the day, was invited to bring the studies of the Anglo-Saxon schools to Charlemagne's empire (781). At the new educational center Alcuin established at Aachen, the emperor himself, and his relations and friends and their sons, were taught in an atmosphere of sharp and witty discussion. In 796 Alcuin retired to preside over St. Martin's monastery at Tours. There he and his monks developed the bold and attractive script known as the Carolingian minuscule, which became the principal alphabet of western Europe and is the source of our printed script today.

Charlemagne's domed, octagonal royal chapel at Aachen was based on an imperial hall of state at Constantinople. Moreover, Charlemagne looked still farther back, and at this "Second Rome" at Aachen deliberately emulated Roman glories. It was a resuscitation and not a continuation, because no direct contact with ancient Rome any longer existed—his nobles, for example, spoke German, and could not read and mostly did not want to. But Charlemagne himself felt very differently, as the heads on his silver pennies show, for they are deliberately given an ancient Roman appearance. And yet, at the same time, the Carolingian art of the day also shows unbroken continuity with the immediate

sweeping boldness with solid commonsense and meticulous tenacity, he very rapidly became an undying legend: the legend of the strong man, extrovert, and hedonist leader of a rowdy and scandalous court, who recreated the western empire and was the invincible champion of Christendom.

His reign overshadowed the entire future. Most of the problems with which his successors were confronted, for many centuries to come, were latent in the heritage he left them. But so were their achievements, too. For by his vigorous, violent methods he had laid the foundations of Europe as it is today.

Rabanus (Hrabanus) Maurus, the most important of the abbots of the monastery at Fulda (822–842), and later archbishop of Mainz (from 847), from a ninth-century manuscript (Bibliothèque Communale, Amiens). Rabanus, Alcuin's best student, composed poetry and many commentaries and theological and pedagogical writings, and was the leading cultural personality of the epoch following Charlemagne's death.
The gold and jeweled orb with cross is part of the regalia of the Holy Roman Empire, and is traditionally associated with the name of Charlemagne himself.

THE JEWS IN ASIA AND EUROPE

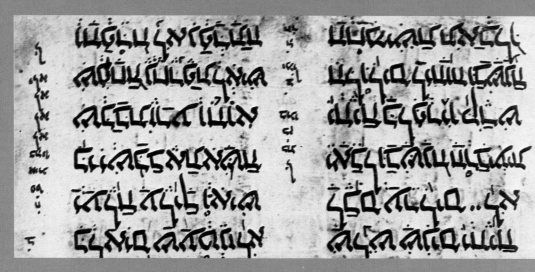

In this age of great migrations, the Jewish Diaspora or Dispersion represents a unique experience. As minorities wherever they went, literate and peaceable amid so much violence, they mustered no armies and conquered no territory. And except in Russia—where the Khazar kingdom became Jewish—they sought and made few converts, thereby differing from the Christians and Moslems of the time. Indeed, as outsiders and scapegoats, with their civil rights always restricted, their very survival in this period—let alone their economic and cultural contribution—was an arresting phenomenon. Their host countries seemed torn between respect and loathing for the Jews. If they flourished at first under the Sassanian Persians, in academies where they elaborated the Talmudic commentaries, that government subsequently went over to a policy of persecutions like those practiced intermittently by the Byzantines. Admired by Mohammed, who sought unsuccessfully to win them over to his own mission, they were destined to play a brilliant role in medicine and philosophy under Islamic Spain. In Christian Europe, however, they gradually fared far worse.

Behold, I will take the children
   of Israel from among the heathen,
whither they be gone, and will gather
   them on every side, and bring them into
their own land: and I will make them
   one nation in the land upon the mountains
of Israel, and one king shall be king
   to them all: and they shall no more be
two nations, neither shall they be divided
   into two kingdoms any more at all.

Ezekiel 37:21–22

Following the Romans' suppression of the Jewish revolt in A.D. 70, most of the Jewish population came to be dispersed throughout the empire. This glass dish decorated with gold leaf, of the fourth or fifth century A.D., is from the Jewish catacombs at Rome, where a very important community was established, from which the city's early Christians seceded. Israel Museum, Jerusalem.
Opposite: Part of the Torah or Pentateuch (the first five books of the Jewish Bible, referred to by Christians as the Old Testament). This ninth-century manuscript is probably the oldest existing copy of any substantial part of the Bible in Hebrew. British Museum, London.

135

THE JEWS
OF THE MISHNAH
AND TALMUD

One of the unique features of Jewish history was, and is, their Dispersion (Diaspora) into many other lands. This began in the late eighth century B.C. when the kingdom of Israel (the more northerly of the two states into which the empire of David and Solomon had split) was attacked and then annexed by kings of Assyria, who removed many of its more prosperous inhabitants—whereupon the "Ten Lost Tribes" were swallowed up and vanished without a trace. Next, the southern kingdom of Judah and its capital Jerusalem succumbed to a Babylonian monarch (597–586 B.C.), who destroyed the Temple that Solomon had erected, and took away a great part of the local population to what is now Iraq. Subsequently, the founder of the Achae-

Part of the Arch of Titus, Rome *(right)*, showing the triumphal procession held in A.D. 70 by Vespasian and his son Titus to celebrate the suppression of the First Jewish Revolt. The relief shows the Menorah (seven-branched candlestick), which formed part of the spoils—and has never been traced again. Only Masada, on the Dead Sea, continued to hold out until 73. Later, with encouragement from the first Christian emperor Constantine I the Great

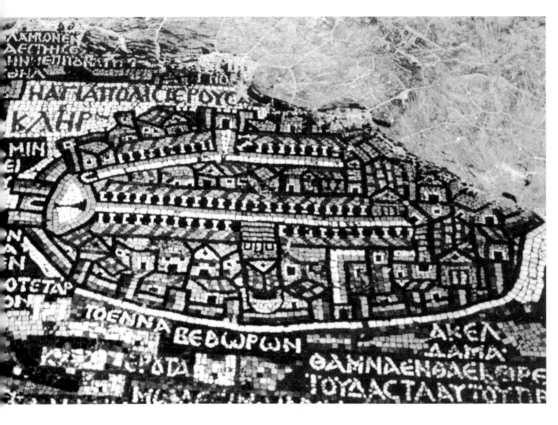

and his successors, the city of Jerusalem was adorned by splendid churches. This plan of Jerusalem *(above)* is part of a world-map on a sixth-century floor mosaic in the synagogue at Madaba. Some of the city's streets can be recognized, also buildings, including the Church of the Holy Sepulcher.

Right: A burial in Beth Shearim (southeast of Haifa), Israel. The cemetery here served a very large area and was in use until the 450s, but it is chiefly famous as being the burial-place of the patriarch Judah I ha-Nasi (d. ca. 217), revered not only for his leadership of the Jewish community, but as the reputed principal editor of the Mishnah, the commentary that dominated subsequent Hebrew thought.

menid Persian empire, Cyrus I the Great (559–530), allowed fifty thousand of their descendants back to their country, where they built the Second Temple at Jerusalem. It was at this period of national consciousness that the term "Jew" first came into use, meaning at first a descendant of the tribe of Judah, though subsequently the word was used in a religious sense as well. The Jews were the people of the Bible, the people who, despite all appearances, enjoyed God's special favor.

The Dispersion steadily continued and increased. The Jews freed themselves from the Greeks, the successors of the Persians, in 164–142 B.C., but subsequently became the

*At the time of the Afternoon Offering on the
last Festival-day they used to make the
Avowal. How used a man to make the
Avowal? [He said] "I have removed the
Hallowed Things out of my house"—that
is Second Tithe and the fruits of
Fourth-year plantings: "I have given them to
the Levite"—that is the Tithe of the
Levites; "and also"—that is the
Heave-offering and Heave-offering of the
Tithe; "to the stranger and the fatherless or
widow"—that is the Poor man's Tithe,
Gleanings, the Forgotten Sheaf, and Pe'ah
[Although these do not render the Avowal
invalid]: "from the house"—that is the
Dough-offering.*

Mishnah. Ma'aser Sheni 5:10

Meanwhile the Jews of the Dispersion, numerically increased by refugees from the Judaean revolts, still lived on, and many of them prospered. Out of the approximately eight million Jews in the world at that time (as against fourteen million today), nearly seven million seem to have lived in one part or another of the Roman empire, where they constituted between six and nine percent of the total population.

The emphatic monotheism of the Jews, which they in due course bequeathed to the Christians and Moslems, is enshrined in the Torah (the first five books of what Christians call the Old Testament) and the books of the Prophets. The Mishnah (from *shanu*, "to repeat"), compiled in the time of the Roman

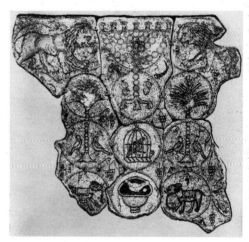

These two floor mosaics illustrate and date a significant change in the pattern of Jewish religious decoration. That on the left, from the early sixth century synagogue of Beth Alpha, depicts Abraham preparing to sacrifice his son Isaac. That on the right, from Maon in the late sixth century, shows no human figures, but only the Menorah and various animal motifs. It is debated whether this iconoclastic shift was due to the Islamic invasion (638—640) or to an independent change of policy by the Jewish religious leaders.

subjects of the Romans, who created the minor province of Judaea (A.D. 6). After the failure of the First Jewish Revolt against the Romans (A.D. 66—70), Jerusalem was destroyed and the Temple burnt down, never to be restored, but a center of Judaism survived at Jamnia (Yavne) on the coast. Following two further revolts, the first throughout the Near East (115 117) and the second in Judaea (132—135), the nucleus of Jewish life shifted to Galilee, where the Romans recognized a succession of Patriarchs as the leaders of their people. One of them, Judah I ha-Nasi (the Prince, d. ca. 217), achieved a powerful nationwide prestige and authority.

empire in Mishnaic Hebrew, accepted oral interpretations of the Biblical texts, of which the validity had been emphasized earlier by the most progressive of Jewish sects, the Pharisees. The principal editor of the Mishnah, in its final form, is believed to have been Judah I ha-Nasi, whose eminence accorded the work immediate recognition. Next only to the Bible itself, it has exerted greater influence on Jewish thinking than any other book, forming the basis of all the vast rabbinical literature of later epochs.

In due course, perusal of the Mishnah encouraged a series of rabbis to prepare the way for a further enormously influential work. This

was the Talmud, completed by the end of the fifth century A.D., which constituted an entire literature in itself, and was the formative element that gave Judaism cohesion and resilience in all the hard times which lay ahead. In its complete form, the Talmud consisted of the Mishnah together with the Gamara, a commentary on the Mishnah containing interpretations of its contents. The Gamara comprised first the Palestinian (Jerusalem) Talmud and then the even more far-reaching and useful Babylonian Talmud. These works were written in Aramaic, the common Semitic spoken tongue of the Near and Middle East, using its western and eastern dialects respectively.

Very few men like Abraham has the sun looked upon. From his youth he served his Maker and walked upright before Him, and from his birth even unto the moment of his death his God was with him.

The Talmud

Babylonia was not part of the Roman empire, but belonged to the Parthians; and then, from the third century onward, its people came under Sassanian Persian rule. It was a country where the Jewish communities, dating back for nearly a thousand years, enjoyed a remarkable efflorescence. By 200, they already numbered almost a million people, thus providing the greater part of the world's Jewish population that was not under Roman rule; by 500 the total had risen to two million. The transference of the nucleus of the Jewish community away from Roman territory, at a time when things were bad for them there, is a characteristic and in their view providential aspect of their history—the development of a "reserve" area whenever the previous center is in danger. Until the foundation of modern Israel, the Jews never again had another center as impressive as ancient and medieval Babylonia. In its academies, Hebrew scholarship flourished, first at Nehardea on the Euphrates, founded in about A.D. 212, and then downstream at Sura (219). When Nehardea was destroyed in a war (262), Pumbeditha took its place, and then Machuza, too, was established beside the Tigris. "In Babylonia," declared Huna (d.297), "we consider ourselves exactly as if we were in the Holy Land"; and throughout the period discussed in this book the country retained its leadership of Judaism throughout the world.

The Torah, meaning "Law," consisting of the first five (Mosaic) books of the Bible—Genesis, Exodus, Leviticus, Deuteronomy, and Numbers—forms the basis of Jewish faith. Its teaching is viewed as forming a perfect unity, combining faith and morals, doctrine and religious practice. Its contents are believed to embody not only the essential beliefs, but also day-to-day observances and morals, including penalties for infractions. The Torah scrolls *(siphrei torah)* shown here were made by "oriental" Jews who played such an important part in the transmission of Hebrew civilization during later Roman and medieval times. The scroll to the left is from Iraq, and the one at right from India. Behind is a silk Ark curtain from Persia.

A MINORITY IN THE PERSIAN AND CHRISTIAN EMPIRES

The countries of the Near East often displayed a high degree of religious tolerance. The city of Dura Europos, on the Syrian bank of the Euphrates, contained buildings where thirteen different faiths conducted their worship, including a very early synagogue (third century A.D.), which was adorned with many wall paintings of Biblical scenes. The detail below is from the series devoted to the raising of dead bones by God (Ezekiel 37:1–14): "And ye shall know that I am the Lord, when I have opened your graves, O my people, and brought you up out of your graves, and shall put my spirit in you and

you shall live." *Opposite:* Two scenes from the childhood of Moses in Egypt. In keeping with Jewish writing, the picture sequence goes from right to left. The pharaoh's daughter, bathing in the river (bottom right), saves the baby, as her servants stand by. In the scene at left, the child is being handed over to his own mother, upon orders of the princess, for nursing. Non-Jewish influences are evident in the clothing of the Ezekiel scene, and in the frontal view of the figures (from a convention that developed in the Parthian empire of Mesopotamia and Iran and its fringes). Further details from these cycles are shown on page 145.

These Babylonian Jews had their own official leaders, the "Princes of Captivity" or exilarchs (Resh Galuta), who received conspicuous privileges from the Sassanian Persian government and lived in great state in their own palatial quarter at the Sassanian capital, Ctesiphon. Most of the Jews of Babylonia strongly supported Persia in its recurrent wars against Rome, and although the Zoroastrian church went through a militant phase of persecuting minorities in the later third century, the Jewish communities remained, at most times, pro-Persian. But persecutions returned, in a more severe form, when Yazdegerd II (ca. 438–457) and his son Firuz (ca. 457–483) became very hostile to their Jewish subjects. The academies at Sura and Pumbeditha were temporarily closed, and the exilarch of the time was condemned to death, though his son Mar Zutra II escaped and set up a small independent state for seven years.

More permanent were the Jewish communities in India (Cochin and the region of Bombay), which probably developed because of Persian trade and were augmented when Sassanian persecutions caused migrations from Babylonia. There were also settlements in China, possibly dating back to the same epoch; there have been Jews at Kaifeng Fu (Honan) right up to modern times.

In the Roman empire the status of the Jews worsened sharply. The turning point came when Constantine I the Great (306–337) replaced paganism by Christianity as his favored religion. For Christian theologians and historians condemned the Jews as corporatively responsible for the death of Jesus Christ. And yet this condemnation was framed in ambivalent and qualified terms, since it had been the Jews, after all, who produced Jesus and unconsciously prepared the way for his mission. They must therefore be protected from extinction. But at the same time, because they had supposedly killed Jesus, it also seemed right in the view of a large part of the Christian clergy that they should be reduced to a miserable existence.

Constantine himself remained contemptuously tolerant, but under his son and successor, Constantius II, the situation worsened when Jewish rebels in Palestine proclaimed a king of their own people named Patricius—in an attempt to exploit the strained relations between Romans and Persians. Thereupon the Roman government began to impose penal laws that assumed an ever more drastic appearance, and respites, notably under the

anti-Christian emperor Julian (361–363), only proved temporary. In 429 the patriarchate was abolished, and the law-code of Theodosius II systematized the numerous restrictions which the Jews by now had to endure. Rebellions (including risings by the dissident Samaritan sect) continued to take place at intervals, and Christian churchmen became increasingly hostile.

It is true that the imperial government consistently protected Jewish freedom, up to a point; for example, synagogues were regarded as immune from billeting, and people who burnt them down had to pay for their reconstruction. Nevertheless, Jews were excluded from the civil service and then from the legal profession as well, and the fervently orthodox Justinian I (527–565) classified them with pagans and thus deprived them of the right to make wills, receive inheritances, or be witnesses in a court of law; he also prohibited the reading of the Mishnah.

Maurice (582–602) even coordinated his anti-Jewish measures with the Sassanian monarch Khosrau II. But during the great wars between the two empires that followed, the Jews rallied to Persia and were said to have massacred nearly 100,000 Christians. When, therefore, the Byzantine army returned to Jerusalem, the Jewish community suffered terrible losses in its turn. Heraclius I, disturbed, it was said, by a prophecy that the empire would be destroyed by a circumcised race, ordered the baptism of every Jew throughout his empire, though it was a saving grace of all such measures that they could never be effectively enforced.

Later Byzantine rulers increased the taxes imposed on Jews, and persecutions recurred from time to time. Eighth-century emperors, eager to prove their own contested orthodoxy, drove many of the Jewish population away from Constantinople and the nearby regions to the areas surrounding the Black Sea. If, however, a Jew decided to abandon his religion and become a Christian, there was nothing to stop him and his descendants from rising high in the Byzantine state: for example, the sister of the empress Irene married a descendant of a renegade Jew from Tiberias in Galilee.

THE JEWS AND MOHAMMED

There were also many thousands of Jews in Arabia. Most of them were the descendants of refugees from the failed Palestinian revolts against the Romans, though some may have been there much longer, and others were Arabs converted to Judaism. In about 400 one of the monarchs of the region, Abu Kariba As'ad, the king of the Himyarites in the Yemen, appears to have adopted Judaism himself, together with many of his subjects. Then his son or grandson Dhu Nuwas (or Yusuf Ashab) conducted a severe persecution of the Christians in his kingdom, culminating in a massacre at Najran. This caused profound shock in the Christian world, prompting a martyrological literature in several languages. Moreover, it gave the Byzantines a chance to intervene. They were eager to secure southern

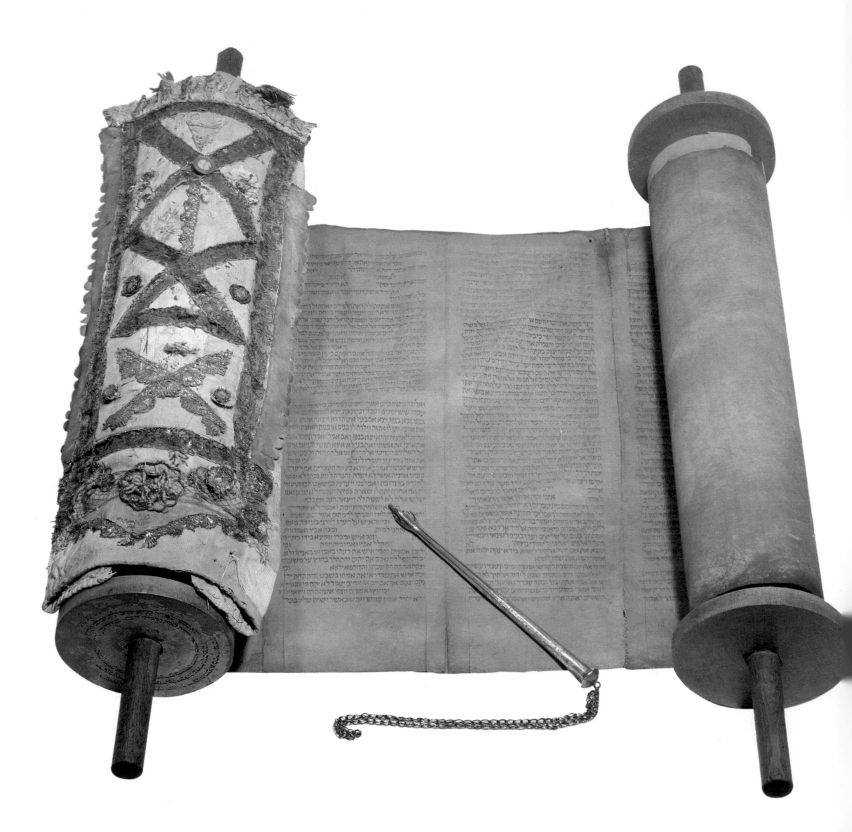

Arabia as a staging point for Indian trade—by which they could bypass Sassanian Persia—and now they saw an opportunity to do so. They therefore instigated the king of the flourishing Christian state of Aksum (Ethiopia) to invade the Yemen. Dhu Nuwas was overthrown, and his Jewish regime came to an end, but a large community of Jews remained in the area; their descendants emigrated to Israel from 1948 onward.

Before his conversion to Judaism, Abu Kariba As'ad had visited Yathrib (Medina), the home of three important Jewish tribes, which formed half the population of the place and controlled some of the best land in the oasis. Moreover, Jewish agriculturalists, craftsmen, and especially goldsmiths prospered at several other Arabian oases as well, including Khaibar (north of Medina), where they formed the entire population. And Jews could not fail to be attracted to Mecca, the halfway house for merchants between the Yemen and Syria.

The different Jewish communities of Arabia were jealous of one another, and did not coalesce in any union. Nevertheless, they dominated the economic life of the country, and Arab poetry praised their poets and chieftains alike. Moreover, their reverence for the Bible strongly influenced the monotheistic beliefs that were developing in seventh-century Arabia, first among the ascetic preachers known as the Hanifa, and then in the fervent teaching of Mohammed.

Mohammed, in return, was convinced that his belief in the one God, shared by the Jews, would prompt them to accept his mission. Indeed, he even pronounced that Abraham and Moses were his own predecessors—sent by God with similar messages to his own. Furthermore, it was an Islamic belief (perhaps based on an independent cult which was later suppressed) that an angel had saved the lives of Abraham's concubine Hagar and their son Ishmael (Ismail)—whom the Arabs revered as their forefather—by showing them Mecca's sacred well, the Zamzam; and Abraham was said to have built the Kaaba as their burial place. Mohammed also adopted Jewish dietary regulations, and fasts, and prayers—and the Moslem faithful, when pronouncing them, were required to turn toward Jerusalem.

Yet in spite of all these measures, most of the Jews of Mecca and the other centers of the region showed no desire to reciprocate; his urgent appeals that they should accept his teaching, and change their way of life, met with little response. On the contrary, they fa-

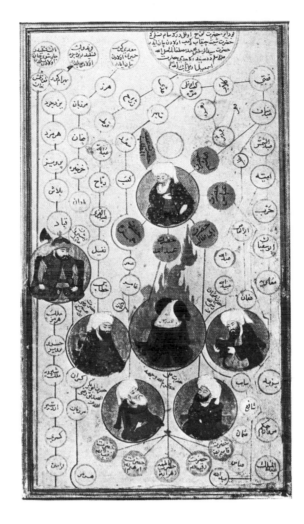

vored the cause of the Meccan Arabs, whose hostility had caused Mohammed to leave their city. However, the disunity of the Jews proved their downfall, for as soon as the Prophet felt he was safe from Meccan attack, he struck a decisive blow against them by attacking and conquering Khaibar; and a mass Jewish emigration from Arabia followed.

These events provided Mohammed with abundant loot—and also gave him occasion to point out to the Jews that their defeat at his hands meant that God was not on their side after all, but on his own. And he went on to declare that they had falsified and corrupted their own scriptures, and perverted the true monotheism of Abraham, the ancestor they shared in common. Yet he never felt able to ignore their existence; and although he did not countenance their forcible conversion by his own followers, the Koran subjects them to searing rebukes, denunciations, and curses.

It was a disappointment to Mohammed that the Jewish communities in Arabia rejected his mission and had to be coerced. This Turkish genealogical table of Mohammed's ancestry lays stress on his descent, through Noah, from Adam's son Seth—thus emphasizing the ancestry he shared with the Jews. On either side of the Prophet, and below, are shown the early caliphs, and above is his grandfather. Chester Beatty Library, Dublin.

The Jewish influence on the Koran was very strong. Jews from the Ghassanid and Lakhmid kingdoms in northern Arabia migrated to Mecca around the year 600, bringing with them their monotheistic beliefs and their law. The Koran, which refers regularly to the Jews as "the People of the Book," displays a thorough knowledge of the Torah or Pentateuch (first five books of the Jewish Bible). The Torah is considered by Moslems to be consistent with their teaching, so that the Jewish rejection of Islam seemed a distortion of the Torah. Jewish communities survived in Islamic countries, as can be seen from these Torah parchment rolls (opposite page) of fifteenth-century date, from Cairo.

Below: Another Jewish sacred text from an Islamic land: a Torah binding, from San'a in the North Yemen (southern Arabia). This intricately decorated cover contains designs resembling flowers and fishes (in the lighter-colored portions) made up of Hebrew texts from Psalms 119 and 121. In the period immediately preceding Mohammed, the kings of the rich land of the Yemen adopted the Jewish faith for a time, and Yemenite Jews have formed a considerable proportion of immigrants into the modern state of Israel.

PRESTIGE UNDER THE CALIPHS

After the Jewish Revolts against the Romans in the first and second centuries A.D., Jerusalem virtually ceased to be a Jewish city, but Judaism recovered and flourished in the peripheral areas of the Holy Land. This door lintel is from the synagogue at Nabratein, probably third century A.D. In the middle of the Hebrew inscription is a wreath containing the Menorah, which had been captured from the Temple by the Romans when Jerusalem fell to them following the First Jewish Revolt.

Sixth-century floor mosaic from Galilee in northern Israel. The design shows the Menorah and other Jewish ritual objects. When Palestine was captured from the Byzantines by the Arabs in the seventh century, the position of the Jews in the country somewhat improved, as in Babylonia after the Arabs had conquered the Sassanian Persians.

In spite of Mohammed's break with the Jews, the wars in which the caliph Omar I (634–644) destroyed the Sassanian Persian empire found them strongly on his side; and their leader the exilarch Bustani welcomed the Arab armies into Babylonia. Nor did their support go unrewarded. Henceforward, they were allowed to enter Jerusalem and stay there, and to worship unhindered in the holy places; while the Babylonian exilarchs, their office recognized and confirmed, lived on in their palace as the princes of a tributary nation, and maintained this position and rank for more than three centuries.

Moreover, the academies of Sura and Pumbeditha soon enjoyed a revival when their directors were raised to the rank of supreme religious dignitaries under the title of Geonim (Excellencies) and were accepted with reverence as authoritative spiritual guides throughout the Jewish world. In Egypt, and Tunisia too, the extensive local Jewish communities awoke to new life. The Arab empire was, on the whole, a bearable place for the Jews. It was true that the "Pact of Omar," gradually developed over the centuries, made it clear that, like other tolerated infidels, they were only second-class citizens. Nevertheless, provided that they paid their taxes—which could at times be harsh—most of the Caliphs did not restrict their freedom very severely.

The Jews had a leading cultural part to play in the Arab empire. In particular, they led the way as teachers in medicine. The oldest known medical work in Hebrew is the *Book of Healing*, written in about 625. Then, half a century later, Masarjawaih, a Jewish doctor of Basra, translated Syriac medical books into Arabic, thus becoming the first of a long line of such translators and laying the foundations of Arab medical studies. Mashallah (Manasseh), by origin a Persian Jew although he had been converted to Islam, was one of the two men instructed to select the site of the new Abbasid capital of Baghdad. He also made a collection of all the sources of ancient astrology. The best-known of all the astrologers in the Arabic world, Abulmassar (Abu Masher), was likewise of Persian Jewish extraction.

Theological ferment pervaded these Jews of the Arabic empire—and like their Moslem and Christian counterparts they did not escape schisms. Above all, the eighth century witnessed the appearance of an increased number of self-styled miracle-working, Messianic redeemers. Notable among them was Abu

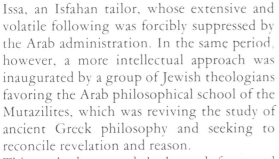

Saadia ben Joseph (882–942), head of the Sura Academy. After Saadia's death, however, Sura fell into disrepute with the government and was closed, and Pumbeditha suffered the same fate in 1040, when its director was executed.

Yet it was also in those same years, at the other end of the Arab dominions, that the Jews experienced their Golden Age in Moslem Spain (which they had helped to establish), conducting much of its international trade and enjoying an extraordinary, climactic efflorescence of scientific, philosophical, and poetical achievements. At the outset of that period, it may have been an eighth-century Jew, "Joseph from Spain," who introduced Indian, known as "Arabic," numerals into that country, from which they spread into western Europe. Joseph was also said to have translated Sanskrit classics into Arabic.

Seen here are additional details from the wall paintings in the third-century synagogue at Dura Europos (see also pp. 140–141). The first scene from the Moses cycle *(below)* shows the pharaoh, seated on his throne, commanding the midwives to kill all newborn males born to Hebrew women (Exodus 1:16). *Left:* From the Ezekiel paintings on the raising of the bones: the prophet is shown prophesying as directed by God. Behind him stand the faithful, and the foot of an angel can be seen at bottom left.

Issa, an Isfahan tailor, whose extensive and volatile following was forcibly suppressed by the Arab administration. In the same period, however, a more intellectual approach was inaugurated by a group of Jewish theologians favoring the Arab philosophical school of the Mutazilites, which was reviving the study of ancient Greek philosophy and seeking to reconcile revelation and reason.

This method attracted the learned, frustrated Jew Anan ben David, who left Babylonia for Jerusalem and founded the Karaite movement (from *qara*, "to read the scriptures"). Karaism was a fundamentalist sect which rejected the authority of the Geonim and declared that the Talmud had falsified Judaism: only the Torah, the Karaites maintained, could be accepted as authority, and religious life must be governed by the literal meaning of its words. The new movement spread rapidly, but was vigorously attacked by the greatest among the Geonim, the Egyptian

WESTERN EUROPEAN JEWRY

These enameled panels are from the imperial crown of the Holy Roman (German) Empire, made for the coronation of Otto I (962) who thus succeeded to the heritage of Charlemagne. The figures represent the Jewish kings David and Solomon, who are recognized as the forerunners of Jesus and of the Christian empire, although the Jews among its population were viewed with heavy official disfavor.

In the Christian kingdoms of western Europe during this period, the Jews generally fared no better than under Byzantine rule, and sometimes even worse: and, apart from short-lived exceptions, a good deal worse than under the Arabs. It is a tale of strange contrasts. Considerable prosperity was possible; yet it was more than counterbalanced by governmental and ecclesiastical sanctions, ranging from covetousness to lethal persecution.

Visigothic Spain, with its dependency in southwest France, provides a vivid example of the paradox. In these lands, where the Jewish communities were large and widespread, the kings treated them at first with relative tolerance, but then, before long, began to try to take over their property, and showed signs of resenting their lack of interest in national unification. Next, after 587, when King Reccared was converted to Catholicism, a series of really tough and terroristic measures came into force, throughout a period of sixty years and more. Humiliated, impoverished, and finally proscribed and enslaved, the Jews of Spain, not unnaturally, welcomed and assisted the Arabs when they came to overthrow the Visigothic kingdom.

In southern Gaul, the Jews were particularly numerous at Marseille, so that it even became known as the "Hebrew City." There and at Narbonne and Montpellier many shipowners were Jews, employing Arles as their emporium. Jewish merchants in such cities exchanged the grain, wine, and manufactures of France for herbs, spices, drugs, and textiles from the east. Among many other communities, they also flourished in the Auvergne, where a hill was known as the Jewish Mountain. A distinguished fifth-century bishop of the area, Sidonius Apollinaris, wrote to a colleague recommending a Jew who was in legal trouble, since these were people, he said, who "from the standpoint of earthly business and jurisdiction commonly have quite good cases," even though he could not condone their beliefs.

This was a characteristically grudging tribute, and yet the Jews in France at this time engaged successfully and unrestrictedly in a wide range of occupations, including not only public offices and all manner of crafts and professions, but above all agriculture and winegrowing. Moreover, they distinguished themselves as soldiers in a siege of Arles, and were in considerable demand as mercenaries. There had also been Jewish communities in the Rhineland from at least 321 (when an edict of Constantine to Cologne testifies to their presence), though how many of them survived continuously during the ensuing stormy centuries is uncertain.

At all events, the Merovingian Frankish monarchy, backed by successive Church Councils, made increasingly oppressive efforts to convert their Jewish subjects to Christianity. From about 568 onward even harsher pressures began to be exerted, culminating in the persecutions of Dagobert I (629–639), who, prompted by the Byzantine emperor Heraclius, expelled the Jews from most parts of his kingdom.

However, Charlemagne insisted on protecting their religion and property, and allowed them to own slaves. The first Jew whose name reaches us from German lands is Isaac of Aachen, whom Charlemagne sent in 797 as interpreter to a pair of envoys dispatched to visit the Abbasid caliph Harun al-Rashid at Baghdad. The Carolingian Royal Annals give an account of the journey. Neither of the envoys survived its rigors, but in October 801 Isaac returned to Europe, landing at Porto-venere in western Italy. His arrival was a sensation, because he brought with him an elephant (named Abu'l Abbas, after the first Abbasid ruler), which he had somehow suc-

Wall-painting from a Jewish catacomb at Rome, of ancient Roman imperial epoch. There were a number of Jewish as well as Christian catacombs in the city, representing an early stage in the long and continuous story of its Jewish community, despite the adjacent presence first of the Roman emperors and then of the Popes.

This anti-Semitic illuminated manuscript illustration *(right)* dates from the period after the eleventh century, when Jews' activities in western Europe were sharply restricted. Moneylending, one of the few pursuits still allowed, became a pretext for further censure from the Christian community. Biblioteca San Lorenzo, Escorial, near Madrid. The branding iron *(below)*, inscribed "kosher," was used to mark cattle slaughtered according to the rules laid down in the *Hulin* treatise in the Mishnah. Jewish Museum, Basel. The inscription *(bottom)* dating to the eighth century, found in Kurdistan, contains a Persian text written in Hebrew script. The document, a business letter, recalls the important part played by the Jewish population in the Islamic Abbasid empire. Though not possessing full citizen rights, they were not persecuted as were their co-religionists in Europe.

ceeded in transporting all the way from the east. He was too late to cross the Alps that year because of the snow, but in July of the following year he reported back to Aachen, and delivered the Caliph's gifts, including the elephant, to the emperor.

keep popular feeling against its practitioners below the boiling point by emphasizing that only nonforcible methods should be used to convert them to Catholicism; and he defended their right to worship according to their own faith, provided that no new synagogues were

Charlemagne's son Louis I the Pious (813–840) issued the Jews with a passport of a type which would continue to govern their lives for a millennium to come. But although this sort of document excluded the Jews from citizenship—regarding them, instead, as the property of their protectors—it still proved too tolerant for some contemporary Frankish churchmen.

In Italy the Ostrogothic monarch Theodoric (493–526) had been inclined to look tolerantly on the Jews, whose strict monotheism he respected; thus, contrary to Roman (Byzantine) law, he recognized the right of their communities to self-government. Pope Gregory I the Great, on the other hand, detested Judaism. Even he, however, tried to

founded. Although subsequent Popes were sometimes more intolerant, the Papal States continued to be full of Jews; and Rome itself has remained almost the only city in Europe to preserve its Jewish community without a break.

The other trading centers of Italy tolerated or harassed the Jews, according to their own local interests in any given epoch. In the south, Jews abounded in sixth-century Naples, and two and three centuries later, when Hebrew learning revived in the Arab empire, the revival spread to other cities of south Italy, which for a time took the lead as exponents of Jewish culture in Europe.

In western Europe in general, during the centuries immediately after the fall of the west

Roman empire, the Jews possessed as yet no definable economic identity. As we have seen, a considerable number of them were still landowners and farmers. But before long they increasingly abandoned such professions. This was because farming needed slaves, whereas contemporary legislation, which became stricter as time went on, limited the extent to which Jews could own slaves belonging to the Christian faith. For example, Pope Gregory the Great, despite the measure of tolerance he displayed, revived a law forbidding such ownership, which brought ruin to many Jewish agriculturalists; and he also commended the same sanction to rulers outside Italy. Later, too, a further development completed their abandonment of the land. This was feudalism, which inevitably involved tenants in military duties on behalf of Christian masters: when the tenants were Jewish, this was a situation that feudal leaders could not welcome, so that the Jews were gradually forced off the land.

In consequence, more and more of them became traders. It was good luck for their communities when the Arab conquest of Syria

eliminated its merchants from their dominant role as traders and carriers in the west. The Jews took this business over, until their name became almost synonymous with "merchant." Apart from some Frisians and, later, Venetians, they were nearly the only people of the time whose living depended almost entirely on commerce. It was they who renewed the Arab dealings with western Europe that the Islamic expansion had imperiled, and who thus did more than anyone else to unite the two alien worlds.

In particular, they played a dominant part in the management of the slave trade, which had attained a huge scale during and after the great movements of the peoples. The laws against their possession of Christian slaves did not, in the end, prove effective, because the regulations could not be thoroughly enforced. And besides, many of the prisoners of war and other slaves whom they acquired—notably the tens of thousands of Slav captives—were not Christians at all, so that their Jewish masters were able to keep possession of them.

One result of the Jews' preoccupation with trade was that they played a large part in the gradual reestablishment of the urban communities which had been shattered in the age of the Germanic migrations. In the end, however, the growth of these very same cities told decisively against them, since in many regions it led to the creation of a native mercantile class which resented them as rivals. This became especially conspicuous in Venice, where the Christians, by playing on religious hatreds directed against the Jews, were active in pushing many of them out of commercial life altogether.

As a result of such pressures, the Jews turned from trade to the lending of money at interest—the money they had accumulated during those centuries of business. This was the occupation which brought them so much of their subsequent unpopularity. It is easy to resent moneylenders—and the Christian church was able to fuel the flames by marshaling theological arguments against usury. For this and other reasons the troubles the Jews had hitherto undergone were nothing to the appalling terrors of persecution that lay ahead. In one European country, however, the position of the Jews, during the period discussed in this book, was entirely different and superior. This was the great state of the Khazars in southern Russia. The pagan rulers (Khagans) of that country, who probably came of Turkish race, were strongly urged to accept Christianity or Islam by the many Christians and Moslem traders who flocked to their capital at the mouth of the Volga. In about 740, however, in order to evade these competitive attempts at coercion, the Khazar ruler Obadiah adopted the Jewish faith, and so did many of his nobles. The great interest which this unusual development aroused in other parts of the European and Jewish world is illustrated by a letter from the Spanish Jew Hasdai ibn Shaprut to a Khazar ruler (ca. 955), and by his supposed reply (though this second document may not be authentic). The state of the Khazars remained Jewish until, in the eleventh or twelfth century, it came to an end.

Jewish marriage contract *(top)* and wedding ring *(above right)*. According to Mosaic law the man was permitted polygamy, but this was changed by rabbinical regulation in the Middle Ages. *Above left:* Jewish children's top of the ancient kind given as Hanukka (Dedication) presents. *Left:* Bishop freeing Christian slaves from a Jewish master. *Below:* A tombstone, A.D. 829—one of the oldest Jewish funeral records in Europe.

THE PEOPLES OF THE NORTH

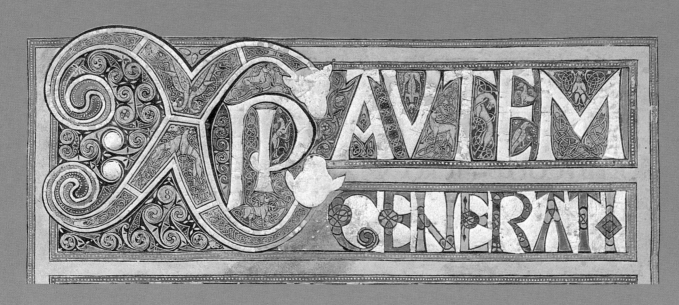

Europe's northern fringes were agitated and turbulent, but productive. The British Isles acted as a magnet upon a great variety of mainland peoples. From the coasts of the continent, wave after wave of Germanic invaders crossed the Channel and the North Sea, stormed the islands and mingled with the local populations. These Angles, Saxons, Jutes, Frisians, and Franks were joined by more peaceable invaders: missionaries from Rome who also seemed drawn irresistibly to these pagan shores. Christianized Celtic Ireland soon sent out a counter-current of its own missionaries across the Irish Sea, and joined the English in producing dynamic and original works of art. But the invasions of Britain were not over: northern neighbors in Scandinavia also set their sights on British conquests, as part of their far-flung migrations and trading and raiding ventures. Traveling farther than any Europeans ever before, Norwegian and Danish Vikings raided many European coasts, set up states of their own—and eventually made their way across the Atlantic to America: while the Swedes penetrated deep into Russia. Moreover, the Scandinavians produced artistic masterpieces, including many surviving objects.

We and our forefathers
    have lived here for three hundred
and fifty years, and never
    has Britain known such terror
and such affliction
    as these; until present times
no one could even imagine
    devastation such as this.

Alcuin of York, on the Viking raids

Two of the characteristic art forms of the North: for the men of God, the Incarnation initial of the Canterbury Codex Aureus, representing a vast tradition of illuminated manuscripts beginning in Northumbria and Ireland and later spreading to monasteries in Europe; for the men of war, an elaborately manufactured helmet of iron, bronze, silver, and gilt from Sutton Hoo in England, seventh century. The excellent technique of this metalworker is closely analogous to that of boat burials of the same period in Scandinavia.

THE COMING OF THE ANGLO-SAXONS

In the late third and fourth centuries A.D.—considerably before the fall of the western Roman empire—Saxons and Franks had been invited into England by the Romans as mercenaries, to repel invasions from other "barbarians," and they had stayed in the country. Next, after 400, when the Roman garrisons had evacuated Britain, waves of further German immigrants arrived across the lower reaches of the North Sea.

What they found was a land which had fallen apart into fragments controlled, in imperfect fashion, by the great landowning families left over from the old system. It was reputedly one of these local magnates, Vortigern—perhaps a chieftain in Kent—at whose invitation three shiploads of Germans arrived in England in the 440 s, under the leadership of Hengist and Horsa. Like their predecessors, they came as mercenaries; but then they turned against Vortigern to assert their own independence. And they were followed into England by further waves of Germans, who harbored equally hostile and predatory intentions

An Anglo-Saxon's view of war is shown on this intricately carved Northumbrian whalebone casket (ca. 700). On the right is the defender of a castle under siege, firing arrows at its attackers; he is the legendary archer Egil from *Egils saga* (Örvandill in Scandinavian mythology). Beneath the circle in the center, where the handle of the casket was attached, a woman weeps over the body of a warrior. British Museum, London (the Franks Casket).

During the fifth century Britain became the center of attraction for numerous waves of Germanic invaders, most of whom had come to stay. Chief among these were the Angles (whence the name "England"), Saxons, and Jutes, whose migrations are shown on the map.

against whatever local leaders still retained any authority.

These fifth-century immigrants to the eastern districts of England comprised Angles, Saxons, Jutes, Frisians, and probably Franks.

The racial distinctions between these various Germanic peoples were not always very sharp, and they were profoundly intermingled one with another. The Angles—who eventually gave their name to the whole country—seem

to have been Scandinavians from Jutland and the lands round about, who came for the most part to the middle parts of England, and to East Anglia and the north. The Saxons were a group of peoples of similar origins, who had moved down to the shorelands around the Elbe and the Weser and farther west; when they came to England, they settled in the southerly areas, where place-names from Essex to Wessex still reflect their presence. The Jutes had originated from northern Jutland, but had left there to mingle with the populations of Frisia and neighboring territories. After arriving on the English coast, they occupied Kent, the Isle of Wight, and adjoining portions of Hampshire. A number of Frisians too (after merging to some extent with both Saxons and Jutes) migrated to England in their company or at the same epoch: the language that came to be spoken in Anglo-Saxon England was very close to theirs. Franks too may well have joined in these invasions, since excavations in Kent, in the extreme southeast of the country, display archaeological affinities with Frankish territory around the Rhine. However, Hengist, who reputedly founded the kingdom of Kent after the death of his fellow-chieftain Horsa in battle, was believed to have been a Jute.

The invaders did not have things all their own way. There are persistent stories, for example, of a British victory in about 500 at Mons Badonicus—probably a hill outside Bath, or perhaps Badbury Rings in Dorset—which temporarily halted their expansion. One leader whose name became associated with this British resistance to the invaders was Aurelius Ambrosianus. Another was Arthur, who seems not to have been a monarch, as later legends made out, but an energetic military commander. Battles in southern and northern England alike are associated with his name, but certainty about the localities in which he operated is unattainable, since most of the stories relating to these engagements date from at least seven centuries later. Nevertheless, Arthur seems to have been a historical figure, who played some notable part in trying to restrict the immigrants' advances. After his time, further attempts to stem the tide continued to be made. But it was all in vain, for by the mid-sixth century the whole of England except the far west was in the hands of the Anglo-Saxons, who divided the country into about a dozen minor, independent principalities.

Metalwork had reached an extremely high standard in Anglo-Saxon times, and in some places at least the blacksmith enjoyed a special place in society. This sword hilt *(top left)* was found in a grave at Coombe in Kent, while the sheath *(below left)* is from Jutland, fifth century (Schleswig-Holsteinisches Museum, Schleswig).

Written records of this period are both scarce and conflicting, but this extract from the Easter Annals of the *British Historical Miscellany*, although perhaps compiled as late as the tenth century, is now taken by most scholars as historical testimony to the existence of Arthur—the hero of numerous well-known legends. By no means all the fabulous tales, however, are backed up by this single reference, which merely refers to the "Battle of Badon in which Arthur carried the cross of Our Lord Jesus Christ on his shoulders for three days and nights and the Britons were victors."

THE CONVERSION OF KENT

Kent, Jutish and perhaps Frankish as well, was the most civilized and Romanized area of the German settlement of England; moreover, at a time when livestock meant a great deal, its Weald provided the best swine pasture in the country. Kent quickly became an independent political unit, and the chieftain or monarch who reigned over its people, Ethelbert I (560–616), was "Bretwalda," that is to say, "ruler of Britain," exercising a loose overlordship of the other Anglo-Saxon states south of the River Humber.

Ethelbert's marriage to the daughter of a Merovingian king helped to make him adopt a tolerant policy toward the Christian religion. This had probably survived, in greatly diminished form, in various parts of England, despite the arrival of so many German, pagan immigrants during the previous century; and Celtic churchmen coming over from Ireland may also have been able to exert some influence. But a decisive step toward the revival of Christianity took place when St. Augustine (the second of that name) led a mission to England on the instructions of Pope Gregory I. Augustine landed on the Kentish island of Thanet in 597 and sought an interview with Ethelbert. The king, it was said, was at first only prepared to hold the meeting out of doors, where he would be less affected by the visitor's magic powers. Yet, before long, Ethelbert accepted conversion. Thereupon Augustine, his mission enlarged by reinforcements from Rome, built a richly endowed abbey outside the walls of Canterbury, a foundation which later became known by his name and ranked as the second Benedictine house in all Europe; and soon afterward he established the cathedral, which came to be for ever the principal see of the country. He himself became the first archbishop, and was invested by the Pope with the power to appoint twelve bishops under him. This Kentish mission had been skillfully planned by Gregory, so that the church it set up would be not national but apostolic, subject to direct papal control; this meant that the English church was destined to turn its back on Celtic isolation and return to the main traditions of Europe. Ethelbert's conversion also revived literacy at the Kentish court, so that he was able to put into writing a code of ninety laws, which not only dealt with secular matters but established the legal position of the church and its clergy.

Nevertheless, the success of Augustine's mission was only of limited scope and duration,

because the next Kentish monarch reverted to paganism; and a major plague in 664 killed many churchmen and caused numerous apostasies. A second and more lasting attempt to establish Christianity in Kent was made by Theodore of Tarsus, a Syrian Greek, sent by Pope Vitalian in 668 to become Archbishop of Canterbury. Although already sixty-six years old at the time, Theodore retained that office until his death twenty-two years later. During this period, he found time to intervene in political affairs. But his great achievement was to arrange for the various churches of the country—since Christianity had by now become established in the various other Anglo-Saxon princedoms as well—to amalgamate within a single ecclesiastical organization. The Synod at Hertford in 672 firmly established discipline and theological uniformity on a Roman basis, and Celtic customs and practices were dropped.

The new, unified church was destined to play a major part in the eventual evolution of England from a group of weak and barbarous little tribal states into a single national unit. Moreover, it was the church, based on sees and cathedrals in the remnants of the Roman towns, which followed up the initiative of St. Augustine and succeeded in acquainting England once again with international learning and ideas. In this process Kent continued to take the initiative, for Theodore endowed

This ornate, jeweled fish was fixed, on its stand, in the bottom of the handbowl shown below, so that it seemed to be swimming when the bowl was full of water. This item was one of the finds at Sutton Hoo (see also pp. 156–157), considered to be the burial place or memorial of King Raedwald of East Anglia. The fish, although it had rarely appeared outside Coptic Egypt by this time, was a symbol of Christ; and Raedwald, though a pagan, had close associations with the Christian court of Kent.

Top right: Detail from an English illuminated book, eighth century. It shows Christ at center, with symbols of the four Evangelists—one of the favorite motifs of early medieval art. Matthew is symbolized by an angel, because his Gospel emphasized the Incarnation. Mark, who wrote of Jesus' royal lineage, is the winged lion; Luke's attribute is the ox, the symbol of sacrifice, because he stressed the Crucifixion and Resurrection; John's is the eagle, signifying inspiration.

Canterbury with an important monastic school, where the subjects taught included scripture, church music, arithmetic, Latin, Greek, and medicine.

The superior cultural and economic level of Kent was once again displayed by its fine garnet-ornamented jewelry of the later sixth and seventh centuries, employing Merovingian Frankish techniques. A little later the same region produced the first English silver pennies *(denarii)*. From about 550 onward Merovingian gold coins had been coming across the Channel, and these provided models for the first English issues, which were minted in several parts of the country beginning in the second half of the seventh century. But these gold coins were almost immediately superseded by silver pieces *(sceattas,* struck in continental Europe as well), which in their turn were replaced in about 775 by thinner

A view of Canterbury cathedral, showing the remains of St. Ethelbert's tower and St Augustine's monastery. When St. Augustine, dispatched by Pope Gregory I the Great, converted King Ethelbert of Kent to Christianity, he established his archbishopric at Canterbury. Later, York was made into a second archepiscopal see.

and broader "pennies," imitated from the Carolingian empire. The first of these pieces bore the name of a Kentish king and were evidently issued at Canterbury, though other English royal centers soon followed suit; and shortly afterward archbishops of Canterbury also minted some coins.

Left: The Gospels of St. Augustine were kept in the cathedral in Canterbury until presented by Archbishop Matthew Parker to Corpus Christi College, Cambridge, in 1575. The page shown here precedes the Gospel of Luke. It shows twelve scenes illustrating the early phase of Christ's Passion, taken from other Gospels in addition to Luke's.

EAST ANGLIA: SUTTON HOO

The kingdoms which acknowledged Ethelbert of Kent as Bretwalda or overlord included East Anglia, whose king Raedwald became a Christian in the course of a visit to Ethelbert's court; on his return home, however, Raedwald, whose wife was vigorously pagan, found it convenient to hedge, by placing altars to Christ and pagan divinities together in one and the same house of worship. He also asserted himself as overlord of southern and central England in succession to Ethelbert and carried his influence beyond the Humber as well, by defeating the king of Northumbria. It is with Raedwald's name that it seems best to associate the finds at Sutton Hoo near Woodbridge in Suffolk, the most lavish, spectacular, and surprising treasure ever to have been discovered on British soil. The place has a group of fifteen burial mounds, of which the largest, when excavated in 1939, was found to have been superimposed on a trench containing a wooden Anglo-Saxon boat, eighty-nine feet in length, which had been hauled up from the estuary of the nearby River Deben.

The illustrations on these pages show some of the remarkable objects found in the excavation of the Sutton Hoo ship in 1939, believed to be the grave or cenotaph of King Raedwald of East Anglia. *Right:* A richly ornamented purse, apparently made at a local workshop well aware of artistic trends in other lands. *Below right:* Jeweled gold buckle; this object is also probably of English manufacture, but displays influences from Sweden and the Merovingian and Mediterranean worlds, blended into a masterpiece of the jeweler's art. British Museum, London.

Above: A sword belt-mount or clasp from Sutton Hoo, made of gold decorated with admirably cut garnets, pieces of mosaic glass, and filigree ornament, now in the British Museum. To this day the moving parts of the mount or clasp are still capable of operating smoothly and precisely.

With the exception of two baptismal spoons and a bowl, the objects found are of markedly pagan character. It is uncertain whether the vessel served as a tomb—originally containing a body—or whether it was merely a memorial or cenotaph. In either case, to judge from the wealth of the finds, it must have been the monument of a king, belonging to the Wuffinga dynasty of East Anglia. And the dates of thirty-seven Merovingian coins which came to light suggest that the king for whom the East Anglians made this memorial was Raedwald, who died in about 625.

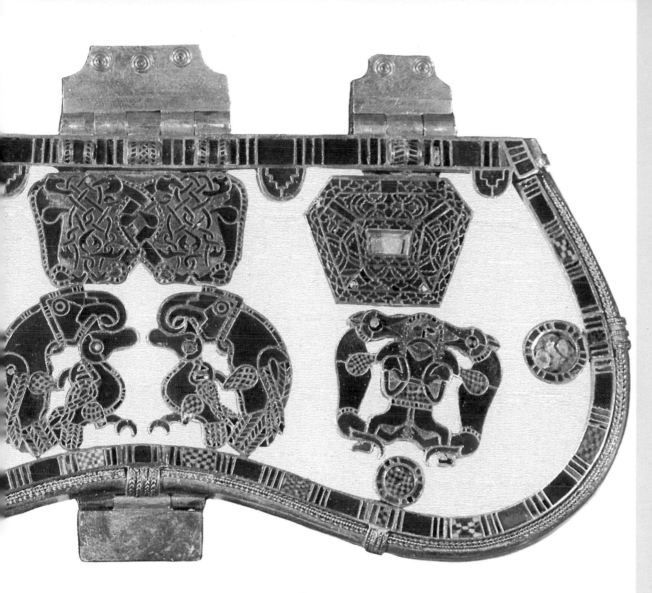

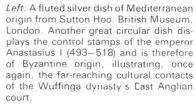

The discoveries at Sutton Hoo are fabulously handsome and varied. A decorated shield, and gilt-bronze helmet of rich and superb workmanship, exactly recall the styles of Vendel and Valsgärde in eastern Sweden (Uppland) — places where boat burials occur at the same period. The presence of such objects at Sutton Hoo recalls that royal East Anglian genealogies include names found also among a people known as the Geatas. This was a Scandinavian tribe which figures prominently in the old English heroic poem *Beowulf*. The Geatas described in that work belong to southern Sweden, or northern Jutland. Thus it would appear that Raedwald and his East Anglian dynasty were either linked to Scandinavia by marriage ties, or even, perhaps, originated from that country themselves.

Two further objects, in which German and Celtic mythological allusions and artistic themes appear to be blended, were evidently symbols of royalty. One is an iron standard, and the other a sort of scepter in a curiously shaped bronze casing. The scepter is a great stone bar in the formalized shape of a whetstone, with bronze mounts. At its extremities are eight carved human faces, and the scepter was originally surmounted by a stylized figure of a stag standing on a bronze ring. The East Anglian monarch in whose honor such outstanding works of art were created must have been a potentate of hitherto unsuspected grandeur.

From the Sutton Hoo ship: a spoon inscribed "Saulos" and "Paulos." British Museum, London. The two spoons which have come to light here—perhaps connected with baptismal ceremonies—are Christian in character, in contrast to the markedly pagan nature of other Sutton Hoo objects, which correspond more closely to Raedwald's sympathies.

Left: A fluted silver dish of Mediterranean origin from Sutton Hoo. British Museum, London. Another great circular dish displays the control stamps of the emperor Anastasius I (493—518) and is therefore of Byzantine origin, illustrating, once again, the far-reaching cultural contacts of the Wuffinga dynasty's East Anglian court.

157

NORTHUMBRIA

A large part of northeast England, from the Humber up to Hadrian's Wall, was settled, in the fifth century, by German mercenaries, followed by further German (Anglian) invaders. The region was known as Deira, and its chief center was York. Next, in about 547, a further group of Anglians, under a chieftain named Ida, established themselves north of the wall at Bamburgh on the coast of Northumberland and founded the royal house of Bernicia, which eventually extended upward through southern Scotland as far as the Firth of Forth. However, the previous, Celtic, populations of Deira and Bernicia alike remained numerous and fused extensively with the immigrants, so that, although these imposed their language, the place names, personal names, and general culture of the territory remained British.

Edwin was the first Christian king of Northumbria. Even before his day, Christianity had been present in adjoining regions of north Britain. In particular, during the course of the fifth century (not earlier, as legend suggested), a Cumbrian Christian named Ninian, of the Roman branch of the faith, had built a stone church at Whithorn (Candida Casa), beside the Galloway coast, and became its bishop. But Saint Ninian may not have been so much a missionary to pagan lands as a churchman called in to oversee Christian communities which, despite all the changes occurring in Britain, had still continued to exist. Whithorn, no doubt, exercised some influence on Northumbria, but Edwin accepted conversion from another source. A condition made by the king of Kent, when

The Franks Casket, made in Northumbria, about A.D. 700, after the conversion of the kingdom to Christianity by a succession of mainly Roman-based missionaries. The scene shown here is the Roman capture of Jerusalem, A.D. 70, with a legend in Runic and Latin characters. Named after Sir A. W. Franks who presented it to the British Museum, London.

Right: From Hexham Abbey in Northumbria: the Frith Stool, dating from the 670s, was taken from Byzantine models. This was one of the objects of foreign and Mediterranean inspiration included in Wilfrid's great church and monastery in the valley of the Tyne.

Ethelfrith, king of Bernicia (593–616), gained possession of Deira as well, and united the two areas into a single Northumbrian state. He also broke through to the west coast, thus cutting off the Celtic principalities of Wales from those in southwest Scotland. Ethelfrith's successor, Edwin (616–632), belonged to the royal house of Deira. An impressive commander and personage, he attacked the islands of Anglesey and Man, and was eventually recognized as overlord of all England—with the single exception of Kent, though the ruler of that kingdom, too, gave him his daughter in marriage.

Edwin married his daughter, was that she should be allowed to continue the practice of her Christian faith: and consequently, when she went north, she was accompanied by Saint Paulinus, whom Pope Gregory I had sent from Rome to England in 601 to assist Augustine in his mission. It was as a result of Paulinus' efforts that Edwin was baptized in 627. The baptism took place in a wooden church built for the occasion at York, which was henceforward both the ecclesiastical as well as the civil capital of Northumbria.

From there, Paulinus traveled north to the royal palace at Yeavering beside the Cheviots, where he preached and carried out mass baptisms for thirty-six days. Excavations at Yeavering have provided an idea of what this sort of Anglo-Saxon residence was like. A series of large timber halls occupied the center of the site, and another wooden structure, with a concentric arrangement of pillars, has been identified as a place of assembly, while a smaller building nearby seems to have been a pagan temple converted into a church.

In 632 Edwin was defeated and killed by his southern neighbors, the Mercians, supported by their allies from Gwynedd in northwest Wales. Deira and Bernicia split apart, and

An Anglo-Saxon view of one of the Viking "dragon" ships which were to transform the face of Britain, first by damaging raids from 793 onward, and then in the following century by systematic invasion and settlement. Northumbria, with its rich monastic foundations, was invaded from 865 onward, and greatly reduced in size. From a tenth-century manuscript in the British Museum, London.

Above left: The prophet Ezra, from the Northumbrian Codex Amiatinus, about A.D. 700. In its design the picture shows close stylistic affinity to contemporary Roman frescoes, suggesting that the artist came from the continent; but the use of color is wholly Anglo-Saxon.

In the early seventh century the territories of Bernicia and Deira were again united to form Northumbria under Oswald and then his brother Oswy. They had come from exile in the Irish monastery of Iona, and brought with them the Celtic version of Christianity. Under these Irish influences, Northumbria was the place of origin of richly illuminated manuscripts such as the Book of Durrow, of which a page is shown here—one of a number of pages devoted to these remarkable abstract designs.

their rulers reverted to paganism. Paulinus fled back to Kent, but two of the sons of the former king Ethelfrith fled to the Celtic, Irish monastery of Iona in Dalriada. Subsequently, they returned home to Northumbria, and one of them, Oswald (634–642), united its two territories once again and asserted an even more effective and far-reaching overlordship than his father, extending his authority not only throughout England but over a number of peoples in Wales and Scotland as well.

Oswald was also encouraged by his stay at Iona to introduce its monks and missionaries into Northumbria, and they came bringing their own Celtic brand of Christian holiness instead of the Roman version that had been favored by Paulinus. The most notable of these visiting churchmen, Saint Aidan, was appointed to a

bishopric and established a monastery on Lindisfarne or Holy Island (635). Thereafter, until his death sixteen years later, he continued to spread Christianity of the Celtic type throughout Northumbria; and Irish monasticism also gained ground in other parts of Anglo-Saxon England as well.

In 641 Oswald, like his father before him, lost his life to the Mercians, and the kingdom of Northumbria again split up into its two component parts. But his brother Oswy (641–670) united the two regions once more and restored the general overlordship exercised by Northumbria, fighting the Mercians off and even annexing their kingdom for a time. He also overawed the Scottish principalities north of his borders. But the principal event of his reign was the Synod of Whitby (664), which was summoned to judge between the claims of the Roman and Irish-Celtic church systems. The issues officially in dispute were mainly ritualistic, but the underlying confrontation was between the more unworldly, unorganized Celtic conservatism and the more tightly controlled and centralized system of Rome. It was the latter cause that prevailed. Its leader was Wilfrid, who during his long and combative career as a bishop of various Anglo-Saxon sees (interrupted by imprisonment and exile) introduced and spread a version of the Benedictine Rule, and firmly resisted any weakening of papal power by Celtic or other regional interests. Moreover, while occupying the see of York, Wilfrid employed foreign craftsmen to build the monastery of Hexham in the watermeads of the Tyne valley, and endowed it with a splendid basilica-church of Mediterranean style.

His slightly older contemporary, Benedict Biscop, was a man of intense religious enthusiasm and impressive education, who vigorously carried on the task of bringing his country, for all its individual characteristics, into the cultural mainstream of Europe. A nobleman of Oswy's court, he took the vows of a Benedictine monk, accompanied Wilfrid on a journey to Rome in 652, and went to Kent in 668 with Theodore of Tarsus, who made him abbot of one of the monasteries at Canterbury. Then Benedict Biscop moved on to Northumbria, where, with the support of King Egfrith and the help of masons from Gaul, he built monasteries at Wearmouth and Jarrow (674, 681–682). The seven hundred monks who belonged to these foundations were all literate and equipped with special skills. For their guidance, Benedict Biscop laid down a Rule of his own, based on the practice of seventeen institutions in other countries. He remained in constant touch with the affairs of the continent, and made no less than five visits to Rome, from which he brought panel paintings and vestments for his monasteries. From the same city, too, came more than two hundred books. He also succeeded in acquiring the services of the arch-chanter of St. Peter's in Rome, and himself taught his monks music, as well as theology, astronomy, and art; so that their abbeys became major intellectual centers.

Benedict Biscop died in 689 or 690. But by then the political supremacy of Northumbria was already a thing of the past. Oswy's son and successor Egfrith had been killed by northern enemies, the Picts, in 685 and Yeavering was destroyed at about the same time. Thereafter no Northumbrian was overlord of England ever again. Nevertheless, in 735 the see of York became England's second archbishopric, after Canterbury. This was a divisive step that delayed the process of national unification. All the same the church school at York did a great deal to preserve classical culture. One of its

The most famous of all the great Anglo-Saxon stone crosses *(left)*, in the church at Ruthwell in Dumfriesshire, stands seventeen feet high. There are five panels of figure sculpture on each of the two broad faces of the shaft. Notably Mediterranean in style and influence, and wholly lacking the curvilinear patterns so typical of northern art, it reflects the influence of the Roman church following the Synod of Whitby in 664.

heads (778–781) was the great Alcuin, who moved from York to the palace school of Aachen, where he became Charlemagne's adviser and richly repaid the Mediterranean importations of Wilfrid and Benedict Biscop by spreading the advanced, sophisticated Northumbrian learning throughout western and central Europe.

It was therefore a terrible shock—expressed eloquently by Alcuin himself—when the Norwegian Vikings made their first appearance on Northumbrian shores. In 793 they raided and sacked the monastery of Lindisfarne and a year later it was the turn of another Northumbrian center, probably Jarrow. These were ominous preludes to the invasions by the Danish Vikings that shattered England in the following century.

Benedict Biscop, a former nobleman of King Oswy's court, became a Benedictine monk and a companion of St. Wilfrid. He was the founder of the monasteries of Wearmouth and Jarrow and, by virtue of his close contact with the continent, one of the men most responsible for the Romanization of the English church in the seventh century, and for the establishment of abbeys as the chief centers of learning in a turbulent land.

161

ILLUMINATED MANUSCRIPTS

Although the monks who went to Italy and France, before and after 600, brought back a number of Latin volumes, the great illuminated Gospels (and lives of the saints) in Britain and Ireland displayed a beautiful writing of their own that is Irish and Celtic rather than Roman. Their designers sought to produce a

The first page of the Gospel of St. Matthew, from the Lindisfarne Gospels, late seventh century (British Museum, London). The upper half contains the elaborately formed letters XPI, which stand for "Christi" in the opening sentence of this first Gospel.

script which seemed worthy of the sacred texts, no matter what the cost and labor. The "uncial" lettering they devised—a great improvement on the shabby cursive writing of the later Roman world—was large, rounded, and legible, drawn with admirable firmness and artistry, and worthy to rank with the finest calligraphy of Islam or China.

At the start of each of their sections these volumes habitually include, on the right, an introductory page with a large, decorative initial letter, and on the left, a "carpet page" covered all over with astonishingly elaborate, interlaced, convoluted designs. Original features abound in each successive book. And yet this remains an art which is strikingly homogeneous from one volume to another. Paradoxically, however, its homogeneity derives from a remarkable blend and variety of formative influences. Some of the models are of Mediterranean origin, drawing upon the mosaic floors of local Roman villas, and various motifs and styles imported from Gaul or Spain (directly, or by way of Ireland); others again are strongly reminiscent of Byzantium and its eastern provinces, particularly Coptic Egypt. But the predominant elements are Anglo-Saxon—with certain Scandinavian overtones—and Celtic.

The artists who created by far the greater proportion of these books appear to have worked in Northumbria. But although this was an Anglo-Saxon state, its people, as we have seen, continued to retain strong Celtic (British) elements, which were further reinforced by close contacts with Celtic (Irish) Iona. So the books are sometimes called "Hiberno-Saxon"; though some prefer to describe them as "insular," since they were made on the two islands, Britain and Ireland, and are quite different from anything made on the continent (despite all its growing links with Northumbria).

These paintings display an inexhaustible wealth of curving or geometrical, never repetitious, rhythmical patterns, which recall the techniques of metalwork and strike a piquant balance between explosive dynamism and elegant conciseness. The designs are anything but static: their spiral and curvilinear figures and adornments wind and oscillate in an incantatory atmosphere of unstable, evasive transformation. Despite all their Mediterranean debts, these illuminators hated and rejected classical naturalism. So, too, had many other northern craftsmen, Celtic and German, long before the establishment of Christian culture. But now, in these attempts to celebrate the great central mysteries of the Faith, we have a great Christian art that goes far beyond any Byzantine models in its retreat into stylization—the first major achievement in the interplay of artistic forces which was creating a new culture in northern and western Europe. At first, these kaleidoscopic mazes of twisted shapes and interwoven coils and audaciously dismembered animal forms arouse bewilderment in the viewer. But then, on further examination, they disclose a cohesive aesthetic harmony, which makes this one of the outstanding abstract arts of all time.

The Book of Durrow was made in about the 670s, probably at the monastery of Lindisfarne, to which monks had come from Ireland. Its illuminated pages, colored in contrasted deep greens, glowing reds, and bright yellows on white backgrounds, combine formalized figures of apostles with a wealth of animal and plant shapes, rectilinear patterns, and intricate networks of scrolls, straps, and knots. Yet the overall patterns, however elaborate, are notable for their restraint and balance. The Book of Durrow is the earliest in this series of books that has come down to us; but it gives the impression of a long preceding tradition, of which no trace any longer survives.

The Echternach Gospels, taken to Echternach in Luxemburg by the Northumbrian missionary Willibrord in about 700, may come from the same workshop as the Book of Durrow. However, they are less exuberant and even more stylized; interesting themes from Pictish art from beyond Northumbria's northern border can be noted. The Lindisfarne Gospels were probably written and illuminated by Bishop Eadfrith (698–721), who had spent six years in Ireland. But in this work Irish and Germanic ideas are even more evidently supplemented than heretofore by influences from all parts of the Mediterranean area—influences derived from the antiquities brought by Benedict Biscop and others from Italy, which confer a new, elaborate, and striking richness. And the Codex Amiatinus, the oldest complete manuscript of the Vulgate (Jerome's Latin Bible) now in existence (taken back to Rome from Northumbria in 716), offers still more emphatic echoes of Benedict Biscop's models.

But the greatest of these volumes was the Book of Kells (ca. 800), which belongs to the same "Hiberno-Saxon" series, though it seems to have been made not in Northumbria but at Iona. Its superb, colorful, intricately woven designs blend iconographic motifs derived from every source of which the artist and his staff could have had any knowledge—and yet total originality is triumphantly achieved.

The other major Northumbrian art that has survived is that of stone carving, displayed in magnificent crosses. Outstanding among them is the eighteen-foot Ruthwell Cross on the Scottish side of the Solway Firth. Its figure reliefs are probably copied, in part, from illuminated books, though the intrusion of a more sober and naturalistic note suggests the additional influence of the Roman sarcophagi

that must have survived in the area. These towering crosses stood out of doors at places of religious assembly, for example where the local community could not afford a church, or where the church was too small to house the entire congregation.

The symbol of Matthew in the Echternach Gospels, about A.D. 700 (Bibliothèque Nationale, Paris). "Imago hominis" ("the image of a man"). Produced in Northumbria, this Gospel is painted in an even more abstract style, and more limited range of colors than the Book of Lindisfarne seen opposite.

Shown at right are two complete pages, reduced to half their actual size, from the Book of Kells (ca. 800, Trinity College, Dublin), believed to have been made by the Irish monks of Iona (western Scotland): one, an impressively decorated full-page initial from St. Mark's Gospel *(opposite)*, and the other *(right)* a page of text from the Beatitudes (Matthew 5:3–10). This text page, which begins

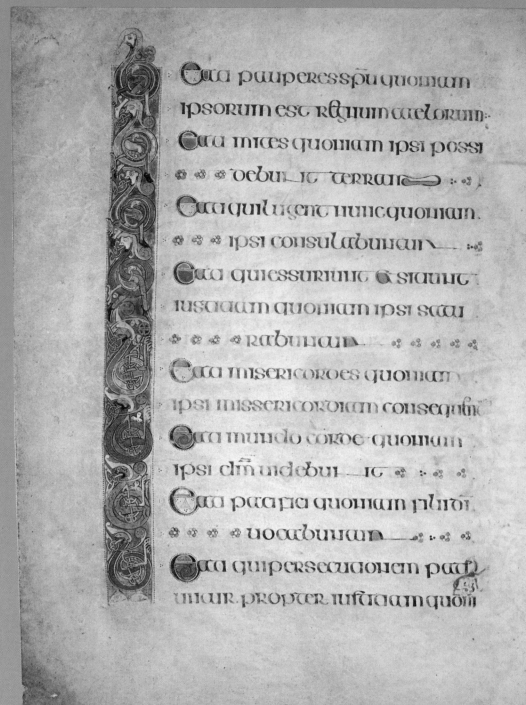

"Beati pauperes spiritu" ("Blessed are the poor in spirit"), contains richly colored and shaped initial B's (for Beati) in each second or third line, the first of which are reproduced in this detail *(above)* in full scale. The first four initial B's on the page contain human figures, and the last four consist of serpent-like animals. This unbroken chain of ornamental initial B's forms a visual counterpart to the repetition of the word "Beati" in the text.

Seen at left in full size are the seventh and eighth lines of the page shown above (Matthew 5:6): "Blessed are they which do hunger and thirst after righteousness: for they shall be filled." (In Latin "Beati qui essuriunt et...") The "uncial" script is rounder, larger, and more legible than the lettering used in manuscripts of previous centuries. It is a model of regularity and neatness, almost suggesting the modern use of printed capital type.

Enlarged to double size, this human figure in profile, with part of a gargoyle head also visible, is taken from the top right-hand corner of the folio at left. *Below:* Enlargement of a detail from a border of an initial page, Book of Kells.

Above: Full-page initial at the beginning of the Gospel of St. Mark in the Book of Kells. The page is reproduced here in half-size. It consists of the words ''Initium Evangelii Ihu (the traditional way of writing Jesu) XPI (Christi)'' (''The beginning of the Gospel of Jesus Christ''). The small letters XPI, for Christ, are visible at bottom center of the page. Evidently, in such pages the emphasis was on ornament rather than legibility; it was assumed that readers knew the beginnings of their texts well enough not to be impeded by this.

These letters *(above)* are an enlargement of the line of text from the bottom right-hand corner of this initial page. The last three letters—''Ihu'' (''Jesu'')—are preceded by ''Iii,'' the ending of the word ''Evangelii.'' Words could be combined or broken up according to the requirements of the overall design.

The profusion of detail in the illuminations from the Book of Kells is endlessly fertile as the two enlarged details at left illustrate. They are from the bottom left corner and the bottom center of the border decoration.

THE UNIFICATION OF ENGLAND

In due course the ten or twelve kingdoms in England diminished to less than half that figure—to the advantage of many of the population, because border harassments became less frequent.

The process of unification gathered strength when the general role of overlord passed out of the hands of the kings of Northumbria, only to assume, some four decades later, a more powerful form under the Mercians, whose hegemony is the most important fact of the English eighth century. Originally based on the upper reaches of the Trent, Mercia had profited from the spread of more advanced economic conditions by expanding its control over most of the central region of the country. The first Mercian monarch to enjoy this new overlordship was Ethelbald (716–757). But he was far outshone by his cousin and successor King Offa (757–796). A strong and ruthless man of wider interests and abilities than any of his forerunners, Offa created what was virtually a single state comprising all England up to the Humber. He reduced some of the other kingdoms to mere shires, in which grants of land needed his personal consent; and he succeeded in extending his authority northward into Northumbria, by the marriage of one of his daughters to its ruler.

Offa was described, or described himself, as

The opening of King Alfred's preface to his translation (A.D. 894) of Pope Gregory I the Great's *Pastoral Care*, an indispensable guide for medieval bishops and priests *(left)*. King Alfred steadfastly resisted the Danish Vikings and thus prepared the way for the final unification of England. The other great uniting factor was the Christian church, firmly established by the missionaries of Gregory, who is portrayed *(below)* on this thirteenth-century Italian fresco. *Below left:* The collaboration of King and Church is the subject of this tenth-century miniature. The monarch is Athelstan (924—939) of the house of Wessex, who was to extend his effective rule over all England. Corpus Christi College, Cambridge.

"King of all the land of the English." In this capacity, he was the first Anglo-Saxon leader to carry political weight abroad; and it was a conspicuous sign of his enhanced position that even Charlemagne had to deal with him on more or less equal terms, so that after a series of disputes, the two rulers came to an agreement embodied in a commercial treaty (796). Offa was also able to persuade Pope Adrian I to create a third (temporary) English archbishopric at his own see of Lichfield. Nearby was the king's fortress-palace of Tamworth, the virtual capital of England, and farther west he constructed a substantial earthwork, "Offa's Dyke," stretching for a hundred and twenty miles between the Dee and Wye estuaries, to keep the Welsh tribes across the frontier at bay.

Offa also improved on the recently introduced Kentish currency by issuing a massive new series of pennies on his own account, at the same Canterbury mint, which was now under his own control. These coins are unique, in the period, for their fine execution, imaginative variety of design, and artistic portraiture, in which German and ancient Roman styles are blended to impressive effect. In Roman fashion, again, Offa portrayed his wife, Cynethryth, on some of his coins. His pennies are found widely on the continent and were even imitated as far afield as the Italian city of Lucca, and he issued a gold piece that must have been intended for the Arab trade, since it copies a coin of the caliph Al-Mansur.

Early in the following century, however, the overlordship of England, which under Offa's house had passed from the north to the midlands, shifted once again from the midlands to the south. The new rulers were the kings of Wessex, a territory which had developed from origins in Hampshire and on the Upper Thames into a state comprising the greater part of southern England. Finally one of these monarchs, Egbert (802—839), completed the incorporation of all the southern part of the country, and he even conquered Mercia as well. Yet these annexations only proved temporary; and before the process of unification could be set on foot once again, half the national territory had fallen to the invasion of the Danish Vikings. It was not until 927 that the kings of Wessex became kings of all England, a position they held until the conquest by the Normans (1066)— who continued to govern the land from the south.

Opposite page: Offa's Dyke in Shropshire (western England) as it still stands today. The fortification was built by King Offa of Mercia (757—796) in order to keep out the Welsh, whose tribes and small principalities had remained independent of the Germanic invaders. In earlier times the local British Kings of Kent, East Anglia, and Northumbria had successively been "overlords" of large English territories, but Offa extended his rule over almost the whole of the country. To symbolize his position as king of all England, Offa issued a novel and extensive silver coinage, which greatly exceeded all precedents in impressive appearance and excellence of design, and circulated far and wide across the Channel into Europe. The penny shown here is now in the British Museum, London.

ANGLO-SAXON SOCIETY AND LITERATURE

The England to which the Anglo-Saxons came was a territory of many virgin forests and undrained marshes, infested with wolves, boars, deer, and wild cats, in addition perhaps to some lynxes and brown bears. The invaders cleared parts of the forests, using what remained to provide fuel and game, as well as acorns and beech-masts for their pigs; and they brought the heavier valley soils under cultivation. Except in Kent with its special Gaulish links, the Anglo-Saxons retained their ancient pattern of single-family home-steads, which they shared with their animals; the houses were built round a headman's communal hall, with outworks attached. The major chieftains ruled as autocratically as they dared, over a population of nobles (earls) and commoners (churls). One chief distinction between these two classes lay in their differing obligations of *wergild*. the compensation price for killing. At the lowest level of society there was a tendency, as on the continent, for slaves to be replaced by serfs.

The other side of this picture is a verse and prose literature unique among the contemporary Germanic peoples of Europe, composed both in Old English and in Latin. The earliest Christian poet in Old English was reputedly Caedmon, a Northumbrian monk of Streanae-shalch (Whitby), who may have been the author of the poignantly religious *Dream of the Rood*. But the most splendid and eloquent poem in the language is *Beowulf*. We do not know who the poet was, or where he worked. It is probable that he lived in the seventh or eighth century: though the legendary actions narrated in the poem are ascribed to the years before 600. Against a Scandinavian background, the author of *Beowulf* tells a story of epic sweep and scope about the mythical hero of that name who overcame the monster Grendel, ravager of the palace of King Hrothgar of Denmark. The only long heroic poem in Old English to have come down to us intact, *Beowulf* marks the true inauguration of English literature. It had originally been handed down by word of mouth; but then its traditions succeeded in surviving transplantation into literary shape. Like many other Anglo-Saxon poems, the work strikes a note of brooding tragedy, dwelling on the superhuman glories of the past and the transient vanity of earthly joy. But there is other beautiful secular poetry, too, much of it Northumbrian in origin, which strikes a much lighter, and even humorous note.

Beowulf was written in Old English because in contrast to continental countries seized by the Germans, the language of England, which had been the least Romanized of Rome's provinces, and the most thoroughly overrun by the subsequent invaders, did not remain predominantly Latin. Yet revived contacts between England and the Mediterranean region ensured that Latin still remained the language of the country's greatest intellectual figures. Outstanding among them was Bede (672/3–735), who was born near Wearmouth and became one of Benedict Biscop's pupils at Jarrow. He wrote extensively and influentially on Biblical and grammatical and other themes. But his *History of the Church* (in England), based on wide and erudite reading in the library of Jarrow, supplemented by first-hand personal knowledge and consultation, is a remarkable original achievement. Bede accepts miraculous interventions in the course of events, and his gentle, unworldly liking for stories of fantastic asceticism goes back to his Celtic boyhood memories. But, in other respects, he displays a high degree of calm and unobtrusive detachment, together with an inspired gift for selecting and integrating an enormous quantity of facts and traditions within a single homogeneous framework.

Bede's scholarship was unsurpassed in Latin literature for four centuries; and his wide reputation earned him the title of Venerable.

A page of the manuscript of *Beowulf*, tenth century. This is the only surviving manuscript of this great Old English poem, probably of seventh- or eighth-century date, which told of heroic, legendary happenings in Denmark. British Museum, London.

The manuscript of the Durham edition of the works of Cassiodorus (the sixth-century Italian scholar who formed one of the most important cultural bridges between ancient and medieval times) was, according to medieval tradition, written down by Bede (d. 735); and he may well, at least, have been one of the six accomplished scribes who seem to have had a share in its production. This picture *(right)* shows King David trampling on a prostrate monster with an animal head at either end. David is also seen *(opposite)* playing a five-stringed, lute-shaped harp with a rounded sounding board—a type of instrument of which fragments were found in the seventh-century Sutton Hoo treasure (discussed on pp. 156–157).

IRELAND AND
ITS CHURCH

Metalwork was one of the most distinguished secular arts of Celtic Ireland, but its use also sometimes extended to the church, as in this eleventh-century bronze relief *(above)* from the Moylough Belt reliquary, a bronze shrine for a leather belt, probably that of a saint. The preservation and veneration of such religious relics was characteristic of the medieval Christian church throughout Europe. The St. John's Crucifixion *(opposite page)*, from Athlone in Westmeath, a cast bronze plaque made in about the eighth century, would have been fastened to a wooden book cover; the plaque is all that now remains. This and the relief above are to be seen in the National Museum of Ireland, Dublin.

Beehive huts from the hermitage of Skellig Michael on the Great Skellig Rock off County Kerry (southwest Ireland). This island rock pinnacle was one of the remotest places to which the Irish ascetics retired in their dedication to a life of "white martyrdom" in the service of God.

Unlike the Anglo-Saxons of England, the Celts in Ireland did not move gradually from political fragmentation toward a single state, but remained disunited, their political evolution falling far below their cultural development. There were many subordinate "kings," who accepted a measure of protection from a smaller number of more influential rulers. Owing to the power that these wielded, the island early showed signs of a division into the historic four quarters, Connaught in the west, Ulster in the north, Munster in the south, and Leinster in the east, with a separate central area of Meath bordering on each of the four.

In Roman times the most powerful chieftains had been those of Connaught, but at the turn of the fifth century they were eclipsed by the occupants of the fortress of Tara in Meath, where Niall of the Nine Hostages (d. 405) became the most powerful monarch the country had hitherto seen, so that certain chroniclers could even ascribe him, with some exaggeration, the title of "King of Ireland." Under his direction, his sons and relatives established themselves in strong positions in Ulster. But his descendants also fanned out over a much wider area of Ireland, and more than forty members of the clan became "kings" of different regions.

Within this kaleidoscopic political scene it is possible to detect a general antagonism between the northern and southern halves of the island. In the south, Munster had been in touch with the continent from the earliest times; and a royal site in Leinster, Lagore, has produced finds of arms and weapons, dating from about 700, which may well have been the property of mercenaries imported from Frankish Gaul.

Outside his or her tribe, an Irishman or Irishwoman had no legal personality. Within the tribe, land was the common property of the family and could not be alienated by an individual; the kingship group, rather than citizenship of a state, was the basis of such stability as existed. The monarchies were elective within those groups, with no member of a royal house able to lay claim to an automatic succession. In Irish society, which was heavily stratified, clientship of two different degrees, free and base, was the fundamental framework providing the poorer people with the protection, and the nobles with the status, they demanded.

Pagan Ireland had been a land of animal and river deities. But then Christianity was brought to the country, by slaves captured in raids on the British coasts, or by Irish migrants

to Britain who had returned to their native land. In 431 a Roman churchman named Palladius made a brief stay in Ireland. Very soon afterward St. Patrick, too, came there as a bishop from his home on the northwestern borders of England. We know of his career from two of his own works, the *Confession* and *Coroticus*—a letter to a Celtic king of Strathclyde (Dumbarton) of that name—and from a biography written by a priest in about 700. Though this latter work is by no means reliable, the hypothesis that the Patrick we know was not a single person, but two or more, seems unnecessary. Indeed, it may even be possible to build up a better picture of him than of any other contemporary figure of northern Europe.

Introducing the Latin tongue for ecclesiastical usage in the island, Patrick also established the Roman episcopal type of church. But, for all the balanced outlook and realism to which our sources bear witness, this proved a mistake, since the Roman formula had been created to serve an urban set-up with which Irish society, founded on rural life, had little in common. Not long, therefore, after his death, the episcopal system was progressively superseded by a structure based on monasteries instead; and by the end of the sixth century the process was complete. The Irish monasteries, such as Clonard, Clonmacnois, and Lismore—institutions which dominated this Age of the Saints—were self-contained and self-sufficient, maintaining themselves on the land, like the rest of the population; and they were governed by abbots just as the families and tribes of the country were ruled by their headmen and chieftains. The abbots took over most of the administrative functions of the bishops, and the Irish church assumed a distinctive character of its own, based on these great monastic centers. They contained hundreds and thousands of ecclesiastical and lay inhabitants who, as time went on, extended their activities far beyond their religious and agricultural duties into various forms of craftmanship and erudition, for which the major monasteries became renowned. And meanwhile the Irish were also carrying asceticism to far more rigorous levels of sanctity, importing from Egypt, by way of Gaul, the taste for austere withdrawal into remote solitude; so that their small, isolated communities of "white" martyrs—men who were wholly dedicated to God without needing to shed their blood—became a well-known, deeply revered feature of the scene.

In the course of the seventh century, the antagonism between northern and southern Ireland was reflected in ecclesiastical conflicts. In general, the less insular south showed a greater desire for conformity with Rome, and at Adamnán's Synod of Birr (696/7), the Romanists, and their cause of organizational discipline and unity, prevailed against the more parochial Celtic traditions, though several further decades were to pass before papal authority effectively prevailed.

Overleaf: The monastery of Clonmacnois (Offaly), founded by St. Ciaran in the later 540s, with its splendid cross. Many of the other stone crosses, which constituted one of the major arts of early medieval Ireland, were formed under the influence of this influential monastery, which passed on artistic motifs of which it had learnt from eastern Mediterranean sources.

IRISH POETRY AND PROSE

Seen below are two stones inscribed with the Ogham alphabet. That on the left is from Tirmahally, County Kerry (length 70 inches, 175cm), and that on the right from Montaggart, County Cork (92 inches, 230cm). The stones date between the fourth and seventh centuries, and are now in the National Museum of Ireland, Dublin. The angled short lines stand for the Latin letters (see key), a type of writing which began in about 400 in the southern part of Ireland where contact with the continent was not lost. But the alphabet was not used to record the early Irish literary works, which were not written down until Roman letters subsequently came into use.

The Ogham script, which represents letters of the Latin alphabet by groups of short lines set at different angles on either side of a central spine, originated in Munster, where people kept up contact with the remains of Roman culture. The script appears from the fourth or fifth century onward, on rough memorial and boundary stones. It was not, however, employed for literary works, which were orally transmitted.

This transmission was the task of a branch of the *aes dana*. These were men of special talents who were believed, like the hermits, to possess certain supernatural powers. They occupied a place of their own in the Irish social hierarchy, and enjoyed the unusual privilege of being allowed to circulate freely round the country. They included jurists, historians, physicians, skilled craftsmen, and above all the *filid*—"seers" or poets, including, or supplemented by, a group known as "bards." These *filid*, entitled to notable rewards that they were rarely slow to claim, exercised a considerable influence over the monastic movement, which thus in some degree became the heir of the pagan druidic and bardic schools. The vernacular literature it developed, the oldest known to us north of the Alps, ceased to be oral when its productions began to be recorded in the Roman characters which replaced Ogham from about 600 onward.

By that time, the primitive Irish language had evolved into the tongue known as Old Irish, and rhyme was beginning to appear in its syllabic, alliterative verse. Most of what has come down to us is in later (Middle Irish) versions, but the *Cry of the Deer* and *Eulogy of St. Columba* appear to go back to originals of sixth-century date. There are also Biblical and court and historical poems; but the theme that dominated all others was nature, lovingly sought out and perceived by poets who showed an unparalleled gift for depicting its grandest and minutest manifestations alike. These men were often monks secluded in lonely places, and a note of mystical melancholy is often to be heard. But the dialogue between one such hermit, Marbán, and his half-brother, King Gúaire of Connaught (who died in 663), displays a happy blend of spiritual feeling, sensitiveness to beauty, and adventurous fantasy laced with self-deprecating humor.

```
Q
C
T
D
H
N
S
F
L
B
I
E
U
O
A
R
Z
NG
G
M
```

My father gave me a whole province of Ireland, this province ruled from Cruachan, which is why I am called "Medb of Cruachan." And they came from Finn the king of Leinster, Rus Ruad's son to woo me, and from Coirpre Niafer the king of Temair... and I wouldn't go. For I asked a harder wedding gift than any woman ever asked before from a man in Ireland—the absence of meanness and jealousy and fear.

The Táin

Other kinds of dialogue, more or less rhetorical in nature, appear in early works of epic character, in which the principal narrative medium is prose. The most important cycle of these sagas comes from the Ulaid, the people of Ulster in the north of Ireland, whose *Cattle Raid of Cooley (Táin Bó Cúailnge)* is designed to be a sort of Irish *Aeneid*: the poem appears to have originated as early as the fourth century, though it was extensively worked over in subsequent epochs. Such sagas may, on occasion, have a tenuous historical basis; but for the most part their contents are mythical. They are the work of men who create a magical, fanciful world of resplendent heroes, which remains profoundly alien to the dour everyday realities of time and place, or of cause and effect.

By the seventh century, this imaginative gift was also abundantly displayed in the creation of Lives of Saints. But there was also quite another type of composition, consisting of Irish law tracts. These treatises, some of which may originally have been composed in verse, were produced by a special class of jurists, going back to the seventh century or before. The tracts provide, in their most primitive strata, our best evidence for the early society of Ireland, and they are the oldest legal compositions, unaffected by either Roman or Mediterranean law, to have come down to us from anywhere in Europe.

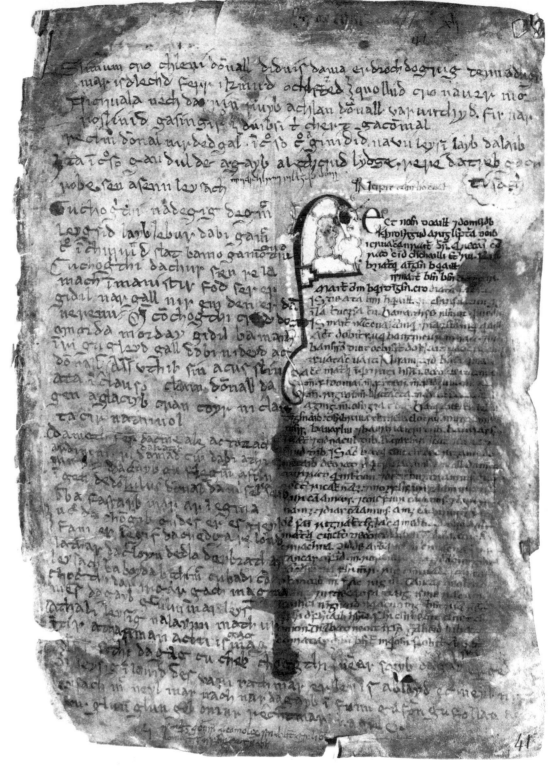

If I married a mean man our union would be wrong, because I'm so full of grace and giving. It would be an insult if I were more generous than my husband, but not if the two of us were equal in this. If my husband was a timid man our union would be just as wrong because I thrive, myself, on all kinds of trouble. It is an insult for a wife to be more spirited than her husband, but not if the two are equally spirited.

The Táin

A page from the Book of Leinster, twelfth century, containing a version of the "Pillow Talk," part of the *Cattle Raid of Cooley (Táin Bó Cúailnge)*, an epic that may have originated eight hundred years earlier, though it had been frequently altered during the intervening period. The *Táin* belongs to a very prominent branch of early Irish saga, composed by the Ulaid of Ulster (Northern Ireland). Trinity College, Dublin

The Ogham script was used to inscribe the name of the owner of these seventh- or eighth-century Irish brooches *(left)*. Its use, for inscriptional purposes, may have been more widespread than our evidence suggests, since so few works of art survived the depredations of the Vikings. National Museum of Ireland, Dublin.

THE ART OF IRELAND

After the collapse of Roman rule in Britain, it was chiefly in Ireland that the Celtic artistic traditions were perpetuated without a break, though Ireland soon exported them to Iona and Northumbria, where they reappeared in impressive form. The arts of Iona and Northumbria, as we can see, blend Irish-Celtic motifs with many other influences. But so, in fact, from the very beginning, had the art of Ireland itself, in which diverse themes from Gaul, Italy, Byzantium, and Coptic Egypt were clearly apparent. They arrived on Irish soil by several distinct channels. First, use was made of the direct sea route through the Straits of Gibraltar. Second, the small Germanic kingdom of the Suevi in Galicia (northwest Spain), suppressed by the Visigoths in about 585, has been identified as fulfilling an

kings, when they established a state on Irish territory in the ninth century, took away, or destroyed, very much else as well. That is probably why not a single one of the great illuminated books that have come down to us appears to have originated from Ireland. Since, however, the volumes made in Northumbria and Iona were so strongly guided by Irish artistic conceptions, it is likely that others, no longer extant, were designed and made in Ireland itself.

The position about Irish metalwork is different. Once again, the Vikings left relatively little of it behind; but what they have left is of a quality and refinement unique in all Europe. One such masterpiece, the richest surviving piece of Celtic jewelry, is the "Tara" brooch, wrongly named because it was found

Below right: The Ardagh Chalice, named after the place of its discovery in County Limerick (western Ireland), now in the National Museum of Ireland, Dublin. It dates from the eighth century. The chalice is almost entirely Celtic in character, although its filigree technique is imported, with improvements, from Anglo-Saxon art, and the traditional curvilinear patterns have been relegated to a subsidiary role.

Opposite: The "Tara" Brooch, about A.D. 700 (National Museum of Ireland, Dublin). Such superb jewelry must have been a major art of early Ireland, though most examples were carried away by the Norwegian invaders. However, the later Vikings came as settlers, forming their own kingdom based on Dublin in the ninth century. This eleventh-century silver brooch *(above)* is in the "Hiberno-Viking" style which developed on the island.

intermediary role. And another link was probably provided by the seaports of Brittany (Armorica), of which the Celtic populations, augmented in the fifth century by emigrants from Cornwall, long remained more or less independent of Frankish rule.

The difficulty about assessing early Irish art is that so much of it has vanished. Woodwork, leatherwork, and textiles could not have been expected to survive, but the Norwegian Vi-

not at Tara but near the mouth of the Boyne, on the northern Meath border. The brooch consists of a closed ring of cast silver, with an ornamental pin attached to it by a smaller, loose ring. Both the main ring and the pin are decorated with gold filigree panels covered with curling and intertwining animals. These patterns and the filigree technique are improved versions of Anglo-Saxon models, so that this style, like that of the illuminated

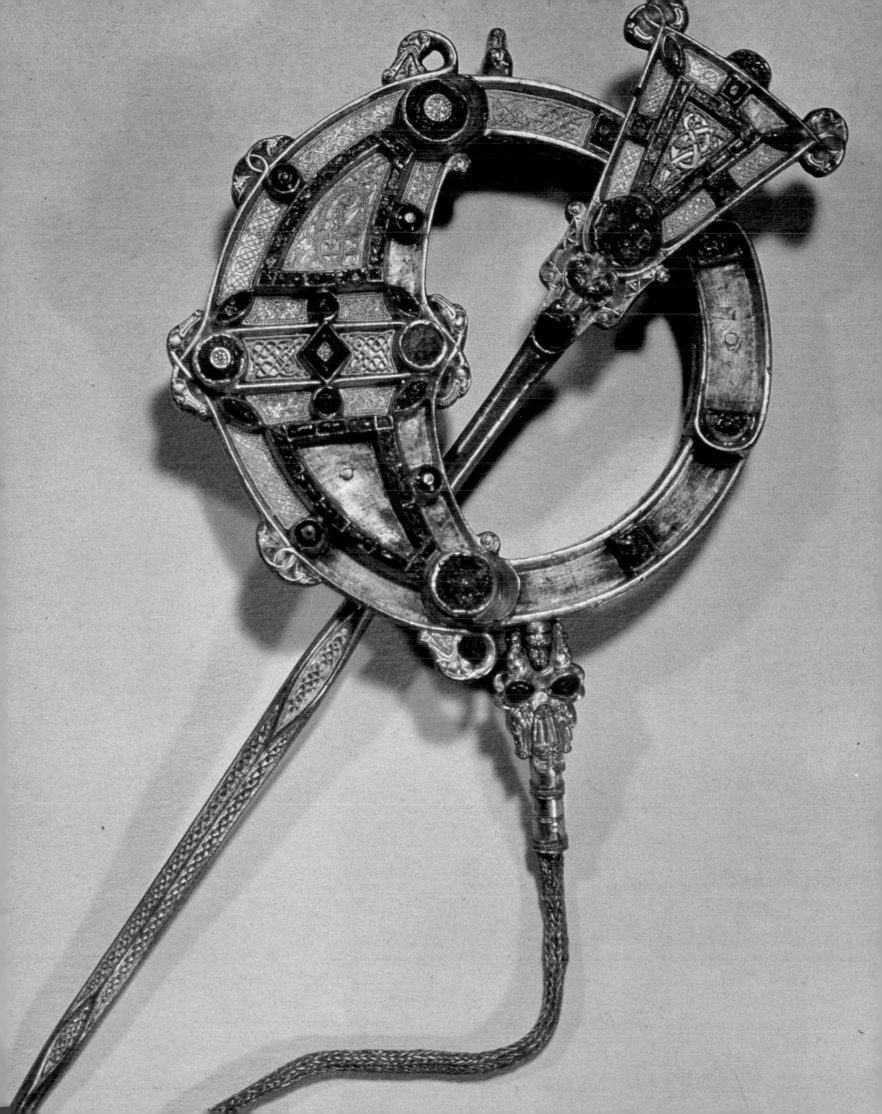

books from Northumbria and Iona which it strongly recalls, can be described as Hiberno-Saxon.

Very close to the brooch in design is the Ardagh chalice (eucharistic wine cup), part of a hoard found concealed in a Munster ring fort. Its silver bowl and foot are linked by a gilt-bronze stem, and around the bowl runs a ring of filigree-ornamented panels; the heavy silver contrasts powerfully with the exquisite decoration. Like the Book of Durrow, the chalice represents a brief moment of balance between the simplicity of the past and the complexity of the future. But the chalice is more purely Celtic that the Book of Durrow —though its filigree has once again, like that of the Tara brooch, been learnt from Anglo-Saxon artists.

High Crosses. Built of stone and standing at waysides or on graves or other holy places, they resemble the crosses of Northumbria, but are far more numerous and varied, and were made over a much longer period of time, extending between the sixth and the tenth centuries. Like the designs of the North-umbrian illuminated books, the interlaced reliefs of these Irish crosses often seem to be modeled on ornamental metalwork. Indeed, strips of decorated metal had presumably been fixed to the wooden crosses, now lost, which were the prototypes of these stone master-pieces, and which, in their turn, had taken their inspiration from prehistoric pagan Standing Stones.

One of the earliest free-standing Irish stone crosses is the highly complicated North Cross

Much of the art of the early Middle Ages everywhere was devoted to religon, but this was all the more likely in Ireland, as its religious life was so particularly intense. Religion in this Age of the Saints, based on the great self-supporting monasteries under their abbots, provided the only stable organizational framework. *Left:* The silver bell-shrine of Conall, eighth century, British Museum, London. *Right:* Shrine of the church of St. Ailbhe at Emly (Tipperary), which was the principal ecclesiastical center of Munster before the rise of Cashel.

Another chalice of equal quality, dating from about 800, was discovered in 1980 in a bog near Thurles (Tipperary), not far from Cashel, the capital of Munster. Taller, more conical, and less full-bodied than its Ardagh fore-runner, it is decorated and encircled with interlaced gold filigree panels and amber settings. Found with it was an object of slightly earlier date, a paten or eucharistic bread dish (with its stand), the first object of this kind ever to have been discovered in Ireland; it is ringed by a band of filigree panels alternating with elaborate glass studs in silver grills. A strainer of gilt bronze in the form of a ladle also came to light at the same time.

The other most remarkable element in the early Christian art of Ireland is provided by its

of Ahenny (Tipperary in Munster), attribut-able to a date before 800. It was probably in one of these southern valleys that the crosses originated. However, most of those which survive today are to be found somewhat farther north, erected under the influence of the great monastery of Clonmacnois. They draw on various artistic models, but particu-larly echo motifs and techniques of eastern Mediterranean origin; so that it seems that the sculptors of these monuments may have been trained by Egyptian (Coptic) or Syrian refugees from the Arabs who had occupied their countries.

The North *(left)* and South *(right)* Crosses of Ahenny, in Tipperary, Ireland, made of granite in the late eighth century. These are some of the earliest of the great free-standing crosses that constituted one of Ireland's most important arts. The designs are in many ways comparable with the almost contemporary Book of Kells, but the crosses place particular emphasis on artistic themes derived from the eastern Mediterranean area. The technique is influenced by metalwork; the earlier wooden crosses, which have, not surprisingly, disappeared, had apparently been decorated with ornamental metal strips.

Fair woman, will you go with me to a wonderful land where music is? The hair is like the primrose tip there, and the whole body is the colour of snow...
The ridge of every moor is purple, a delight to the eye are the blackbird's eggs; though the plain of Ireland is fair to see, it is like a desert once you know the Great Plain.
Fine though you think the ale of Ireland, the ale of the Great Land is more heady; a wonderful land is the land I tell of, the young do not die there before the old.

Above: The Book of Durrow is the earliest of the memorable series of "Hiberno-Saxon" Gospel Books. It dates from the years after 670 and was probably made at the Northumbrian Monastery of Lindisfarne (Holy Island), which had been founded in 653 by St. Aidan who came from Celtic Iona and was accompanied and followed by Irish artists. The Book of Durrow displays an austere style in comparison with what was to follow; contrast this symbol of St. Matthew with the other illustrations on this page. Trinity College, Dublin.

Sweet mild streams flow through the land, choice mead and wine; matchless people without blemish, conception without sin, without guilt.

We see everyone on all sides, and no one sees us; it is the darkness of Adam's trespass that screens us from being counted.

Woman, if you come to my mighty people a crown of gold shall be on your head; honey, wine, ale, fresh milk, and beer you shall have there with me, fair woman.

Midir's Invitation to the Earthly Paradise, Irish poem, author unknown, ninth century

Above: The Book of Kells, about A.D. 800. This was the last and greatest of the Hiberno-Saxon illuminated books, made not in Northumbria like the earlier manuscripts, but at Iona in the Celtic (Irish) kingdom of Dalriada in western Scotland. The design derives elements from a variety of foreign sources; and yet at the same time it achieves effects that are dazzlingly original. Trinity College, Dublin.

When the Irish left their homelands for Europe, they took their great skill of manuscript illumination with them—and taught it to others. The double-page *(left)* is the beginning of the Gospel of Luke at the monastery of St. Gallen in northeast Switzerland. The monastery was founded in 612 by the Celtic missionary St. Gall—a companion of St. Columbanus—and converted into a Benedictine abbey in about 720, becoming a leading center of the art of illumination and the most influential educational institution north of the Alps.

Ireland, during the first millennium A.D., was more densely inhabited than Britain, and the later centuries of the western Roman empire witnessed population pressures, and disturbed conditions, which brought about a very extensive series of migrations from Irish shores to the west coasts of Scotland, England, and Wales. Although extremely little is known about the details of this phenomenon, it represented a movement quite as extensive as the influx of the Anglo-Saxons who arrived on England's opposite, eastern shore.

The Irish immigrants, known as "Scotti," occupied the maritime regions of Britain from south Wales to the Solway Firth. Moreover, they planted even more important colonies farther north, on the isles and lochs of Argyllshire (meaning "land of the Gaels of the west"). This region became known as Dalriada—the name of Ulster, from which these settlers had come. The first of the Irish visitors to Argyllshire may have arrived as early as the third or fourth century A.D., but a definitive settlement was made in about 500 by Fergus Mor and his two brothers. They established three small principalities, which in the later sixth century became united under King Aidan.

The power of this Scottish Dalriada was based on a fleet and on fortresses at Dunadd and Dunolly, but its principal religious center was Iona, in the Inner Hebrides. On that island was the monastery founded in about 563 by St. Columba (Columcille) from Donegal in Ulster. From Iona, Columba sent missionaries all over Scotland, so that the monasteries they established recognized Iona as their mother house, and its abbots as the country's chief ecclesiastical rulers. It was from Iona, too—formerly their place of refuge—that the Northumbrian kings Oswald and Oswy invited many visitors, including Aidan who founded Lindisfarne. Such were the reasons why the great illuminated books made in Northumbria exhibit such very strong Irish characteristics, while the greatest of these volumes, the Book of Kells, was apparently designed in Iona itself.

Columba's successor as the leading Irish missionary, Columbanus (543–615), though a man of Leinster, was likewise brought up in Ulster at the monastery of Bangor. His travels

took him not to Britain but to the continent, where he inaugurated a powerful and far-reaching revival of religious life. Among his principal memorials were the monasteries of Luxeuil in France and Bobbio in Italy, where he died. Columbanus felt an ardent passion to spread his own rigorous brand of Christianity, and his impact on the outside world was greater than that of any other Irishmen of any time. Many other itinerant Irish monks followed in his missionary wake—and went farther afield still. They reached the Faroes not long after 700, and Iceland by the 790s; when the first Norwegians arrived there in 874, they found Irish hermits already installed. This prolonged, unparalleled, and fervent outburst of missionary journeying to spread the Faith was based on the same concept of "white" martyrdom which had caused hermits to settle

on remote islets: except that now the severance was to be more complete still, since the missionaries were to live and die far from their beloved native soil.

I have a shieling in the wood,
None knows it save my God:
An ash-tree on the higher side,
   a hazel bush beyond,
A huge old tree encompasses it . . .

Swarms of bees and chafers,
   little musicians of the wood,
A gentle chorus:
Wild geese and ducks,
   shortly before summer's end,
The music of the dark torrent . . .

The voice of the wind against
   the branchy wood
Upon the deep-blue sky:
Falls of the river,
   the note of the swan,
Delicious music . . .

In the eyes of Christ,
   the ever-young, I am no
Worse off than thou art.

Song of the Hermit Marbán to his brother King Gúaire

Opposite: Reconstruction of the monastery of Kells in Ireland, founded by St. Columbanus (543–615). It was designed like an Irish farm. The Book of Kells is named after the place because it was taken there after the destruction of Iona by the Vikings. Following his Irish activities, Columbanus founded monasteries in France (Luxeuil) and Italy (Bobbio) that exercised enormous influence. *Bottom left:* Pictish inscription on the pedestal of a memorial stone from St. Vigeans (Angus, Scotland). The name "Drosten Voret Forcus" appears, but the rest of the inscription is indecipherable. Picts' Museum, Arbroath.

The map shows the main migration patterns of the Celts following the Anglo-Saxon invasion of mainland Britain. A large part of the Celtic population of Cornwall fled across the sea to Brittany (northwest France), where a Celtic language is still spoken by some today.

"St. Columba's House," still standing above the ruins of the monastery at Kells (reconstructed opposite). The walls are more than a yard thick, surrounding a single room.

A Pictish stone from Dunnichen, Angus, Scotland. The Picts, apparently of mixed Celtic and pre-Celtic race, controlled much of central and eastern Scotland. It was at Dunnichen that King Brude defeated and killed King Egfrith of Northumbria in 685.

SCANDINAVIA AND ITS ART

The ancient peoples of Sweden, Denmark, and Norway were of mixed race, partly blonde and "Nordic," partly shorter and round-skulled and dark. The nature of their beliefs about the universe is hard to determine, because so much of our information comes from sagas composed toward the end of the Middle Ages. The *Prose Edda* and *Heimskringla* (history of Norway) and *Egils Saga* by the outstanding epic historian of Iceland, Snorri Sturluson, are particularly important, though he lived as late as the twelfth and thirteenth centuries and introduced many anachronisms. But it seems clear that the early Scandinavians shared the German belief in the World Ash-tree, Yggdrasill—whose branches reach the sky and cover the earth—and in Ragnarök, the heroic conflict and doom that will come at the end of the world. They also worshiped the same gods as the other Germanic peoples. Preeminent among the deities was Odin (Woden), the universal father, highest of the gods, the lord of kings and warriors and poets, supremely wise but also magically grim and sinister. Tor (Thor), the immensely strong blacksmith, whose hammer was the thunderbolt, became the divinity of farmer and peasant, the patron of ordinary people: red-haired and red-bearded, a mighty eater and drinker.

The language of the Scandinavians, too, was Germanic. But when the other Germans, who lived farther south, migrated to distant lands in the fourth and fifth centuries A.D., they left an empty border region that caused the Scandinavian communities beyond it to develop on separate lines; and between 500 and 700 their speech moved away from continental German. At first, except for minor local differences, it evolved as a single "Common Scandinavian" language, within which national distinctions between the three countries did not become apparent until after the turn of the millennium. Nor, for a long time, was there any sense of three separate nationalities, though burial customs and artistic techniques began to develop on variant lines from one country and region to another.

Woodwork, which has only survived in rare examples, must have been one of the principal arts of Scandinavia. Its peoples were also advanced workers in metal. In particular, the animal (zoomorphic) style already evolved in Roman times made extraordinary progress in their hands. Their artists owed debts to the Merovingians, Northumbrians, and Irish. But the Scandinavians who drew upon these sources did so with vigorous and varied origi-

nality, employing the chip-carving technique, by which the flat surface was cut with the corner of a chisel into a series of glittering facets. It is a dexterously acrobatic, sophisticated art, in which the semi-naturalism of late Roman motifs is cunningly offset by intricate processes of abstraction; and the balance shifts gradually in favor of ever more abstract themes, as the animals, prancing in their kaleidoscopic patterns, become ever increasingly disjointed and capricious, and more and more teasing to the eye.

The stages of this transformation can be approximately identified. Objects of the early fifth century found in a large bog at Sösdala in southern Sweden show early, tentative attempts to rework the Roman animal designs. "Style I," of the sixth century, was based on elaborate single animals, that became progressively more and more distorted. "Style II," reaching its climax at the principal centers of the Swedish mainland, favored interlaced animals of ribbon-like form. "Style III," which characterizes the Viking Age that followed, was more complicated and fussy; its principal feat was to display a new sort of animal, a powerful, fantastic, "gripping beast."

The interwoven lines and symmetry of this fifth-century picture-stone from the island of Gotland, off the Swedish coast, show the foundations of the animal (zoomorphic) style that was to follow, where the geometrical figures were replaced by animal motifs linked in ever more complicated patterns.

Right: The bronze figure of the god Tor, seated on a throne and clasping a curious hammer, was discovered in Iceland. Tor and many other gods, notably Odin the universal father, were common to all the Scandinavian peoples.

Opposite: A sword-hilt from Snartemo, Norway, late sixth century. The highly sophisticated style of this metalwork (based on animal forms unrecognizably dismembered and distorted) provides a reminder that the Vikings were not only destroyers, but the inheritors of a great artistic tradition—though many of their finest products are lost, because they consisted of wood and leather. Universitets Oldsaksamling, Oslo.

SWEDEN

From the last years of the fifth century, a stream of late Roman and Byzantine coins was flooding into the Swedish Baltic isles, by way of Germany and the Rhine. First they came to Öland and then to Gotland, where massive gold neck-rings (torcs) and other objects have been found in very large quantities; also bracteates, great gold pendant amulet disks with increasingly stylized adaptations of the portrait-heads on imperial coins and medallions.

many years carved large limestone grave slabs, which display fresh and vivid reliefs of mythical or historical scenes. But the gold finds on the two islands only belong to brief periods, at Öland from about 480 to 490 and at Gotland from 500 to 520. Thereafter the communities came to an abrupt end, probably at the hands of raiders or invaders.

The same period saw the erection of fortresses on the Swedish mainland, which was divided

"Bracteate" (thin gold plate) from Hammenhög parish, Skåne, south Sweden, fourth century. These engraved disk pendants, made over a considerable area of southern Scandinavia and worn as amulets, draw upon the coin and medallion portraits of the late Roman emperors—redesigned according to Germanic tastes, infusing elements of Scandinavian myth.

An aerial view of Eketorp, the great fifth-century stronghold on the island of Öland, off Sweden, where a vast hoard of gold was buried between about 480 and 490. The community seems to have come to an abrupt end at about that time.

On Öland, a distributing center for suppliers and purchasers of goods, the circular, powerfully fortified settlement of Eketorp is the earliest permanently inhabited Scandinavian stronghold of which we have any knowledge. Gotland, a little to the north, maintained a farming community, and businessmen, too, became wealthy from the transit trade, operating from its natural harbors and anchorages. At one of them, Paviken, they repaired their ships and made beads; and their sculptors for

into more or less independent tribal units. In particular Uppland (to the north of the modern Stockholm) enjoyed a deep protected inland waterway system (Lake Mälaren) which provided a natural center for early settlement and trade. Thus at Valsgärde and Vendel (after which this pre-Viking archaeological epoch is often named), from the sixth to the ninth century, the chief men of the great families were buried in their boats near the sea, together with lavish arms and treasure which testify to a wealthy economy; and the recurrence of identical styles at Sutton Hoo on the east coast of England hints revealingly at international contacts. A few miles south of these Uppland centers was the capital of the state, Old Uppsala, where four huge grave mounds of the sixth century are probably those of the local rulers. This country of the Sviar or Svea (from whom comes "Sverige," the name of Sweden), was the oldest and most powerful Scandinavian monarchy, and it expanded its territory considerably in the years following 700.

A little to the south of Uppsala, on the small island of Lillön (Ekerö) in Lake Mälaren, was the settlement of Helgö. Founded after 400, on a site well hidden from the perils of the open sea, it expanded rapidly into a major town during the two centuries that followed. Under the control of the princes of Uppland, the place became not only an agricultural center but also a new sort of trading post, importing wares from across the Baltic and North Seas and even from as far as north India, and exporting slaves, dairy produce, furs, hides, sealskin ropes, and local ironwork.

By 800, Helgö was beginning to be superseded by a place on the neighboring island of Birka (Björkö), which became the northernmost mercantile center of Europe and the busiest and most cosmopolitan of all Scandinavian markets. Visitors intent on trading came to Birka on ships, skis, skates, and sledges; in its streets jostled men wearing the patterned linen shirts of the eastern Slavs, and the kaftans of the Arab and Persian worlds. St. Ansgar, who had been given his training at Corbie in Picardy, came as a missionary to Birka (853–854) after first visiting Schleswig, but Christianity did not win its final victory in Sweden for another three hundred years or more.

A bridle mount of gilt bronze—two and a half times actual size—executed in a version of the animal style. This and other similar mounts from Bro, Gotland, Sweden, are the work of an extremely competent Viking jeweler. Gotland's position as one of the first Swedish centers to attain high prosperity is dated by such gold finds, which belong to the early sixth century.

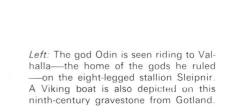

Left: The god Odin is seen riding to Valhalla—the home of the gods he ruled —on the eight-legged stallion Sleipnir. A Viking boat is also depicted on this ninth-century gravestone from Gotland. Statens Historiska Museum, Stockholm.

THE SWEDES IN THE EAST

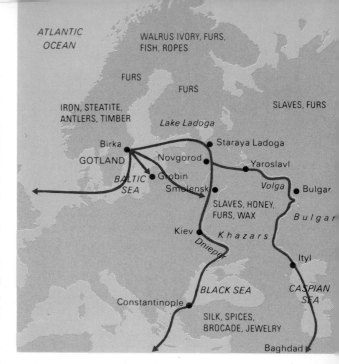

The Vikings established vast trade routes covering most of the known world. To the Christian west the Norwegians and Danes came mostly by sea—sailing through the Straits of Gibraltar into the Mediterranean, and across the North Sea, and to Iceland, Greenland, and even North America. But the trading journeys of the Swedes in the east were just as extensive, extending by land and river far into Russia and southeast to Baghdad, for silk and spices.

In the course of their far-reaching overland travels the Vikings must often have had recourse to the use of wagons. One such vehicle surviving is this ceremonial carriage found at Oseberg, dating from the ninth century—part of the rich finds from a well-preserved burial ship (shown on p. 192).

The wares from the Swedish ports traveled far and wide. But the main thrust was toward the east, and in the last decades of the eighth century groups of Swedes began to settle on the east coast of the Baltic, as a first step toward further explorations. Their first important base was at Grobin (Grobina) on the Latvian coast, where excavations of a large burial place reveal the existence of a dual settlement, in which traders from Gotland and adventurers or warriors from Uppland lived together. Grobin was not far from the mouth of the River Dvina, from which there were facilities for portage (the overland carrying of boats) to the headwaters of the Dnieper that reached right down through Russia.

But the settlement at Grobin was only the prelude to another and more important drive which led the Swedes through the Gulf of Finland to Aldeigjuborg (Staraya Ladoga), situated in a protected position up the River Volkhov six miles before it runs into Lake Ladoga. The previous occupants of the place had mostly been Finns, but Aldeigjuborg was visited by Swedish merchants (as well as Frisians and Slavs) as early as the eighth century; and then, from shortly after 800, material excavated from a fortified site covering 160 acres indicates the presence of a substantial Swedish community. The settlement was mainly important because of its easy access to the Dnieper and Volga, the rivers upon whose waters extensive commerce made its way to the Black and Caspian Seas.

Russian history is essentially river history, and in its development the role of the Swedes was

quite as remarkable as the contemporary activities of Norwegian and Danish Vikings in the west. First, farther up the Volkhov, the settlers from Aldeigjuborg came to Novgorod (Holmgardr in the Scandinavian language) near Lake Ilmen and played a part in the foundation of this future major kingdom in the early or middle ninth century. Novgorod was located near the Volga, down which the next step was Jaroslavl (northeast of Moscow), where large mound-cemeteries display strong Scandinavian elements, along with Slav material.

Lower down the Volga at the Bulgar bend,

Fadlan, got a view of them and admired their fine physique, though deploring their highly defective personal hygiene.

Meanwhile, at the point where the Black Sea and the Sea of Azov meet, Swedes had joined Slavs to form the stronghold of Tmutarakan (825), which challenged Khazar control of the Don-Constantinople route. Also, yet another group of Swedes moved in the direction of the Black Sea by an alternative route, down the Dnieper. Extensive Swedish material of the epoch appears in large cemeteries at Smolensk and Gniezdovo, and lower down the river rose the foundations of Kiev. This was the future capital of the second great kingdom (together with that of Novgorod) which the Swedes helped to found in the course of

Of all the gold bracteates which have come down to us, this specimen of sixth-century date from Gotland is surely one of the most imposing, and gives some idea of the wealth accumulated by the Scandinavians in the course of their raiding and trading.

A reconstruction of the tapestry discovered in the Oseberg ship. The scene is almost certainly mythical, but its exact interpretation has not yet been ascertained beyond doubt. However, the picture does provide us with some details of Scandinavian life in the ninth century; horsedrawn wagons are seen—possibly inspired by

Swedish and other traders struck out across the wastelands to reach the Silk Route to Baghdad and China somewhere near the Aral Sea: nearly a hundred thousand Islamic coins have been found beneath the soil of the Scandinavian homeland, showing that this activity was fully under way by the early ninth century. Other traders, however, preferred to stay on the Volga, where they formed and exploited a bridge between two powerful kingdoms, the Bulgars to the north and Khazars to the south. Swedes came down as far as the Khazar capital, Ityl, at the mouth of the Volga on the Caspian. There, in the tenth century, an Arab, Ibn

the ninth century, extending as far north as the Gulf of Finland and even dominating Novgorod itself for centuries to come.

The relative parts played by Swedes and Slavs in the early settlements is hotly disputed—and in any case it varied from place to place. Yet it seems clear that the designation "Rus," from which Russia takes its name, referred originally not to Slavs but to northmen, particularly Swedes. The term was apparently borrowed, by way of the Slav language, from the Finns, whose name for Sweden is Ruotsi—a word that probably comes from Roslagen, a coastal district of Uppland.

the overland eastern traders—and the men are wearing loose-fitting trousers. Whether or not the Vikings actually wore horned helmets, like the figure shown here top left, has been the subject of much debate. But they are depicted so infrequently that they must have been very rare; probably they were of religious significance, rather than normally worn by the warriors.

DENMARK AND NORWAY

Hedeby in Denmark was the largest northern town of the age, and well situated to become a center for international trade and industry. Shown below is a part of the reconstruction of the town to be seen in the Schleswig-Holsteinisches Museum, Schleswig. Houses were constructed by splitting tree-trunks lengthways and planting them vertically in the ground to form a continuous wall which was then packed with mud; but other dwellings were made of buttressed wattle and daub. Inside, the larger houses were divided into separate rooms.

The Scandinavians were accustomed to cremate their dead, and their burial sites were fairly elaborate. This bronze figure *(below)* was found in the grave of a warrior, together with an iron sword, two lances, a spear and shield-mounts. But not all such hoards were associated with honoring the dead; the Vikings as looters and traders amassed large quantities of imported silver as coins, hacked-up silver objects, or jewelry, which they subsequently buried, in many cases without ever reclaiming them. This find *(above right)* is from Birka in Sweden.

Denmark, like parts of Sweden, formed an early political unit, because of its relative uniformity, and the accessibility of all its regions one to another. People of Germanic speech had migrated at an early date from southern Sweden onto the Danish islands, including Zeeland, where a sanctuary was established at Leire. Denmark seems to have been the original home of the Runic alphabet, adapted from Mediterranean forms of lettering in the third century A.D.; the script was believed to enjoy occult powers, and in due course made its appearance on commemorative inscriptions. Two large golden horns (now lost), of fourth century date, found at Gallehus in Schleswig (Slesvig), display remarkable abstract scenes ultimately derived from Romano-Celtic art.

Schleswig, the narrow neck of land linking the North Sea with the Baltic, provided Denmark with its major lines of communication. On the west coast of the isthmus, at its narrowest point, the Danes had an active market harbor at Ribe, which, by the eighth century, if not

earlier, was receiving imports from across the North Sea in exchange for agricultural goods. More important, however, was Hedeby ("the town of the heath") on the opposite, eastern coast of Schleswig just south of the modern Danish-German frontier, on an arm of the narrow but navigable Schlei (Slie) Fjord. Hedeby, founded in the years before and after 800 by the amalgamation of three smaller communities, possessed easy and protected access to the sea and developed a road across the isthmus which eliminated the long and perilous sea route round the north of the Jutland peninsula. Thus Hedeby was able to supersede Frisian Dorestad as the main center for the transit trade between northwestern and northeastern Europe. In consequence, the place grew rapidly into the largest Scandinavian town of the age. Its activities included iron smelting, bronze casting, glass-making, weaving, and the manufacture of objects of bone and horn; it also became the first Scandinavian mint. However, an Arab visitor, Ibraham ibn Yakub, found the singing of the inhabitants exceptionally untuneful.

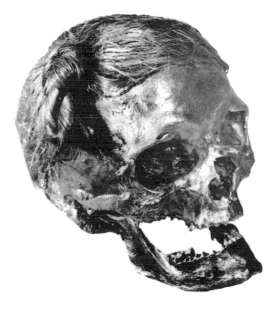

Hedeby's development was prompted by a new political phenomenon, the growth of a strong Danish kingdom. For its formidable and skillful king Godfred (d. 810), who ruled over the greater part of the country, made his principal center at Hedeby, where he built or enlarged a massive frontier fortification, the Danevirke extending from one side of Schleswig to the other. This barrier was intended to shelter the Danish trade route across the isthmus—and to keep out not only the Slavs, but the Carolingian Franks as well. For Godfred was strong and audacious enough to confront Charlemagne himself, and even to bring his

North Sea conquests to a halt. But the final unification of Denmark, and its conversion to Christianity, did not come for another century and a half.

In Norway, the area in closest touch with other countries was the Eastern Region (Østland), which was centered upon the coast of the Oslo Fjord and its rich agricultural hinterland—and must have achieved a considerable degree of political organization in the fifth or sixth century; this can be deduced from the enormous burial place or cenotaph to be seen at Raknehaugen (in Raumerike, north of Oslo). On the Oslo Fjord itself, during the ninth century, a regional, seasonal market began to develop at Sciringesheal (Kaupang). Another nucleus of population, up on the long west coast of Norway, was the territory of Trondelag round the Trondheimsfjord, ruled by prosperous landowning farmers with a vested interest in social stability. And finally, at the southwestern extremity of the country, there was the mountainous, deeply indented coast of Vestland (round Bergen), overpopulated and Spartan—the breeding ground of Viking enterprise in the age to come.

Early Scandinavian fashions in dresses and hairstyle. There are a number of skulls like this one *(left),* which were preserved in bogs or swamps; the hair is usually brown or fair. The dresses are from Randers in Denmark, and the skull from Schleswig (Germany).

THE VIKING EXPLOSION

As numerous legends suggest, the Scandinavians had long been travelers on the sea, and the name of Norway, "the north way," confirms that this was so. But the enormous Viking outburst only began toward the end of the eighth century. As time went on, it became a many-sided phenomenon, involving expansions of various different kinds—in which the Vikings appeared as looters, pirates, traders, settlers, and creators of states. Some believe that "Viking" comes from a word relating to raiding expeditions. But the most widely accepted etymology derives the term from *vik,* a bay or creek (as in Narvik, Norwick, Lerwick)—the inlets beside which these Scandinavians lived, or where they lay hidden in their ships while waiting to pounce on their victims.

The movement of expansion started among the Norwegians and particularly among the men of their southwestern, impoverished region of Vestland, penetrated by fjords providing numerous harbors. According to heroic tradition, adventurers from this territory were already traveling to Denmark and the Baltic in the course of the seventh century, and—in the other direction—far up their own coast as well, where they sought to intercept competitive shipping.

Then, in the eighth century, these Norwegians from Vestland sailed off across the North Sea and launched trading or raiding expeditions to the various islands, first the Shetlands and Orkneys, and then the Hebrides and Faroes. In about 780 these enterprises were followed by the first settlements, which seem to have been at least partly of a peaceful

The Oseberg ship, Oslo, about A.D. 800. The ship, preserved in a mound, was used for the burial of two women, perhaps a queen (Asa?) and her slave, sacrificed on her tomb. Buried with them was an unprecedented collection of Viking art at its most powerful, among which were the wagon and tapestry seen on pages 188 and 189, and items of foreign plunder such as the Frankish belt-mount and Irish golden arm-ring shown here. The ship itself was made of oak and clinker-built (with the hull planks overlapping); it had fifteen pairs of oars, a mast, and a square sail. It was a general duties vessel: appropriate to a chieftain in the coastal waters of Norway, and built in the grand manner for royal transport.

character, prompted by a desire for better pastures on these islands than could be found at home. In 787 seamen from Vestland came to the south coast of England as well, landing at Portland in Dorset, where they killed the officials sent to inquire the purpose of their visit. Next, almost at once, began violent Norwegian raids on the coast of Northumbria. In 793 the monastery of Lindisfarne was sacked and burnt. In the following year another raid felled a second rich Northumbrian monastery, probably Jarrow; and in 795 it was Iona that suffered. During the following years similar tip-and-run assaults continued steadily.

These attacks on the monastic centers of Northumbria were mainly launched from the bases the Norwegians had established on the Shetlands, though the starting point for the Iona raid was probably their Hebridean settlement at Lewis. From Lewis, too, came similar lightning onslaughts upon the sanctuaries situated on the capes and isles of Ireland. In about 795 the monastery of Rathlinn island off the northeast Irish coast was among places burnt to ashes. Moreover, the list rapidly lengthened. In the next century other victims

grassy coasts of southwest Greenland had received Norwegian settlers, and most remarkable of all, L'Anse aux Meadows on the northern tip of Newfoundland, across the Atlantic, is evidently a Norwegian settlement of about A.D. 1000, half a millenium before Christopher Columbus.

Wondered at and feared for thousands of miles, the Vikings had traveled farther than any Europeans before them, and had played a unique part, by violent and peaceful means alike, in breaking down regional barriers. Overpopulation was one of the reasons for this unprecedented explosion. Another factor was the Scandinavian system of inheritance by which property all went to the eldest son, so that there was a surplus of young landless men of the ruling class *(jarls)*, who consequently migrated, mobilizing free peasants *(karls)* to join them on their overseas expeditions. And these expeditions were all the more alluring because of the recent large-scale growth of commerce in the whole North Sea area, which largely superseded the Mediterranean—controlled by the Arabs—as the principal zone of business activity. This trade in the North Sea had hitherto been in the hands of the Frisians,

Vikings attacking with swords and long-handled axes; the Anglo-Saxon viewpoint on a tombstone of the tenth or eleventh century from the monastery of Lindisfarne, Northumbria, which was raided and sacked in 793. Lindisfarne Priory Museum.

included the Frisians (Dorestad) and Franks (Noirmoutier, Rouen, Quentovic). It was not surprising that the Gallic liturgy included the plea: "Graciously guard us from the disasters of this night!"

Already by this time, however, the true and even more significant Viking Age was under way, marked no longer by mere raids but by determined settlements over extensive and widely separated areas; settlements which actually led to the foundation of new, Viking states in Ireland (source of invaluable slave labor) and also in England and Normandy. Moreover, by the end of the tenth century the

and when the Carolingian monarchy suppressed their state it eliminated the only naval power that could keep the Scandinavians in check.

The western Vikings were able to achieve their success because they built peerless fleets of fast and roomy ships and used them with unparalleled speed and mobility. The development of these slender, flexible vessels through various phases of increasingly skillful construction can be traced from a growing number of examples that have been discovered in recent years in Norway and Denmark, covering a period of several centuries.

Dies for embossing ornamental plaques, from Öland, Sweden. The figures are of gods or heroes vanquishing fearsome monsters. Metalwork of all descriptions was one of the Vikings' greatest skills; excavations of smithies have revealed that their craftsmen knew and used all the tools to be found in modern use.

FROM EUROPE TO THE FAR EAST

Most of the peoples of the east, from central Europe all the way to Asia, were marked at some point in the dawning Middle Ages by contacts with the ferocious, nomadic horsemen of central Asia—Avars, Bulgars, Khazars, and White Huns. They came to dominate the massive Slavic populations who had migrated from their homelands in and around the Ukraine and who failed during this period to achieve durable political or national institutions. The invaders mostly spoke forms of Turkish, and China too had known its invasions of Turkish-speaking peoples. Yet under the Northern Wei dynasty, which was itself of such an origin, Buddhist culture flourished and the state became stronger and more centralized. Under the T'ang emperors (618–906), China formed the most extensive and powerful state in the world. In India's northern empire, vast regions were occupied by the White Huns. In the seventh century, however, Harsha restored unity in the northern part of the Indian peninsula, while strong and artistically active kingdoms were also established in the south. However, the fall of Sind to Arab invaders (712) heralded annexation by Islamic armies.

The Emperor's armies have
grown old and grey,
Fighting hundreds of
miles from home.
The barbarians know
no trade but battle
and bloodshed,
And have no fields
or ploughed lands.
Just wastelands where
whitened bones lie
among the yellow sand.

Li Po, eighth-century Chinese poet

Central Asia was dominated throughout the
epoch described in this book by warlike
mounted tribes of nomadic origin, and their
suzerainty also extended over eastern Europe,
preventing the establishment of a Slavic
state. Later, as illustrated in this fourteenth-
century Slavonic manuscript *(opposite)*, it
was cavalry that formed the main core of the
imperial armies.
In the east, the Chinese were successful in
maintaining adequate defense against the nomads to form the great T'ang empire—the
birthplace of much impressive art, architecture, and lyric verse. It was T'ang China that
produced the two figures shown here: the
guardian of a grave *(left)* and a master of ceremonies *(right)*.

"Slav" is a linguistic expression, describing a family of languages of which the present-day speakers belong to at least five anthropological groups. This ethnic diversity was already, to some extent, foreshadowed in ancient times. However, by the middle or later years of the Roman empire, the speakers of the Slav tongue or tongues had already developed sufficiently uniform customs to become recognizable as a single, though diversified, cultural unit.

The role of the Slavs in the period covered by this book was curiously paradoxical. They achieved a massive population expansion for which Europe, throughout all its history, provides no parallel. And yet, on the other hand, they attained political importance and independence only for fleeting periods of time, or for the most part never at all.

Their place of origin was the forest-steppe zone of the western Ukraine and the southeastern corner of Poland, between the middle Dnieper and Upper Vistula. Finds of third and fourth century date in this area may be signs of their presence. But the earliest certainly Slavic material appears about a hundred years later, on river terraces and slopes of sandy dunes at Zhitomir and other sites west of the Dnieper. The occupants of these settlements manufactured hand-made pottery, cremated

their dead, and lived in square semi-subterranean buildings surmounted by pitched roofs. At Pen'kovka, in the region of the Dnieper rapids, wooden planks were used for lining earthern walls. In general, these houses above ground were inhabited during the summer months, and partially sunken dwellings during the winter. In the River Tjasmin area, there are traces of the massive posts of circular wooden temples.

The typical Slav social institution was the patriarchal, patrilineal joint family house, the

The Slavs variously buried or cremated their dead, generally providing the burial site with food, such as eggs and meat, and small trinkets or items of jewelry. These gilt bronze spurs and the wheel-made pot (and gilt bronze tongue-piece, *opposite page*) were all found in graves in Slovakia.

home of several brothers and their families. In the seventh and eighth centuries, these dwellings were grouped in villages of considerable size protected by ramparts or cliffs and centered upon a headman's residence, to which the other houses might be linked by a covered way. The average village occupied about five thousand square yards of land, though the largest settlements of all could be six times more extensive.

Around the year 800 these families, groups of families, and villages were beginning to coalesce into self-governing tribal communities of substantial dimensions, under a chieftain who directed the affairs of his people with the assistance of an advisory council. The Slavs, Byzantine visitors noted, were rough and primitive people, but hospitable, music-loving, and fond of hot baths. They owned and exported slaves, and their principal occupation was agriculture, which they conducted with the help of the heavy plow (introduced, perhaps, before 600), employing collar harnesses of which they had learnt from central Asia.

They also forged admirable laminated swords. But their tribal units were nothing like extensive or mutually cooperative enough to put up a concerted resistance to the succession of nomad and semi-nomad invaders, mostly of Turkish (Turanian) speech—Huns, Avars, Bulgars, and Khazars—who ruled over enormous East Slav populations. So, too, at Novgorod and Kiev, did the invaders from far distant Sweden, although their descendants became gradually assimilated to the numerically predominant Slav communities. In due course, the East Slavs became differentiated into Great, White, and Little Russians, occupying northern and central Russia and the Ukraine respectively.

Until the eighth century, in the absence of a national state, the eastern Slavs lived in self-supporting village communities governed by an elective tribal chief and council. The villages were generally fortified with earthworks, or else built in naturally fortified places, as exemplified by this reconstruction of Novotroitskoe (Russia). Against the cold of winter the villagers built themselves semi-subterranean houses, shown in this reconstruction (top left), which is likewise derived from the archaeological survey of Novotroitskoe.

THE WEST AND SOUTH SLAVS

The collapse of the Hun empire in the fifth century enabled some of the Slavs of the Russian borderlands to break out of the country of their origin in a series of attempts to satisfy their hunger for land. And so they embarked on the huge-scale, multiple movements which eventually produced the nations of the West Slavs (Poles, Czechs, Slovaks) and South Slavs (Serbs, Croats, Slovenes, and—by amalgamation—Bulgars).

In the west, down the rivers Vistula, Warta, and Oder, a very mixed culture of German, Hunnish, and Slavonic elements developed, and the Slavs eventually predominated to form the kernel of the Polish nation. Meanwhile, many of their kinsmen traveled up the Danube and turned northwestward into the Elbe-Saale region, where they filled the vacuum left by the emigrations of its former inhabitants. These wide plains were known as a "land of forts," of which traces of more than

The Slavs who flooded in great numbers into what is now Yugoslavia from the sixth century onwards eventually became divided into the Serbs, Croats, and Slovenes who form the three principal ingredients in the country's population. Nevertheless, the Byzantine empire's impressive gold currency was still in use in Slavonic lands. This coin of the emperor Constantine V (741–775) was found in the tomb of a Croatian princess at Trilj, Dalmatia. Archaeological Museum, Split.

The Slavs in eastern and central Europe were a war-like race—often fighting against each other as much as against the other inhabitants of the region, the Germans—and this led to a great respect for the horse and its rider. The grave *(far right)* at Holiare (Slovakia), eighth century, shows a warrior buried together with his horse. Among many other equestrian gravefinds are this silver plaque depicting a falconer, from Stare Mesto in Slovakia (to be seen in the Narodni Museum, Brno) and tongue-piece from Nagysurany in Hungary (Hungarian National Museum, Budapest).

two thousand survive today. One of the fort-builders was Charlemagne, who had to organize formidable Frankish frontier defenses against Slav incursions.

West of the mouth of the River Oder lies Germany's largest island, Rügen, on which, in the course of the eighth century, the Slavs founded a permanent settlement and market-harbor at Ralswiek, where numerous Arab coins have been found. The island also possessed a great shrine of the principal Slav deity, Svantevit, god of war and protector of fields. For a long time, Slavs and Germans fought against their own compatriots quite as much as each other, but gradually each of the two

groups united against the other, and by the end of the Middle Ages these northern territories had all passed into German hands.

In central Europe, things turned out differently. For a great many of the Slavs who moved up the Danube in the fifth and sixth centuries did not then turn northward, like the rest, but stopped and settled in Czechoslovakia—that is to say, in Moravia, Bohemia, and Slovakia, regions recently vacated by the Lombards, where the population, after numerous vicissitudes, remains predominantly Slavonic today. Mediterranean contacts helped these West Slavs to improve their technology, and their work on the land benefited

The South Slavs, traveling on foot in vast numbers, migrated from their original homeland in the early sixth century and moved down the rivers Pruth and Theiss (Tisza). The Pruth group or federation included the Antae, who achieved a warlike reputation at the Danube mouth, but succumbed to Bulgar domination. As for the Theiss group of South Slavs, it moved deep into the Balkans. By the middle of the century its warriors had raided as far as the Adriatic on the one side of the peninsula and the Aegean on the other, and had even reached the wall of Constantinople itself; and then between the years 584 and 589 alone further waves of Slavs invaded Greece on no less than ten occasions. Soon they were settling there as well, and the Byzantine emperors, distracted by Persians and Arabs in the east, were powerless to stop them. However, the Heraclian dynasty decided instead to exploit this influx of manpower, seizing enor-

mous numbers of the immigrants as slaves—the word comes from Slav—recruiting many others into the army, and transporting their compatriots in great quantities to Asia Minor and elsewhere.

Among those who remained in the Balkans, three different patterns of settlement eventually developed. In Greece the Slavs remained a minority, and did not succeed in imposing their language. In Bulgaria, they came under rulers of Bulgar (Turkish) origin, though subsequently imposing upon them the Slavonic language and culture. In the western Balkans, on the other hand, it was their own Slav communities that formed the nuclei of what later became the Slovene, Croat, and Serbian nations, which form the modern Yugoslavia.

from the introduction of rye in the years after 500. However, they remained politically dependent on the Avars, until in 623 a slave-dealer named Samo, probably Frankish in origin, arrived in Czechoslovakia with a group of fellow adventurers and led a revolt which enabled him to establish his rule over the mixed populations of the area for fifteen years. The first real Slav state, however, though once again short-lived, was the ninth-century empire of Great Moravia, of which the adherence to Christianity, brought about by Saints Cyril and Methodius, inaugurated an epoch of large-scale Slav conversions to the Orthodox church.

By the ninth century Mikulcice in Moravia, (Czechoslovakia), which had long been an important fortress, was probably the chief royal residence of the transient Great Empire, although only the foundations of the palace *(above)* remain. But we have more extensive evidence of a long and skilled tradition of metal-working, blending Byzantine, oriental, and Germanic motifs into a Moravian style, displayed by these ornate earrings found in the grave of a "princess" in Mikulcice.

AVARS AND BULGARS

One of the most important phenomena of the time was the activity of various groups and hordes of terrifying horsemen, nomadic in origin, who continuously overran and occupied enormous areas extending from central Asia to mid-Europe. For the most part, their leaders spoke languages of the Altaic group (of the Ural-Altaic family), which includes the tongues spoken today by the Turks and Mongols; so that this group of languages is also known as Turanian, after the legendary founder of the Turkish race.

The short-lived fifth-century European empire of Attila's nomadic-pastoral Huns was followed by that of the Avars, who came from the eastern and central Russian steppes to the Caucasus in about 550, and then spread across the Carpathians into central Europe. The belief that the horse-borne leaders of these hordes spoke a language of the Turkish group, like the Huns before them, is largely based on some of their proper names, though their followers (once again like those of the Huns) comprised a huge variety of ethnic communities, nomad and sedentary alike.

When these masses of Avar riders and their hangers-on irrupted into the middle of Europe, the Byzantine emperor Justinian I enlisted their services in order to put down a host of other barbarian tribes (558-567), and they settled as his allies. Before long, the Avar khan Bayan, an arrogant conqueror of the stamp of Attila, controlled a gigantic area stretching from the Volga as far as the Danube and the Elbe. This robber state, the greatest military power in Europe, dominated massive German, Bulgar, and Slav populations and extorted huge sums in tribute and ransom from Constantinople. On one occasion, they even struck against the strong walls of the city itself (626); and they conducted menacing sieges of the empire's second capital, Thessalonica, though Bayan did not disdain to have baths built by Byzantine architects near Sirmium (Sremska Mitrovica). Thereafter, however, the power of the Avars gradually weakened, until Charlemagne, in three campaigns, was able to overwhelm their circular fortifications (rings) and put an end to their national existence (791-805), in alliance with the Bulgars who proceeded to occupy most of the territory the Avars had dominated.

The Bulgars were originally another Turanian (Turkish)-speaking race, their name being a Turkish word meaning "mixture," which in an ethnic sense they evidently were. They had probably moved from Asia into Europe at some time during the course of the fifth century, in the wake of the Huns—whom they themselves regarded as their ancestors. After the collapse of the Hun empire, the early representatives of this Bulgarian nation, often described as "proto-Bulgars," began to assume an identity of their own, wandering over large areas of the continent and finally settling on either shore of the Sea of Azov, where they engaged in the breeding of horses, to be employed for their fast-moving cavalry. They moved south every year and crossed the Danube, in order to raid the Byzantine empire.

In about 560, however, these Bulgarian communities were suppressed by the Avars. Thereupon, part of the Bulgar population fled up the Volga, as far as its great bend and confluence with the Kama. There, merging with the local populations of Finns and Slavs, they founded their encampment or township of Bolgar, capital of a new state of Black Bulgaria; the place became a bazaar-terminal for caravan routes to the Baltic region and central Asia and China. These contacts gradually improved the civilization and agriculture of the rapidly spreading Black Bulgars. At first they were under the sovereignty of another semi-nomad Turkish people, the Khazars. But in the eighth and ninth centuries, the Black Bulgars threw off the Khazar yoke, and after becoming converts to Islam (before 921) remained their own masters for another four hundred years.

But another portion of the Bulgar peoples had at first remained in the Sea of Azov area after the Avar invasion. This second branch of the Bulgars recovered its independence in the early seventh century, forming a new federation which was centered on the Azov port of Phanagoria (Taman) and extended over the North Caucasian steppe and the Kuban and the Ukraine. This state was subsequently known as Old Great Bulgaria. Under the pressure of the Khazars, however, its chieftain Asparuch led his people, perhaps some 50,000 in number, down into the Byzantine empire (679), where he established a kingdom, roughly coinciding with modern Bulgaria, with its first settlements at Pyuki (Pevka) island (in the delta of the Danube) and near Nicolitel (in what is now the Rumanian Dobrogea). The new unit was recognized by the Byzantine emperor Constantine IV; and Constantine V, in a series of nine campaigns, was unable to suppress it.

Thus was set up the only organized and

This ninth-century Bulgarian drinking cup or bowl comes from the gold treasure of Nagyszentmiklós in the Banat (west Rumania), discovered in 1799. This region formed part of the First Bulgarian Empire from 804 to 896. The Bulgarian origin of the twenty-three vessels found here is confirmed by Bulgar titles of rank *(boilya, zhupan)* inscribed on them. Christian liturgical inscriptions are to be seen as well. Kunsthistorisches Museum, Vienna.

dynamic state to emerge in the Balkans during the whole of this epoch. From its fortified camp, later capital, at Pliska (Aboba), the Sublime Khans, backed by a warlike, centralized military bureaucracy, controlled a number of Slav tribes—which, however, in the course of the two centuries that followed, imposed their own language on their Bulgarian suzerains. The Byzantine emperor Justini-

an II Slit-Nose enlisted the help of the Bulgar khan Tervel in order to regain his own throne (705). But Khan Krum (ca. 802–814), vastly expanding his dominions, defeated and killed a later emperor, Nicephorus I, and besieged Constantinople itself. Thereafter, at the end of the century, followed the creation of a powerful Christianized (Orthodox) Great Bulgarian Empire.

The early Bulgar communities lived a semi-nomadic existence, making ends meet by breeding horses which they then employed in raiding parties against the outlying territories of the Byzantine empire. Eventually, amalgamating with the Slavs, they created the First Bulgarian empire, but still the armored, mounted warriors were the mainstay of their society. The design shown above is on a gold jug from the Nagyszentmiklós treasure, now in the Kunsthistorisches Museum, Vienna.

THE KHAZARS

In the mid-fifth century A.D., Khazar tribes, apparently the descendants of Huns, mixed with Slavs and Finns, were living in the middle of Russia. But in 576–582, when the Turks (of whom more will be said later) came from eastern Asia to invade the Caucasus, they brought many Khazars in their company, and left them behind when they withdrew again. To judge from the single phrases and words of their dialects that have survived, the Khazars spoke a language related to that of their former Turkish masters.

The Khazar immigrants added themselves to the equally mixed populations west and northwest of the Caspian Sea, and there they established a primitive state, which remained subject for a time to a Turkish khanate in mid-Asia, serving it by keeping its western neigh-

The Khazar state, controlling a number of Slavonic tribal groups, stood at the crossroads of many cultures. Together with the Byzantines they provided a bulwark against the rising tide of Islam in the south, protecting the empire's northern border lands and dependencies from the Arab armies. From the ninth century onwards the Khazars also had to confront a new and formidable enemy in the Russians, and in 965 a war against Svyatoslav I of Kiev heralded the decline of Khazar power. A Russian attack by sea is the subject of this illustration from the Radziwill Chronicle.

settlements on the middle reaches of the Dnieper. In 704 the Byzantine emperor Justinian II Slit-Nose, during a period of exile, married a daughter of the Khazar monarch of the time, and in 732 Leo III gave his son, Constantine V, in marriage to a Khazar princess, Tzitzakion (the Turkish word for "flower"), so that their son, Leo IV, was known as "the Khazar." Leo III took this action in order to shore up the Khazars against the Arabs, who in 722 had seized one of their principal capi-

bors the Avars at bay. The Khazars were also employed by the Byzantine emperor Heraclius (610–641) as allies against the Sassanian Persians; and later they fought the Byzantines' Arab enemies as well.

Meanwhile the Khazar people, modifying or abandoning their former nomad habits, were expanding northward up the Dnieper and Don and Volga; and gradually they came to form a powerful nation, dominating numerous Slav-speaking tribes, to which they brought protection and prosperity in exchange for tribute collected at huge fortified

tals, Balanjar (Khir-Zurt on the River Sulak in Daghestan). For the Byzantines relied on the Khazar state to protect their own northern outposts, especially in the Crimea. To show this reliance, the imperial protocol of Constantinople ranked the rulers of the Khazars even above the Carolingian monarchs and the Popes of Rome.

Despite setbacks, the power of the Khazar state reached its height in the latter half of the eighth century; their control extended for many hundred miles up the Black Sea rivers, and all the way from the Dniester to the Urals.

over by the island fortress of Al-Baida, became a thriving commercial center, in which merchants of all races and faiths were allowed to live in freedom and autonomy, dealing in the wax, furs, leathers, and honey that came down the river. The Khazars of Ityl also organized the overland transport of boats between the Volga and the Don; and near the mouth of the Don, Byzantine engineers constructed a fortress for Khazar use at Sarkel ("White House," now Tsymlyanskaya, ca. 833).

"White" Khazars (owing this description to their fairer skins) ruled over "Black" Khazars, an inferior social class. The headship of the government was divided between the Khagan (Great King) and the Beg. The Beg was the commander of the army—one of the earliest salaried standing armies in Europe. But the

The precise origins of the Khazars are uncertain, but it seems that prior to the establishment of their empire in about the seventh century they had lived a nomadic life, speaking a language of the Turkic group. From their earlier period come these fairly crude objects; the iron head of a warrior's axe, and a clay jug for carrying water. The silver coin was issued under Leo IV (775—780), the Byzantine emperor known as "The Khazar." His father had married the Khazar princess Tzitzakion to demonstrate the firm diplomatic links between the two empires, and their military alliance against external threats.

From the end of the eighth century onward, the Khazar rulers followed the Jewish faith, making it the official state religion—a unique phenomenon in the history of this era, when in the rest of the world Jews were despised if not actually persecuted. This tombstone, showing the Jewish symbol of the Menorah, is from Phanagoria on the Kerch strait, at the mouth of the River Kuban.

Partly agricultural in their interests but more particularly commercial, they formed a bridge between the continents of Europe and Asia, obliging the Bulgar states of Russia to concede them a share in their trade, and vigorously exploiting the great route between the Caspian and Aral (Oxus) Seas that led onward to central and eastern Asia.

In succession to Balanjar and Semender (Makhachkala?) in the northern Caucasus, their principal capital was a former winter camp at Ityl, in an unidentified location near Astrakhan at the mouth of the Volga. Ityl, presided

Khagans were the titular rulers, and chiefs of the pagan state cult.

One of their number, Obadiah, reigning at the end of the eighth century, found himself harassed by rival attempts at religious conversion made by the Byzantine Christians and Arab Moslems who flocked to his court; and so he decided to evade the dilemma by embracing Judaism instead. Thereafter he and his nobles, and their descendants, remained Jewish until their state, after gradually diminishing in size, was absorbed by Kiev in the eleventh century.

WHITE HUNS AND TURKS

Before the beginning of this period, the nomads in the eastern regions of central Asia had devised or adopted improvements in cavalry equipment which subsequently became known in the west, where they transformed the warfare and social development of the countries of Europe. The foot-stirrups employed on the steppes were borrowed from China before the sixth century, and probably the horse-collar too. As for horseshoes, our earliest unambiguous evidence comes from nomadic rider graves of the tenth century in the Yenisei valley; but the invention may have been a great deal earlier.

In the fifth century the dominant people in these remote territories had been the Hephthalites or White (white-skinned) Huns. They were nomads related to Attila's Hunnish peoples in Europe. The original home of the White Huns had been in Mongolia, but by the end of the fourth century they had begun to move westward, until they reached the Aral Sea; and then they set up their main headquarters or encampment at Bamyan (Afghanistan). Ruling there, for a hundred and thirty years, they constituted a grave problem for their new neighbors the Sassanian Persians, whose king Firuz (ca. 457–483) they defeated and killed. One of his successors, too, Kavadh I (488–531), had to cede them Merv and Herat, although he also tried, with some success, to deflect them into useful service as mercenaries. In 557, another Sassanian ruler, Khosrau I, managed to destroy their power. Meanwhile a branch of the White Huns had struck southeastward into the Indian kingdom of the Guptas. At the end of the fifth century the White Hun chieftain Taramana had temporarily obtained complete control of the northern part of the Indian peninsula, and even held a large part of central India, too, for a time. His son Mihirakula established his capital at Sakala in the Punjab, but was driven back into Kashmir by a confederation of Indian princes; and soon after his death (ca. 540) the whole dominion of the White Huns fell to pieces.

It was destroyed by the Turks, with the encouragement of the Sassanian Persians. These mounted Turkish nomads had first made their appearance in the eastern regions of central Asia. The Toba (Chinese T'o-pa, Turkish Tabgach) from Siberia, who invaded northern China and set up its Northern Wei dynasty (386–581), probably spoke some form of Turkish. The Wei, it is true, soon adopted Chinese culture. But in the sixth century, another mass of irresistible Turkish horsemen overran Mongolia, and Turkish rule was now established over a gigantic area extending from Lakes Baikal and Balkash down to the borders of Tibet and North India, and across the continent all the way from Mongolia to beyond the Aral Sea. From the outset, this great tract of Turkish territory seems to have been divided into two separate parts, comprising an eastern state and its western offshoot.

The Western Turks had two main headquarters, near Urumchi (Sinkiang) and Tashkent (Uzbekistan). Although they helped Sassanian Persia to destroy the White Huns, it was their general policy to side with Byzantium against the Persians. In 699 the Western Turks became subordinate to the Eastern Turkish

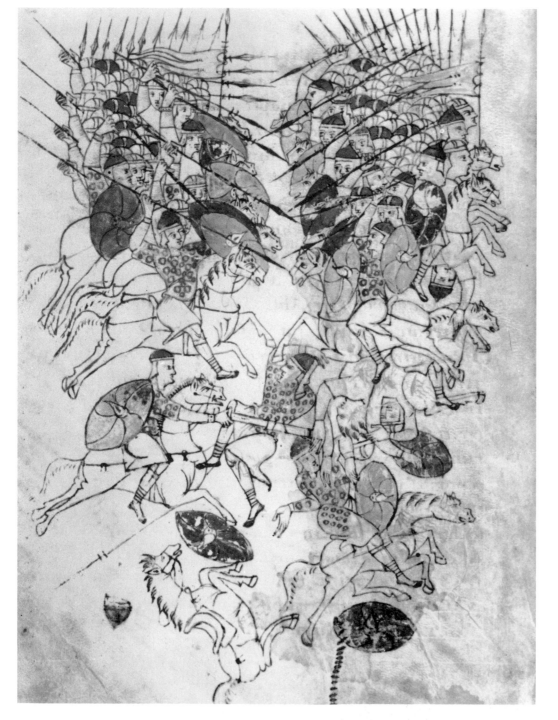

state once again. Their migration to what is now Turkey still lay more than three centuries in the future.

Meanwhile the territories of the Eastern Turks extended southward from Lake Baikal to the Great Wall of China. Inscriptions of 732–735, found in the valley of the Mongolian River Orkhon where the tents of their capital Karabalgasaun were also situated, are the earliest surviving Turkish records. Written in a sort of Runic script, they describe in vigorous epic language how the Eastern Turks, after succumbing to T'ang China, had regained independence under their national heroes Prince Kül and King Bilge. They remained independent until the territory was seized by the Mongols in successive stages during the tenth and subsequent centuries.

In common with most early civilizations, the peoples of the eastern steppes carved stone figures of their gods. These images are from Sagly and Ulaatai, Siberia, seventh to ninth century.

WEI AND SUI CHINA

Chinese cultural advances proceeded apace; yet for nearly three hundred and seventy years after the end of the prosperous Han dynasty (202 B.C.–A.D. 221) much of the vast and densely populated land was in a state of disunity and turmoil. In particular, disturbances in the northern territories caused southward emigrations which increased fivefold the number of Chinese living beyond the River Yangtse.

It was in the north that irrupting horsemen, apparently of Turkish origin, set up the Northern Wei dynasty (386), thus supplementing the large populations of foreign origin who already lived in this part of China. The Northern Wei established their capital first at the frontier-towns of Lan-chou (Kansu) and Ta-t'ung (Shansi), and then (in the fifth century) at two successive cities of Honan—Ping Ch'eng and the ancient metropolis of Lo-yang (494). It was not long before they became a great power, founding their capital in the old Han site of Ch'ang-an in Shensi.

However, the name of the Six Dynasties, which is generally given to the period of China's history between A.D. 221 and 589, applies not to the north but to the south of the country, referring to a succession of royal houses that ruled in that part of the land.

But then Yang Chien (Wen Ti, the "Cultured Emperor"), founder of the Sui dynasty (589–618), reunited the whole of China and restored the stability which has, in general, been a marked feature of its society throughout the ages, reflecting the concept of the Emperor, under heaven, at the center of the world. Residing at Ch'ang-an, Yang Chien introduced the civil service recruitment system which has been a major Chinese contribution to the world. He also tackled grain distribution in northern China with great energy. But his wars against Eastern Turks and others were only partly successful; though his son Yang Ti, who rebuilt Lo-yang as a resplendent subsidiary capital, pushed farther into central Asia than any other emperor since Han times.

Such successes were assisted by the employment of the foot-stirrup which the booted Chinese had, from the third or fourth century onward, adapted from the big-toe stirrups of the bare-footed Indians. Of fifth century date, too, are paintings from Kansu which reveal that the modern type of collar harness was already in use—three hundred years before it became known in Europe. Silk textile manufacture (admired in the west) and hydraulic engineering had long been highly developed

in China, and great progress was made in the manufacture of iron and steel; the Sui dynasty constructed iron-chain suspension bridges and segmental arch bridges as well. These technological advances took place in an intellectual climate which must have been more congenial to scientific research than the atmosphere of Europe, and was to continue to present these superior opportunities for more than a millennium to come.

This atmosphere was encouraged by the prevailing systems of Chinese thinking. Confucianism was particularly concerned with the improvement of things in this world; and Taoism stimulated an enquiring attitude to nature. Buddhist belief, too, was steadily join-

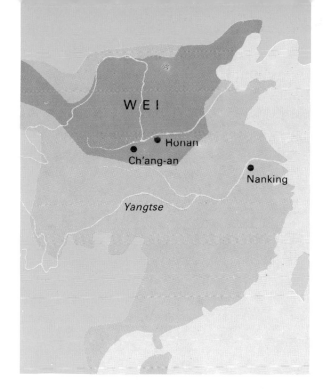

and solemn. In the northwest, at Tun-huang in Kansu, some two dozen cave-temples—a form of construction that had come from north India by way of central Asia—are covered with paintings, while toward the other end of the country, a famous painter, Chang Seng-yu, worked at Nanking for a Buddhist royal house.

History and philosophy were equally active. Two northern writers, Yang Hsien-chih and Li Tao-yüan, composed works about the Chinese present and past which are major documents of social history; and in north and south China alike, throughout the entire epoch, the Buddhist Meditation School (Ch'an in Chinese, Zen in Japanese) flourished in various different forms.

China between the fourth and sixth centuries: in the north, the Northern and other Wei dynasties, established by Turkish invaders from north and west of the frontier, and in the south, where Nanking was the principal city, the last five (succeeding Wu) of the Six Dynasties (Eastern Tsin, Former Sung, Southern Ch'i, Southern Liang and Southern Ch'en, 317—589).

Outstanding amongst the technological achievements dating back to the Sui rule was the building of bridges, some of the iron-chain suspension type, and others of open spandrel construction. The An Ji bridge shown here was the work of the master mason Li Chun (605—616).

ing these schools of thought as the third of the "three doctrines," because it responded to people's needs. Moreover, its monastic institutions were favored by the tax exemption system; and its traditions opened up big, novel possibilities for Chinese architecture and art. Under the Northern Wei rulers, great new Buddhist monasteries were built, and towering pagodas—peculiar to Buddhist architecture—of very varied design, including a particularly splendid example at Lo-yang. Near the same city, in four of the many caves of Lung-men, can be seen some of the first distinctively Chinese examples of Buddhist sculpture, which reached its peak not long after 500; the Sui Buddhas are calm, heavy,

Founders of two great schools of thought which encouraged the intellectual and scientific progress of China during this period: Buddha (Siddhartha, Gautama) (ca. 556—483 B.C.) (far left) subject of a statue of the fifth or sixth century A.D. now in the Rietberg Museum, Zurich, and Confucius (551—479 B.C.), from a manuscript illumination of the sixth century A.D.

207

T'ANG CHINA

The T'ang emperors (618-906) made China, for a time, the largest and most powerful state in the world, and a rival of Byzantium as the greatest center of civilization. The second of these rulers, Li Shih-Min (T'ai-Tsung, the "Grand Ancestor"), who reigned from 626 to 691, was a man of remarkable all-round ability who reformed the entire structure of Chinese society, encouraging, in particular, a rapidly growing bourgeoisie, which was given priority over the peasant class. T'ai-Tsung also ended the threat from the Eastern Turks by conquering all Inner Mongolia up to the Gobi Desert. Moreover, his troops went on to advance throughout Western Turkish territory as well, occupying the Tarim basin and enforcing Chinese suzerainty over Bokhara and Samarkand, stages on a major trade route between east and west.

Many superb artistic objects have come down to us from the T'ang dynasty. This is in part due to their prolific manufacture of decorated, elaborate objects for everyday use, as opposed to mere items of purely functional value. This gold pedestal bowl, of eighth-century date, comes from the ancient city of Ch'ang-an (Sian), the ancient capital of the T'ang rulers at the end of the central Asian trade routes. The white glazed spittoon dates from ca. 850.

Both the internal commerce of China and its trade with other countries was greatly stimulated by the unification of the country and its extensive conquests under the T'ang dynasty. Much of this external trade was in the hands of foreigners, particularly from Persia and the lands adjoining it, who came by land through central Asia or by sea to Kuang-chou (Canton; whose people are known as "the sons of T'ang"), and settled in the principal cities. Foreigners are often depicted on the small pottery figures of the period, such as this merchant, believed to be an Armenian, holding a wineskin. Art Museum, Seattle.

T'ai-Tsung's numerous vassals, whose statues were erected on his tomb, included the king of Champa (Viet-nam). Subsequently, T'ai-Tsung's son and successor on the Chinese throne, Kao-Tsung (the "High Ancestor"), 649–683, reduced to vassal status, at severe economic cost, the whole large and prosperous peninsula of Korea, to which Chinese missionaries brought Buddhist, Confucian, and Taoist ideas and rites. Subsequently Kao-Tsung's former consort was proclaimed emperor (690–704), the first and last Chinese woman to rule in her own right without a titular male colleague; and she performed heroic achievements in consolidating the dynasty.

In the middle of the eighth century, however, the T'ang rulers suffered grave reverses, including a fateful defeat by the Arabs at Talas in 751. Next, four years later, a rebellion caused the flight of the emperor and his court, whereupon the northern regions of the country were overrun by the Uigurs (a successor state of the East Turks), as well as by Tibetans who briefly occupied Ch'ang-an and remained menacing neighbors for the next eighty years. In spite of the revolutionary discovery of the correct formula for gunpowder soon after 800, the T'ang dynasty was never the same again, and before the century was over the country had begun to fall apart.

The T'ang period had been an age of immense artistic vitality. Ch'ang-an boasted innumerable architectural masterpieces. Furthermore, in the years before and after 700, talented artists were active at many important cave sites, both in central China and in Kansu (Tun-huang), where fine sculpture made its appearance and distinguished wall paintings are to be seen in more than two hundred cave chapels. Only copies, however, survive of the works of the most notable painters of the age, namely Wu Tao-tzu, famous for his ample modeling and sweeping linear brush-line, and the landscapist Wang Wei, creator of quiet, contemplative, allusive paintings in ink on silk. Both men were fabulously versatile: Wang Wei was not only an artist but also a scholar, musician, and writer of poetry. This was a Golden Age of lyric verse from which the works of two thousand poets have survived. Preeminent among them was Li Po (701–762), a singer of friendship and wine, who for the most part lived outside the cultured court of his monarch Li Lung-Chi (Hsüan-tsung, the "Mysterious Ancestor"). Leading parts were also played by two compas-

The Wild Goose Pagoda at Ch'ang-an begun in 652 and subsequently much restored. The pagoda is a form of building unique to Buddhist architecture. Starting as a simple one-story structure, it seems to have corresponded at first with the Indian *stupa*. However, before long the Chinese began to add to the height of the pagodas until finally they might be as much as twelve stories high. The earliest pagodas now surviving are constructed of stone and brick; but we know that there were also wooden pagodas in China during the seventh century.

sionate, critical observers of the social scene, Tu Fu (712–770) and his admirer Po Chü-i (772–846)—who was nevertheless happier leading a quiet, withdrawn life.

Po Chü-i was for a time friendly with the great Confucian writer Han Yu, who attacked Buddhism (819); later, the emperor Wu-Tsung (840–846), after a census disclosing that it had 260,000 monks, 4,600 temples and 40,000 shrines, severely restricted and repressed the religion, with the declaration that "its strange ways have become so customary and all-pervasive as to have slowly and unconsciously corrupted the morals of our land."

In Japan, which had received a good deal of Chinese culture by way of Korea, this process of acclimatization continued apace under the energetic guidance of the prince regent Shotoku Taishi (574–622), a great Buddhist apologist, whom a pioneer painting displays in the company of his sons. Soon afterward the revolutionary Taika Edict (645) introduced a theory of absolute government in which the ancient clan institutions were largely super seded by a network of local officials. In the course of the next century, the Japanese land system adopted features which have caused it to become the best-known example of feudalism outside Europe. By this time there were 80,000 Buddhist monks in Japan, including

many at the successive capitals Nara (710) and Kyoto (784). These cities were both equipped with admirable new buildings, and adorned with sculptures displaying a variety of different styles. The ground plan and separate buildings of the walled compound of the Horyuji at Nara faithfully reproduce those of a seventh century temple at Ch'ang-an in China, and the Horyuji pagoda—which is the best surviving early example of this type of structure—likewise preserves Chinese styles.

Pottery figure of a horseman from the tomb of Princess Yung T'ai near Ch'ang-an (706). For the construction of these very popular tomb figures, pottery was the most favored material, because moulds could be employed to produce the various parts of the human figures and animals, rapidly and en masse, and assemble them in sections.

Left. Ink painting of Bodhisattva (Buddha to be) flying on a cloud; eighth century. The work of Wu Tao-tzu was perhaps like this. Shosoin, Nara, Japan.

Happier far the owner of
    a small garden;
Propped on his stick he
    idles here all day,
Now and again collecting
    a few friends,
And every day enjoying
    lute and wine.
Why should he pine for
    great terraces and lakes
When a little garden
    gives him all he needs?

Po Chü-i (d. 846)

During the T'ang period it was the practice to place small sculptures of glazed or
unglazed pottery in tombs. The number,
quality and arrangement of the figurines
depended on the rank of the deceased.
The lively representations of animals (particularly horses and lions), court ladies,
musicians, merchants, and other types
provide an interesting record of the activities and fashions of the day. At their
best, these figurines are the most naturalistic works of Chinese art of the time.
Such, for example, are the saddled camel
and grave watchman shown on these two
pages. Both are from a tomb near
Ch'ang-an, eighth century.

211

INDIA

After a long period of confused local separatisms, a major north Indian power was established in the fourth century by the Gupta family, wealthy landowners from Magadha (Bihar), whose rule as Great Kings of Kings established suzerainty over the greater part of the peninsula. Their epoch is sometimes described as India's Golden Age. The legendary hero Chandra Gupta II (375–415) moved his capital from Pataliputra (Patna) to the sacred city of Ayodha (Uttar Pradesh) and also maintained a brilliant court at Ujjain (Madhya Pradesh).

Skanda Gupta (455–470) offered vigorous opposition to the mortal menace of the White Huns, but after his death resistance weakened when his empire was split up, first into two states with their capitals at Pataliputra and Ujjain, and then into a number of smaller princedoms as well. In these circumstances, the White Huns were able to break through on a massive scale: and by the early sixth century they had occupied huge areas of India, before pressure from the Turks and Persians forced them to contract. Huge movements of populations had followed in their wake, and the subcontinent remained politically fragmented for many decades. Nevertheless, by the early sixth century, Indian ships were regularly crossing the China Sea, while others traversed the Indian Ocean by the southern spice route to the Yemen, from which their cargoes were then transported northward up to Mesopotamia and Syria.

During the Gupta period the patriarchal system became the norm in northern India: the earliest evidence for the immolation of widows comes from about 510. Nevertheless, there was a high degree of religious freedom, which in turn promoted intellectual vigour. The poet and dramatist Kalidasa, who may have worked at the court of Chandra Gupta II, became the most remarkable figure in classical Sanskrit literature, for which he set wholly new standards (his play *Sakuntala* was a major influence on Goethe). Epics were also written in the allied Prakrit language and, in the south, in the independent Tamil tongue as well.

Meanwhile Hinduism was gradually developing new tendencies, including worship of the Mother Goddess. The veneration of images in temples was also introduced; and early Gupta sculpture, presenting for the first time a distinctively Indian style, excelled at gracious, sophisticated depictions of Buddha, such as can be seen at Mathura (Uttar Pradesh).

Buddhist cave-shrines in the cliffs at Ajanta (Maharashtra) and elsewhere display numerous wall-paintings, mainly of sixth and seventh century date, and caves of the Chalukya kingdom of Mysore contain large-scale mythological reliefs of the same period.

A renewed attempt at welding northern India together was made by Harsha (Harsha-vardhana, 606–647), king of Thanesar in the Punjab, who established his capital at Kanauj

The first art and architecture in a truly Indian style was the result of the unification of much of the country under the Guptas in the later fourth century. This Gupta style continued in use and was elaborated in subsequent centuries when large parts of the north were under the yoke of the White Huns. This sandstone figure *(above)*, of about the sixth century, represents the god Varaha (the third *avatara* or descent or manifestation of Vishnu as the Cosmic Boar) and comes from Sarnath, north of the Ganges; the sixth- or seventh-century granite figure of Buddha comes from the south. Buddhism originated with a historical personage, Siddhartha (Gautama), who was born in about 556 B.C. into a family of the warrior caste in the Nepalese foothills. At the age of twenty-nine he renounced the world and taught the "Four Noble Truths" and the "Noble Eightfold Path" to liberation or *nirvana* (literally "extinction," blowing out the flame).

(Uttar Pradesh). Harsha was an important patron of literature, himself being an author of Sanskrit plays; and he was described by a Chinese pilgrim as an admirer of Buddhism and a model of efficiency and justice. Apart from his payments to his soldiers, who received cash, he usually preferred to issue salaries in the form of grants of land.

In the manufacture of goods, as in commercial enterprises of all kinds, autonomous guilds were the rule. For Harsha, like the Guptas, did not aim at a rigorously centralized administration; thus he was satisfied to receive homage from his numerous subject rulers. However, his efforts to move south and conquer the Deccan were repelled by Pulakesin II (608–642), king of the Chalukyas. Pulakesin, who was the greatest warrior of his time—enjoying sufficient international repute to exchange envoys with Sassanian Persia—shared most of the Deccan with Mahendra-varman I (600–625/30), who ruled the Pallavas in the southeast, with his capital at Kanchipuram (between Madras and Bangalore).

However, after the deaths of these powerful personages, India was again split into numerous separate states. In the north, Kanauj became a bone of contention between three of their rulers, who exhausted themselves in the process. Further south, power was seized from a branch of the Chalukyas by the Rashtrakutas of Latur (Maharashtra), who dominated the region from about 757 to 975. However, their aggressively militaristic policy enfeebled the country and contributed to its weakness in face of the Muslim invasions, which had begun with the Arab annexation of Sind (712) and continued until the country was completely engulfed after the end of the millennium.

The origins of these disasters can be traced back to the disunity of the seventh and eighth centuries. And yet these had also constituted a period of great cultural distinction. Ciphering and decimal systems were apparently invented by Indians—and transmitted to the Arabs, who subsequently passed them on to Europe. "Arabic" numerals, too, were of Indian origin; they were said to have reached Islam in a Sanskrit astronomical treatise by Siddhanta, translated by order of the Baghdad caliphate in 773 (although it has been alternatively suggested that the first Moslem state to know of them was Spain, through the agency of a Jew of that country).

During the same period, architecture and sculpture continued to flourish in India. The

gifted Mahendra-varman I developed the construction of stone temples, and commissioned important Hindu reliefs at Mamallapuram, followed shortly after 880 by noble shrines at Kanchipuram, where he resided. This was also the probable place of origin of the architects who built an impressive temple at Pattadkal (ca. 740), in the state of the Chalukyas. Their conquerors, the Rashtrakutas, have left monuments in honor of the Hindu god Shiva, notably an enormous monolithic temple in his honor at Ellora (Maharashtra), and a colossal three-headed relief of the same deity at Elephanta (not far from Bombay). On the opposite coast, in the seventh and eighth centuries, Orissa, under a strong local dynasty, erected the first of a long and continuously evolving series of temples, in a highly individual style which is well represented at the capital, Bhubaneswar. In north India, too, the Hindu temple displayed a remarkable series of developments.

The Indian view is that the world is *maya*, illusion, and that the wise man must liberate himself from its corruption until he attains the happiness of *nirvana*, spiritual serenity. In the period that followed, however, the Hindu doctrine came under examination from the Vedanta philosophers, whose pioneer Shankara (780–820) set out to explain the traditional teaching in rationalistic terms. By reasoning, he concluded, we find that the world must have a transcendent cause, and, once that has been identified, differences between known, knower, and knowledge no longer exist.

The Indians decorated their temples with massive monuments to their numerous gods, including intricate statues and reliefs showing scenes from their legendary lives. The four-faced lingam of Shiva *(above right)* and others like it, represent him as the creator, maintainer, regenerator and destroyer of the universe. The stone relief *(above)* shows Lokanatha or Padmapani ("the one who holds the lotus"), the chief Boddhisatva of mercy, healing the sick.

Mamullapuram, thirty-seven miles south of Madras, was the chief seaport of the trading kingdom of the Pallavas, whose great monarch Narasimha-varman I made it into a major artistic center (ca. 630). The Arjuna Rath (meaning chariot, i. e. vehicle of the gods) *(opposite)* is one of the city's five temples, which are replicas of wooden structures. This Rath, together with three of the others, is carved from a single granite boulder. With its pyramidal roof, composed of three tiers of small pavilions crowned by a cupola, it imitates a *vihara* (monastery). The Shore Temple *(above)* was not carved out of living rock but was made of granite blocks; so that it could be given a high tower. The cell beneath it opens directly onto the sea, to allow the first eastern light of the sun to illuminate its interior, and to let sailors pay homage to the shrine from their approaching boats.

Before the time of the Guptas, Mathura, eighty-five miles south of Delhi——reputed to be the birthplace of Krishna——had already been a notable religious and cultural center, becoming the second capital of the Kushan dynasty; the renowed Gupta sculptural style was derived from Kushan models surviving at Mathura. This relief *(left)* depicts Parvati, the consort of Shiva. Of eighth-century date, it belongs to the post-Gupta period, before Mathura, like other cities, succumbed to the armies of Islam.

EPILOGUE

Early in their history, the Germanic tribes became split following the southward migration of the Goths, Franks, and others to overrun the territories of the former western Roman empire, while the Scandinavian tribes remained in the north until the Viking explosion carried them as far as Greenland and even North America in the west and Kiev in the east. But whereas the southern migrants became converted to Christianity and may be held responsible for the formation of the later Holy Roman (German) Empire, other Germans at home long retained their pagan customs and gods, as evidenced by this depiction of Odin (Woden), the universal father, on an eighth-century tombstone from Hornhausen, Germany.

Charlemagne, crowned as emperor in Rome in A.D. 800, set up a great empire covering most of what is now France, Germany, and Italy. Although this was to prove short-lived, collapsing immediately after the death of its illustrious founder, in later days the kings of France were to claim their inheritance from Charlemagne. The gold sword shown here (called "Joyeuse") was believed to have belonged to the great emperor himself—although it is of eleventh-century manufacture—and was used for many centuries in the coronation ceremony of the French monarchs. Louvre, Paris.

The period that has been summarized in this book is remarkable for a number of developments that exercized an enormous effect on the immediate future—and on the times in which we are living today. In spite of all the abundant signs of continuity with their past, these three or four centuries, in which the Middle Ages dawned, display at least a dozen landmarks that can still be seen across the ages as epoch-making.

A.D. 476: The last Roman emperor to rule in Italy was compelled to abdicate, leaving the whole of what had been the western empire in the hands of various tribal leaders, whose societies would gradually assume the form of Europe's nation states.

ca. 499: This was the time of the completion of the *Talmud*. the great and comprehensive work that was to guide and hearten the Jews in all subsequent epochs and crises.

529: St. Benedict founded the monastery of Monte Cassino, from which spread the network of institutions under the Benedictine Rule that played a huge part in the revival of western European culture along Christian lines.

590: Gregory I the Great became Pope; it was he who ensured that the papacy would become one of the major influences forming the course of European history.

610: The first preaching, at Medina in Arabia, of Mohammed, who created the religion and civilization of Islam.

618: The coming into power of the T'ang dynasty, under which China, for nearly three centuries, achieved a new climax and efflorescence in almost every field of human activity.

718: The second and final rebuff of the Arab army and fleet before Constantinople, which prevented Islam from overcoming the Christian empire of the Byzantines for more than seven hundred years to come.

732: Charles Martel's victory near Poitiers in France: the decisive moment when the Arabs began to be turned back in western Europe as well.

793: The first Viking raid on northeast England: symbol of the emerging Danish, Norwegian, and Swedish attacks and settlements over an area that extended all the way from Kiev to Newfoundland.

800: The coronation of Charlemagne as emperor in Rome: thus the creator of the greatest western state of the age set himself up as a rival of Byzantium, and laid the foundations of the Holy Roman Empire.

LIST OF ILLUSTRATIONS AND PHOTO CREDITS

37 *Top:* Besieged warriors. Illumination. Mss.Grec. 74, fol. 92v. From Constantinople. 11th c. Bibliothèque Nationale, Paris. P: Cliché Hachette, Paris.
Below: Justinian II. Gold solidus. Obverse and reverse. From Constantinople. 8th c. Courtesy Museum of Fine Arts, Boston. Gift of Mr. and Mrs. Edward Jackson Holmes.
38 Fortress of Cotiaeum, Phrygia, Asia Minor. P: Bruno Balestrini, Milan.
39 *Left:* Rider. Statue. Bronze. From Istanbul (?). 4th or 5th c. Gift of J. J. Klejman, 1962. The Metropolitan Museum of Art, New York.
Right: Byzantine defense. Illumination. Ms. Scylites, Greek 5–3. P: Oronoz, Madrid.
40 *Top:* Flora, Goddess of spring. Textile. Fragment. Byzantine. 4th or 5th c. Victoria and Albert Museum, London. P: Claus Hansmann, Gauting.
Left: Chronicle of Byzantine History. P: Oronoz, Madrid.
40/41 Joseph meets Potiphar's wife. Illumination from the Old Testament. Cod. Theol. Grec. 31, fol. 32. 6th c. Nationalbibliothek, Vienna.
41 *Left:* Leo III. Gold solidus. Obverse. 8th c. P: From "Monnaies Byzantines" by P. D. Whitting, Office du Livre, Fribourg.
Right: Ladies preparing newly woven silk. Detail. Ink-and-colors on silk. 11th/12th c. China. Chinese and Japanese Special Fund. Museum of Fine Arts, Boston.
42 *Left:* Saints Sergius and Bacchus, Istanbul. Interior. P: Hirmer Fotoarchiv, Munich.
Right: Virgin and Child between Saints George and Theodore. Icon. St. Catherine's monastery, Sinai. P: Roger Wood, London.
43 *Top:* Byzantine worshippers in Haghia Sophia. Illumination. Ms. Scylites. P: Oronoz, Madrid.
Center: A man holding a sacred volume. Illumination from "Armenian Book of Gospels". 9th c. Freer Gallery of Art, Washington. P: Claus Hansmann, Gauting.
Bottom: Crucifixion of sun and moon. Relief. From Dalmatia. 7th or 8th c. San Donato Museum, Zadar, Yugoslavia. P: Alinari, Florence.
44 *Left:* Qala'at Sem'an. Ruins. Reconstruction after Duthoit. A.D. 1862. P: Elsevier Archives, Amsterdam.
44/45 *Top:* Main doorway, Qala'at Sem'an. P: Lucien Hervé, Paris.
Bottom: Ruins of the Alahan monastery, Isauria, Asia Minor. P: Sonia Halliday, London.
45 *Left:* Plaque. Detail of a reliquary casket. Silver, gilt. 6th c. Musée du Louvre, Paris. P: Réunion des Musées Nationaux, Paris.
Right: Pedestal of the column of St. Simeon Stylites. Qala'at Sem'an. 5th c. P: Elsevier Archives, Amsterdam.
46 Christ being acclaimed by the apostles. Detail of an illumination. Codex Purpureus, fol. 61. 6th c. Museo Arcivescovile, Rossano, Italy. P: Hirmer Fotoarchiv, Munich.
47 Condemnation of Christ by Pontius Pilate. Illumination. Codex Purpureus, fol. 8v. 6th c. Museo Archivescovile, Rossano, Italy. P: Scala, Florence.
48 *Top:* Cross. Mosaic. Apse of St. Irene, Constantinople. P: Dumbarton Oaks, Washington.
Below: Bishops piercing a portrait of Christ with swords. Illumination. Add Ms. 19352, fol. 27v. British Library, London.
49 *Top:* Leo III. Gold coin. 8th c. British Museum, London.
Below left: St. Peter. Icon. Monastery of St. Catherine, Sinai. P: Roger Wood, London.
Below right: Man in a garden. Illumination from Book of Beasts, by Nicander. Cod. suppl. gr. 247, fol. 48. 10th c. Bibliothèque Nationale, Paris.
50 Justinian offering the Virgin his cathedral. Mosaic. Detail. South Vestibule, Haghia Sophia, Istanbul. P: Sonia Halliday, London.
51 Haghia Sophia, Istanbul. P: Ullstein Bilderdienst, Berlin.
52 Dome of Haghia Sophia, Istanbul. P: Anatol/ZEFA, Düsseldorf.
52/53 Haghia Sophia, Istanbul. Interior. P: R. Everts/ZEFA, Düsseldorf.
54 *Left:* Flying angel. Coptic textile. From Akhmin. 6th c. Victoria and Albert Museum, London. P: P. Bernard, London.
Right: Cosmetic box. Silver. 5th c. Musée du Louvre, Paris. P: Hirmer Fotoarchiv, Munich.
55 *Above left:* The Ascension of Christ. Illumination. Ms. Plutarch 1.56, fol. 136. From Zagba, Syria. 6th c. Biblioteca Medicea Laurenziana, Florence. P: Guido Sansoni, Florence.
Above right: Silver plate. From Cyprus. 7th c. The Metropolitan Museum of Art, New York. P: Robert Harding, London.
Below left: Throne of Maximian. Byzantine. Ivory, carved. 6th c. P: Hirmer Fotoarchiv, Munich.
Below right: Necklace. Gold. Byzantine. A.D. 600. P: Claus Hansmann, Gauting.
56 *Top:* Redeemer and angels between San Vitale and Bishop Ecclesius. Mosaic. Apse of San Vitale, Ravenna. 6th c. P: Scala, Florence.
Below left: Justinian surrounded by his court. Mosaic. San Vitale, Ravenna. P: André Held, Ecublens.
Below right: Theodora surrounded by her court. Mosaic. San Vitale, Ravenna. P: Scala, Florence.
57 *Top left:* Child and donkey. Detail of a mosaic. Great Palace, Istanbul. P: André Held, Ecublens.
Top right: Eagle and snake. Floor mosaic. Great Palace, Istanbul. P: André Held, Ecublens.
Above from left to right: Tiger. Detail of a mosaic. Damascus. P: André Held, Ecublens.
Cup. Detail of a mosaic. Fanlight. San Vitale, Ravenna. P: André Held, Ecublens.
Rivers of Paradise. Detail of a mosaic. Apse. San Vitale, Ravenna. P: Leonard von Matt, Buochs.
Flowers of Paradise. Detail of a mosaic. Apse. San Vitale, Ravenna. P: Leonard von Matt, Buochs.
Below: Demetrius, Leontius and John. Mosaic. Church of St. Demetrius, Thessalonica. 7th c. P: André Held, Ecublens.
58 Head of Theodora. Detail of a mosaic. Apse. San Vitale, Ravenna. P: Leonard von Matt, Buochs.
59 Head of Justinian. Detail of a mosaic. Apse. San Vitale, Ravenna. P: Leonard von Matt, Buochs.
60 *Left:* Basil II. Illumination. Psalterium. Cod. Marc. Gr. Z. 17, 421. 11th c. Biblioteca Nazionale Marciana, Venice. P: Foto Toso, Venice.
61 *Top:* Saint Cyril. Fresco. Detail of the façade, church at Bereda, Bulgaria. 13th or 14th c. P: The Bulgarian Artists, Sofia.
60/61 Basil I imprisoning Leo. Illumination from the Scylites. Biblioteca Nacional, Madrid. P: Oronoz, Madrid.
61 *Center:* A Seljuk prince. Bowl. Persian. 13th c. Harris Brisbane Fund, 1951. The Metropolitan Museum of Art, New York.
Bottom: Group of nuns. Painting. 15th c. The Bodleian Library, Oxford. P: Hirmer Fotoarchiv, Munich.
62 Mounted horseman. Fresco. Detail. From Qasr-al-Hair-al-Gharbi. 8th c. National Museum Damascus. P: Editions d'Art Albert Skira, Geneva.
63 Mihrab. Algaferia mosque. 11th c. Saragossa, Spain. P: Jean Mazenod, from *L'Islam et l'Art Musulman*, Editions d'Art Lucien Mazenod, Paris.
64 *Top:* Sassanian king. Seal. Sard in modern setting. 3rd–6th c. H. L. Pierce Fund. Museum of Fine Arts, Boston.
Center from left to right: Southeast gate. Takht-i-Sulaiman. Sassanian fortress. Azerbaijan, Iran. P: Rudolf Naumann, Affolterbach.
Fire god. Intaglio. Sassanian. Cabinet des Médailles, Paris. P: Bibliothèque Nationale, Paris.
Fire altars. Sassanian. Naqsh-i-Rustem, Iran. P: Robert Harding, London.
Bottom: Byzantine emperor with prisoners. Textile. From Syria. 4th or 5th c. Victoria and Albert Museum, London. P: Claus Hansmann, Gauting.
65 *Left:* Dancing girl. Detail of a bowl. Sassanian. From Iran. 5th c. Purchase John L. Severando Fund, The Cleveland Museum of Art.
Center: Khosrau II at his court. Illumination. Ms. Suppl. Persan 1029, fol. 100. Bibliothèque Nationale, Paris.
Right: Detail of a bowl. Sassanian. Silver, gilt. 5th c. Gift of Katherine Holder Thayer. The Cleveland Museum of Art.
66 Portrait of a Sassanian king. 4th or 5th c. P: Ronald Sheridan, London.
66/67 A Sassanian hunter. Detail of a plate. Silver. 6th c. P: Ronald Sheridan, London.
68 *Left:* Himyarite silver coin. Obverse. Male head with monogram. Reverse: Head with inscription. British Museum, London.
Right: The Black Stone. From Mecca. P: Philip K. Hitti.
69 *Top:* Desert landscape. P: Ruth Ruedi, Lucerne.
Left: The Kaaba shrine. Detail of an illumination. Ms. Hazine 1222, fol. 151. Topkapi Sarayi Museum, Istanbul.
Right: Lamp. Bronze. From Arabia. 1st c. British Museum, London.
70 *Above:* The banner of Mohammed. Topkapi Sarayi Museum, Istanbul.
Center left: Birth of Mohammed. Illumination from "Universal History" by Rashid al-Din. 14th c. University Library, Edinburgh.
Center right: Christ on a donkey and Mohammed on a camel. Illumination from "Universal History" by Rashid al-Din. 14th c. University Library, Edinburgh.
Bottom: Mohammed preaching of the new religion. Illumination. Ms. 3 Siyar-e Nabi, fol. 448v. Spencer Collection. The New York Public Library.
71 *Above:* Mohammed visited by angel Gabriel. Illumination. Ms. Hazine 1222, fol. 158. Topkapi Sarayi Museum, Istanbul.
Below left: Mohammed and his followers putting the Black Stone into the Kaaba. Illumination. From "Universal History" by Rashid al-Din. University Library, Edinburgh.
Below center: Mohammed declaring Ali his successor. Illumination. From Tabriz. A.D. 1307. University Library, Edinburgh.
Below right: Mohammed's ascension on the mare Buraq. Illumination. Ms. Sup. Turc. 100 fol. 840. Bibliothèque Nationale, Paris.
72 *Left above:* Al-Haris meets an old man. Illumination. Maqamat of Al-Hariri. Ms. Arabe 3929, fol. 54v.
Left below: Letter said to have been written by Mohammed. P: John R. Freeman, London.
Right above: Two musicians. Plate. Ivory. From Egypt. 11th or 12th c. Bargello, Florence. P: Alinari, Florence.
Right below: Sûrat at-Târiq, LXXXVI, 1–9. Qur'an. From Iraq or Persia. 5th/11th c. Collection of H. H. Prince Sadruddin Aga Khan, Geneva.
73 *Top:* Mohammed as preacher. Illumination from "Chronology of Ancient Nations" by Al-Biruni, copy of Ibn al-Kutbi, 14th c. Ms. 161. University Library, Edinburgh.
Center: Binding of the Koran. 9th or 10th c. P: Jean Mazenod, from *L'Islam et l'Art Musulman*, Editions d'Art Lucien Mazenod, Paris.
Bottom: The Morning Star (see page 72 right below).
74/75 Moslems on horseback. Illumination. Ms. Arabe 5847, fol. 19. Bibliothèque Nationale, Paris.
76 *Left:* Aqueduct. Khirbat al-Mafjah. 8th c. P: A. G. Walls, Amman.
Right: Nilometer. A.D. 861. Rhoda Island, Cairo. P: Erwin Böhm, Mainz.
76/77 Courtyard. Great Mosque of Ibn Tulun, Cairo. 7th c. P: Ronald Sheridan, London.
77 *Left:* Bathroom. Mosaic. Khirbat al-Mafjah. 8th c. By Courtesy of the Israel Department of Antiquities and Museums, Jerusalem.
Right: Christ. Coptic painting. 9th or 10th c. P: Ronald Sheridan, London.
78 *Left above:* Fresco. Detail of the west wall. Room of Six Queens, Qusayr-Amra, Jordan. P: School of Oriental and African Studies, London.
Left below: Great Mosque. Cordoba, Spain. 8th c. P: Peter Witte, Madrid.
Right: Minaret. Great Mosque, Kairouan, Tunisia. 7th c. P: Hans Huber, Garmisch-Partenkirchen.
78/79 Great Mosque, Damascus. Interior. Built under Al-Walid. 8th c. P: Hans Huber, Garmisch-Partenkirchen.
79 Mausoleum of Ismail the Samanid, Bokhara, Soviet Union. P: A. F. Kersting, London.
80 *Left:* Hunting lodge. Exterior. Built under Walid I. 8th c. Qusayr-Amra, Jordan. P: Claus Hansmann, Gauting.
Right: Female figure. Relief. 8th c. Qusayr-Amra, Jordan. P: Claus Hansmann, Gauting.
81 Mosaic. Ummayad. Palace of Hisham, near Jericho. 8th c. P: Ronald Sheridan, London.
Right: Female figures. Fresco. 8th c. Qusayr-Amra, Jordan. P: Claus Hansmann, Gauting.
82/83 The Dome of the Rock, Jerusalem. 7th c. P: Erwin Böhm, Mainz.
84 *Above left:* Stucco decoration. Detail. Palace of Khirbat al-Mafjah, Israel. 8th c. Rockefeller Museum, Jerusalem. P: By Courtesy of Israel Department of Antiquities and Museums, Jerusalem.
Above right: Mihrab. Great Mosque of caliph Al-Mansur, Baghdad, Iraq. P: School of Oriental and African Studies, London.
Center: The Fort of Ukhaidir. Near Baghdad, Iraq. P: Archaeological Institute, Turin.
Bottom: Nude female bather. Fresco. Qusayr-Amra, Jordan. 7th c. P: Claus Hansmann, Gauting.
85 *Left:* Statue of a caliph. Palace of Khirbat al-Mafjah, Israel. 8th c. P: Barbara Grunewald, Berlin.
Center: Entrance gate. Qasr al-Hair al-Sharki, Syria. 9th c. P: Barbara Grunewald, Berlin.
Right: Enthroned ruler. Statue. Ummayad Palace of Qasr al-Hair al-Gharbi, Syria. 8th c. P: Photo Ciné Azad, Damascus.
86 *Above left:* Tariq-chana Mosque, Daghman, Persia. 8th c. P: Josephine Powell, Rome.
Above right: Arcades. Interior of the Abbasid palace, Baghdad, Iraq. P: Jean Mazenod, from *L'Islam et l'Art Musulman*. Editions d'Art Lucien Mazenod, Paris.
Below: Fragment of a Tiraz. Abbasid. From Baghdad or Bishapur. 10th c. Gift of George D. Pratt. The Cleveland Museum of Art.
87 Ewer. Bronze. From a grave in upper Egypt. 8th c. Museum of Islamic Art, Cairo. P: Jean Mazenod, from *L'Islam et l'Art Musulman*. Editions d'Art Lucien Mazenod, Paris.
Right: Armed rider. Chessman. Persian. Ivory. 8th or 9th c. L. A. Mayer Memorial Institute for Islamic Art, Jerusalem.
88 *Top:* Public Library at Hulwan. Illumination. Maqamat of Al-Hariri. Ms. Arabe 2213, fol. 847–5v. Bibliothèque Nationale, Paris.
Center, from left to right: Dirhem. Silver. Abbasid. From Nishapur. British Museum, London.
Dinar. Gold. Obverse: Al-Mutawakkil. Reverse: dromedary. From Baghdad, Iraq. 9th c. Kunsthistorisches Museum, Vienna. P: Meyer K. G., Vienna.
Bottom: Warrior on a dromedary. Illumination from Ms. Arabe. Bibliothèque Nationale, Paris. P: Snark International, Paris.
89 *Above, from left to right:* Plato. Samanid. From Khorasan, Persia. 10th c. Freer Gallery of Art, Washington.
Dish. Silver. From Iran. 7th–8th c. P: Ronald Sheridan, London.
Dish. Glazed. From Nishapur, Iran. 9th c. P: Ronald Sheridan, London.
90 *Left:* Gold coin of Al-Hakam I. A.D. 796–822. Staatliche Museen Berlin, GDR.
Right: Gold coin of Abd-Ar-Rahman II. A.D. 822–852. Staatliche Museen Berlin, GDR.
91 Great Mosque of Cordoba. Interior. Built by Abd al-Rahman I. 8th c. P: Scala, Florence.
92 Box. Ivory, carved. From Cordoba, Spain. 10th c. Musée du Louvre, Paris. P: Réunion des Musées Nationaux, Paris.
92/93 Minaret. Abu-Dulaf Mosque, Samara, Soviet Union. P: Archaeological Institute, Turin.
93 *Right:* Bottle. Glass. 9th c. National Museum of Iraq, Baghdad. P: Claus Hansmann, Gauting.
Bottom: Bowl. Gold. From Persia. 4th–6th c. Kunsthistorisches Museum, Vienna. P: Claus Hansmann, Gauting.
94 Palace of Theodoric I the Great. Mosaic. Sant'Apollinare Nuovo, Ravenna. P: Scala, Florence.
95 Equestrian statue of Charlemagne. Bronze. 9th c. Ancien trésor de la cathédrale, Metz. Musée du Louvre, Paris. P: Réunion des Musées Nationaux, Paris.
96 *Top:* Theodoric I the Great. Gold solidus. 5th c. P: Leonard von Matt, Buochs.
Bottom: Sant'Apollinare Nuovo, Ravenna. P: Fotocielo, Rome.
97 *Above left:* Make-up jar. From Desana, Italy. Museo Civico, Turin.
Right: Two brooches. Silver with niello. 6th c. Schmuckmuseum, Pforzheim, Germany. P: Claus Hansmann, Gauting.
Center: Make-up spoon. Silver. From Desana, Italy. Museo Civico, Turin.
Below: Civitas Classe, Ravenna. Mosaic. Sant'Apollinare Nuovo, Ravenna. 4th–5th c. P: Leonard

von Matt, Buochs.
98 *Above left:* Anonymous coin. Bronze. Ostrogothic. Staatliche Museen Berlin, GDR.
Above right: Queen Arnalasuntha. Detail of a diptych. Ivory. Byzantine. 6th c. Kunsthistorisches Museum, Vienna. P: Lichtbildwerkstätte Alpenland, Vienna.
Below, from left to right: Belt buckle. Bronze, gilt. From Herpes, France. British Museum, London.
Pendant. Gold, glass, garnets. Ostrogothic. Treasure of Cesena, Italy. 6th c. Gift of J. Pierpont Morgan, 1917. The Metropolitan Museum of Art, New York.
Buckle. Bronze. From a tomb in Romagna, Italy. Germanisches Museum, Nuremberg.
99 *Left:* Sarcophagus of Theodoric I the Great. Mausoleum at Ravenna. P: Leonard von Matt, Buochs.
Right: Mausoleum of Theodoric I the Great, Ravenna. P: Leonard von Matt, Buochs.
100 *Above, from left to right:* Consul Boethius. Detail of a diptych. Ivory. 6th c. Museo Civico Cristiano, Brescia, Italy. P: Mansell Collection, London.
Boethius' library. Illumination. Ms. 12, fol. 11r. A.D. 1406. By kind permission of the Master and Fellows of Trinity Hall, Cambridge.
The scribe Ezra. Illumination from Codex Amiatinus. 8th c. Biblioteca Medicea Laurenziana, Florence. P: Guido Sansoni, Florence.
Below, from left to right: Lady Philosophy appears to Boethius. Illumination. Ms. 10109, fol. 2r. 11th or 12th c. Biblioteca Nacional, Madrid.
The Muses of four great arts. Illumination. Ms Class. 5, fol. 9v. Staatsbibliothek, Bamberg, Germany. P: Rheinisches Bildarchiv, Cologne.
Sects of Philosophy. Detail of an illumination. Ms. 12, fol. 6r. A.D. 1406. By kind permission of the Master and Fellows of Trinity Hall, Cambridge.
101 *Above left:* St. Benedict. 6th c. Catacomb of Hermes, Rome. P: Leonard von Matt, Buochs.
Monastery of Monte Cassino, Italy. After the second World War. P: Leonard von Matt.
Below left: Christ in Majesty. Illumination from Codex Amiatinus. Biblioteca Medicea Laurenziana, Florence. P: Guido Sansoni, Florence.
Below right: St. Benedict and an abbot of Monte Cassino. Illumination. P: Leonard von Matt.
102 *Left:* Initial letter Q. From a manuscript by Gregory the Great. Ms. 170, fol. 75v. 11th c. Bibliothèque Publique de Dijon. P: Minirel Création, Chenove.
Right: Pope Gregory at his desk. Ivory. From Trier, Germany. 9th or 10th c. Kunsthistorisches Museum, Vienna.
103 *Top:* St. Luke. Illumination. CCCC Ms. 286, fol. 129v. 6th c. Master and Fellows Corpus Christi College, Cambridge.
Center: Ampullae of Queen Theodelinda. Silver. 6th c. Tesoro della Cattedrale, Monza. P: Arnoldo Mondadori, Turin.
Bottom: Cover of a Gospel of Queen Theodelinda. Tesoro della Cattedrale, Monza. P: Scala, Florence.
104 *Top:* The iron crown of Lombardy. Gold. Tesoro della Cattedrale, Monza. P: Scala, Florence.
Below: Ornamental plaques for shields. Bronze, gilt. From Ischal-Alz, Bavaria. 7th c. Prähistorische Sammlung, Munich. P: Claus Hansmann, Gauting.
105 *Left:* Santa Maria della Valle, Cividale, Friuli, Italy. Lombard. Interior. P: Scala, Florence.
Right: Lombard cross. Gold. From France. 7th c. Bequest of Mrs. Edward Jackson Holmes. Museum of Fine Arts, Boston.
106 *Above:* Brooch. From Rebrin, Slovakia. 5th c. Kunsthistorisches Museum, Vienna. P: Meyer K.G., Vienna.
Below: Visitation of the Virgin. Relief. Stone. From the altar of San Martino in Cividale del Friuli, Italy. 8th c. Museo Cristiano, Friuli. P: Scala, Florence.
107 *Above left:* Cross of Agilulf. 6th–7th c. Tesoro della Cattedrale, Monza. P: Scala, Florence.
Above right: Medallion pendant. Gold, enamel. Lombard. From Comacchio, Italy. 7th c. The Walters Art Gallery, Baltimore.
Bottom left: Christ in his Majesty. Relief. Stone. From the altar of San Martino in Cividale del Friuli, Italy. 8th c. Museo Cristiano, Friuli. P: Scala, Florence.
Bottom right: Three kings of the East. Relief. Stone. From the altar of San Martino del Friuli, Italy. 8th c. Museo Cristiano, Friuli. P: Scala, Florence.
108 *Left:* King Agilulf. Plaque. 7th c. Museo Nazionale, Florence. P: Alinari, Florence.
Three holy women. Stucco frieze. Santa Maria in Valle, Cividale del Friuli, Italy. 8th c. P: Scala, Florence.
109 *Left:* Flight to Egypt. Fresco. Santa Maria Foris Portas, Castelseprio, Italy. P: Scala, Florence.
Right: Altar enclosure. Marble. 8th–12th c. Santa Maria Maggiore in Pergamo, Italy. P: Scala, Florence.
110 *Left:* Eagle brooch. Gold, glass. Barbarian. 5th c. Germanisches Nationalmuseum, Nuremberg.
Right: San Juan Bautista de Baños, Baños le Cerrato, Palencia, Spain. 7th c. Visigothic. P: MAS, Barcelona.
111 *Left:* San Pedro de la Nave, Zamora, Spain. 8th c. Visigothic. Interior. P: MAS, Barcelona.
Right: Fragment of Codex Argenteus. Silver ink on purple vellum. 6th c. University Library, Uppsala.
112 *Left:* Santa Maria del Naranco, Oviedo, Spain. Exterior. 9th c. P: MAS, Barcelona.
Right: Crown of Recceswinth. Gold, jewels. Visigothic. 7th c. P: MAS, Barcelona.
113 The Story of Moses. Illumination from the Ashburnham Pentateuch. Ms.N.Al. 2334, fol. 56. 6th or 7th c. Bibliothèque Nationale, Paris.
114 *Top:* Helmet. Gilt. From the tomb of a Frankish noble. Morken, Germany. 7th c. Rheinisches Landesmuseum, Bonn.
Center left: Warrior combing his hair. Carved tombstone. From Niederdollendorf, Germany. Mid-7th c. Rheinisches Landesmuseum, Bonn.
Center right: Horseman. Plaque. Bronze, silvered. Merovingian. 7th c. Gift of J. Pierpont Morgan, 1917. The Metropolitan Museum of Art, New York.
Below: Casket of Theodoric I the Great. Gold. Merovingian. Trésor de l'Abbaye, Saint-Maurice.
115 *Top:* Model of a Frankish village in 7th or 8th c. Germany. P: Ronald Sheridan, London.
Center left: Finial. Early Christian or Merovingian. 6th c. Fletcher Fund, 1947. The Metropolitan Museum of Art, New York.
Center right: Front of a tombstone. Frankish. From Moselkern, Germany. Rheinisches Landesmuseum, Bonn.
Bottom: Childeric I. Seal ring. Gold. 5th c. Ashmolean Museum, Oxford.
116 Disk brooch. Gold, garnets. From the tomb of Wittislingen, Germany. 6th c. Munich. P: Claus Hansmann, Gauting.
117 *Above left:* Disk brooch. From Castel Trosino, Italy. 7th c. Museo dell'Alto Medioevo, Rome.
Above right: Disk brooch. From Minden, Rhineland. 7th c. Rheinisches Landesmuseum, Trier.
Center: Quatrefoil brooch. Silver, gilt. From Mölsheim, France. 8th c. Carolingian. Hessisches Landesmuseum, Darmstadt.
Below left: Disk brooch. Gold. Rheinisches Landesmuseum, Trier.
Below right: Quatrefoil brooch. Gold. From Humbécourt, France. 7th c. Musée des Antiquités Nationale, St. Germain-en-Laye. P: Réunion des Musées Nationaux, Paris.
118 Mounted warrior. Pressed disk. Gold. From Pliezhausen, Germany. 7th c. Württembergisches Landesmuseum, Stuttgart. P: Claus Hansmann, Gauting.
119 *Above left:* Galloping horseman. Merovingian brooch. 7th c. P: Ronald Sheridan, London.
Above right: Gold solidus. Obverse: Portrait of Lothar II. Reverse: Cross surmounting a globe. 7th c. Merovingian. British Museum, London.
Bottom: Title page from Sacramentarium Gelasianum. Frankish. Reg. Lat. 316, fol. 132v. 7th c. Biblioteca Apostolica Vaticana, Vatican City.
120 *Left above:* Buckle. Merovingian. From Germany. 6th or 7th c. P: Ronald Sheridan, London.
Left below: Denier of Charlemagne. Silver. British Museum, London.
Right: Gravestone. From France. 7th or 8th c. Musées Departementaux de Loire-Atlantique, Nantes.
121 Bust of Christ. Relief from a tombstone. From Gondorf, Germany. 7th c. Rheinisches Landesmuseum, Bonn.
122/123 Moses presenting the Ten Commandments to the Hebrews. Illumination. Ms. Latin 1, fol. 27v. 9th c. Bibliothèque Nationale, Paris.
124 *Above:* Coin of Pepin III. Obverse: PIPI. Reverse: "RP". Frankish. 8th c. Fitzwilliam Museum, Cambridge.
Center: Four-horse chariot. Textile. Byzantine. Found in the tomb of Charlemagne. 8th c. Musée de Cluny, Paris. P: Hirmer Fotoarchiv, Munich.
Bottom: Saint Zacharias. Fresco. Santa Maria Antiqua, Rome. 8th c. P: Sopritendenza Foro Romano, Rome.
125 *Top:* Chalice of Tassilo. Gilt. 8th c. Münster-Abtei, Krems, Germany. P: Fotohaus Westmüller, Linz.
Bottom: Story of Susanna. Crystal of Lothar II. Bronze, gilt. Carolingian. 9th c. British Museum, London. P: Mansell Collection, London.
126 *Left:* Lothar I. Illumination from "Lothar Gospels". Ms. Latin 266, fol. lv. Bibliothèque Nationale, Paris.
126/127 King Offa and King Wermund. Pen-and-ink sketch from "Historia de Offa Rege", by Matthew Paris. 13th c. British Museum, London.
127 Mounted nobleman with seven followers. Plate. Ivory. 6th or 7th c. Rheinisches Landesmuseum, Trier.
128 *Left:* Nydam-ship. Frisian. Found in a peat bog, Jutland, Denmark. Schleswig-Holsteinisches Landesmuseum für Vor- und Frühgeschichte, Schleswig.
Right: Figure of a bearded Scandinavian god. Wood. From Broddenbjerg, Jutland, Denmark. 5th c. National Museum, Copenhagen.
129 *Left and right:* The so-called Pagyndrusis Codex of St. Boniface. 8th c. Treasure of the Abbey at Fulda. P: Leonard von Matt, Buochs.
130 Siege of Pamplona. Cover of Charlemagne's casket. Cathedral at Aachen. P: Ann Münchow, Aachen.
131 *Left:* Charlemagne's throne. Cathedral at Aachen. P: Edwin Smith, Saffron Walden.
Right: Talisman of Charlemagne. Sapphires and fragment of wood. Palais du Tau, Reims. P: Arch. Phot. S.P.A.D.E.M., Paris.
132 *Top:* St. Peter giving the standard to Charlemagne. Detail of a mosaic. From the Triclinio Lateranense, St. John Lateran, Rome. 8th c. P: Mansell Collection, London.
Center: Palatine chapel of Charlemagne. Interior. Aachen, Germany. P: Leonard von Matt, Buochs.
Bottom: Gatehouse, Lorsch, Germany. 8th c. P: Bruno Balestrini, Milan.
133 *Top:* Orb with cross. Regalia of Charlemagne. P: Mansell Collection, London.
Below: Rabanus Maurus. From a 9th c. manuscript. Bibliothèque Communale, Amiens.
134 The Pentateuch in Hebrew. 9th c. British Museum, London. P: Mansell Collection, London.
134/135 Menorah. Gold, glass. Jewish. From the catacombs, Rome. P: Françoise Foliot, Paris.
136 *Left:* Holy City of Jerusalem. Mosaic. From Madaba. 6th c. P: Dayton International, Channel Islands.
Right above: Romans carrying the Menorah. Detail of a relief. Arch of Titus, Rome. A.D. 81. P: Leonard von Matt, Buochs.
Right below: Tombs at Beth Shearim, Israel. P: Schwabe Verlag, Stuttgart.
137 *Left:* Sacrifice of Isaac. Floor mosaic. Detail. Synagogue, Beth Alpha, Israel. 6th c. The Institute of Archaeology, The Hebrew University of Jerusalem.
Right: Mosaic. Synagogue of Ma'on, Nirim, Israel. 6th c. By Courtesy Israel Department of Antiquities and Museums, Jerusalem. P: Francoise Foliot, Paris.
138/139 Torah scrolls of Oriental Jews. Left from Iraq, right from India. P: Ronald Sheridan, London.
140 Vision of the revival of the bodies. Fresco. Detail. Ezekiel 37, 1–10. Synagogue, Dura Europos. Mid-3rd c. P: Jewish Theological Seminary, New York.
141 Story of the childhood of Moses. Fresco. Detail. Synagogue, Dura Europos. Mid-3rd c. P: Jewish Theological Seminary, New York.
142 Torah-coat. Cotton. From Oberrhein, Germany. Late 18th c. Torah scroll. Buckskin and vellum. From Cairo, 15th c. Torah-pointer. Silver, partly gilt. From Vienna. 19th c. Jüdisches Museum, Basel. P: D. Widmer, Basel.
143 *Top:* Mohammed and four caliphs. Illumination. Zubdat al-Tawarich, Turkish. Ms. 423, fol. 21b. A.D. 1600. Chester Beatty Library, Dublin. P: Pieterse-Davison International, Dublin.
Below: Psalms 119 and 121. From Ms. Or. 2348, fol. 39r. From San'a, Yemen. British Library, London.
144 Lintel, synagogue of Nabarta, Israel. 2nd c. P: The Institute of Archaeology, The Hebrew University of Israel, Jerusalem.
Bottom: Mosaic. Floor in the synagogue at Beth Shan. Jewish. 6th c. P: Ronald Sheridan, London.
145 Vision of the revival of the bodies. Fresco. Details. Ezekiel 37, 1–10. Synagogue, Dura Europos. Mid-3rd c. P: Jewish Theological Seminary, New York.
146 King Solomon and King David. Enamel plates from the crown of Holy Roman Empire. 10th c. Kunsthistorisches Museum, Vienna.
147 City of Jerusalem and Menorahs. Fresco. Fanlight, Jewish catacombs, Rome. P: André Held, Ecublens.
148 *Left above:* Brand-stamp for cattle. Iron. From Alsace, France. 18th c. Jüdisches Museum, Basel. P: Thomas Hartmann, Würenlos.
Left below: Letter, in Persian with Hebrew letters. Ms. Ar. 8212. From Kurdistan. 8th c. British Museum, London.
Right: Las Cantigas de Santa Maria. Illumination from an 11th c. manuscript. Biblioteca de San Lorenzo del Escorial, Madrid. P: MAS, Barcelona.
149 *Top:* K'tubba, marriage settlement. Vellum, painted. From Rome. A.D. 1751. Jüdisches Museum, Basel. P: Thomas Hartmann, Würenlos.
Center, from left to right: Representation of Jewish slave-trade. Relief. Bronze. Church of Gnesen. 12th c. The State Jewish Museum, Prague.
Top. Wood. From south-Germany. Early 19th c. Jüdisches Museum, Basel. P: Thomas Hartmann, Würenlos.
Wedding ring. Gold, filigree, enamel. From Venice. 17th c. Jüdisches Museum, Basel. P: Thomas Hartmann, Würenlos.
Below: Tombstone. From Venusa, Italy. A.D. 829. The Institute of Archaeology, The Hebrew University of Israel, Jerusalem.
150 The Incarnation Initial. From the Canterbury Codex Aureus, fol. 11. Royal Library, Stockholm.
151 Helmet. Iron, silver and bronze, gilt. From Sutton Hoo, England. 7th c. British Museum, London.
152 Anglo-Saxons at war. Whalebone, carved. 7th c. British Museum, London.
153 *Above:* Sword-hilt. From a grave at Coombe, Kent. Saffron Walden Museum, Saffron Walden.
Center: Easter Annals, giving the factual evidence for the existence of king Arthur. Ms. Harley 3859, fol. 190a. British Library, London.
Below: Sword-mount. Silver, niello, carved. From the Nydambog, Jutland, Denmark. Schleswig-Holsteinisches Museum für Vor- und Frühgeschichte, Schleswig.
154 *Left above:* Fish. Ornate, jeweled. From Sutton Hoo, England. 7th c. British Museum, London.
Left below: Handbowl, with fish. From Sutton Hoo, England. 7th c. British Museum, London.
154/155 Christ (center) and the Evangelists. Detail from a 8th-c. manuscript. Ms. 4. Bibliothèque Municipale, Autun.
155 *Left:* Scenes from the New Testament. Illumination from the "Gospels of St. Augustine". Ms. 286, fol. 125r. Master and Fellows Corpus Christi College, Cambridge.
Right: Remains of St. Ethelbert's tower and St. Augustine's monastery, Canterbury. Engraving. P: Mansell Collection, London.
156 *Left:* Hinged clasp. Gold, garnets, glass, filigree. From Sutton Hoo, England. 7th c. British Museum, London. P: Ronald Sheridan, London.
Right: Buckle. Gold. From Sutton Hoo, England, 7th c. British Museum, London. P: Ronald Sheridan, London.
156/157 Richly ornamented

purse. From Sutton Hoo, England. 7th c. British Museum, London. P: Ronald Sheridan, London.

157 Spoon with inscription. From Sutton Hoo, England. 7th c. British Museum, London. P: Mansell Collection, London.
Below: Fluted dish. Silver. Roman. Early 7th c. British Museum, London. P: Mansell Collection, London.

158 *Center:* Roman capture of Jerusalem. Casket. From Northumbria. A.D. 700. British Museum, London. P: Mansell Collection, London.
Bottom: Frith stool. Hexham Abbey, Northumbria. 7th c. P: John Webb.

159 *Left:* The scribe Ezra. Illumination from Codex Amiatinus. 8th c. Biblioteca Medicea Laurenziana, Florence. P: Guido Sansoni, Florence.
Right: Anglo-Saxon view of a Dragon ship. 10th c. British Museum, London. P: Robert Harding, London.

160 Carpet with scroll work. The Book of Durrow, fol.3v. 7th c. Courtesy of the Board of Trinity College, Dublin. P: The Green Studio, Dublin.

161 *Left:* Ruthwell Cross. Anglo-Saxon. 8th c. Dumfries. P: Thames and Hudson, London.
Right: A priest holding a model of a church. P: Scala, Florence.

162 The Incarnation initial. From the Book of Lindisfarne, fol. 29. British Library, London.

163 Symbol of St. Matthew. From the Echternach Gospels. Ms. Lat. 9389, fol. 18v. Bibliothèque Nationale, Paris.

164 Illumination from the Book of Kells, fol. 40v. The Board of Trinity College, Dublin. P: The Green Studio, Dublin.

165 Mark I "Initium Evangelii IHU XPI Christi". From the Book of Kells, fol. 130r. The Board of Trinity College, Dublin. P: The Green Studio, Dublin.

166 *Center:* Offa's dyke. Hergan, Shropshire, England. 8th c. P: The Mustograph Agency, London.
Below: Penny of Offa. Silver. Obverse: portrait of Offa. Reverse: inscription. 8th c. British Museum, London.

167 *Top left:* Opening of king Alfred's preface to his translation of Gregory the Great's "Cura Pastoralis". Ms. Hatton 20, fol. Ir. 9th c. The Bodleian Library, Oxford.
Top right: Gregorius I Magnus. Detail of a fresco. Monastery of Sacro Speco, Subiaco, Italy. 13th c. P: Leonard von Matt, Buochs.
Below: Aethelstan presenting Bede's "Life of St. Cuthbert" to the monks of Chester-le-Street. Ms. 183, fol. Iv. Master and Fellows of Corpus Christi College, Cambridge.

168 *Above:* A page from a manuscript of Beowulf. 10th c. British Museum, London. Drawing.
Below: David as Victor. Illumination from "The Durham Cassiodorus", fol. 172v. 8th c. The Dean and Chapter of Durham Cathedral.

169 David as Musician. Illumination from "The Durham Cassiodorus", fol. 81v. 8th c. The Dean and Chapter of Durham Cathedral.

170 *Left:* Male figures. Relief. Detail. From the Breac Baodhóg shrine. 11th c. National Museum of Ireland, Dublin.
Right: Beehive cottage. From the Island of Skellig Mhichill, Kerry, Ireland. P: Franco Cianetti, Italy.

171 Athlone Crucifixion. Bronze plaque. 8th c. Irish/Celtic. National Museum of Ireland, Dublin. P: Mansell Collection, London.

172/173 Stone crosses. Monastery of Clonmacnois, Ireland. 6th c. P: Claus Hansmann, Gauting.

174 Ogham stone. From Monataggart, County Cork, Ireland. 4th–7th c. National Museum of Ireland, Dublin. P: Claus Hansmann, Gauting.
Right: Ogham-stone. From Tirmohally, County Kerry, Ireland. 4th–7th c. National Museum of Ireland, Dublin. P: Claus Hansmann, Gauting.

175 *Left:* Brooch. Silver, gilt. Irish. A.D. 700. National Museum of Ireland, Dublin. P: Claus Hansmann, Gauting.
Right: The Book of Leinster. 12thc. Ms. The Board of Trinity College, Dublin.

176 *Left:* Brooch. Silver, gold and amber. From Roscrea County Tipperary, Ireland. 11th c. P: Lee Boltin, New York.
Right: The Ardagh chalice. Silver, gold, filigree. From Ardagh, Limerick, Ireland. 8th c. National Museum of Ireland, Dublin.

177 The Tara brooch. Bronze, gilt, filigree. A.D. 700. National Museum of Ireland, Dublin.

178 *Left:* Bell-shrine of St. Connel. Silver. Irish/Celtic. 8th c. British Museum, London. P: Mansell Collection, London.
Right: The Emly Shrine. Silver, gold, enamel, yew wood. Irish. 8th c. Theodora Wilbour Fund. Museum of Fine Arts, Boston.

179 *Left:* The North Cross of Ahenny, Tipperary, Ireland. 8th c. P: Claus Hansmann, Gauting.
Right: The South Cross of Ahenny, Tipperary, Ireland. 8th c. P: Belzeaux/Zodiaque, La Pierre-qui-Vire, France.

180 *Left:* Symbol of St. Matthew. Illumination from the Book of Durrow. The Board of Trinity College, Dublin. P: Robert Harding, London.
Right: Beginning of Luke's Gospel. Illumination. Irish Codex 51. 8th c. Stiftsbibliothek St. Gallen, Switzerland. P: Claus Hansmann, Gauting.

181 *Left:* Beginning of Luke's Gospel. Illumination. Irish Codex 51. 8th c. Stiftsbibliothek St. Gallen, Switzerland. P: Claus Hansmann, Gauting.
Right: Illumination. Book of Kells. 8th c. The Board of Trinity College, Dublin. P: Claus Hansmann, Gauting.

182 *Top:* Monastery of Kells, Ireland. Built by St. Columbanus. A.D. 543–615. Reconstruction. P: Peter Harbison, Dublin.
Bottom: Stone from St. Vigeans, Angus, Scotland. P: Scottish Development Department.

183 *Left:* St. Columb's House in Kells, Meath. A.D. 814. P: Franco Cianetti, Italy.
Right: A bull. Slab. Carved. From Broch, Burghead. 8th c. British Museum, London. P: Claus Hansmann, Gauting.

184 *Left:* Picture-stone. From Gotland, Sweden. 5th c. P: Gotlands Fornsal, Vispi, Sweden.
Right: God Thor. Bronze figure. From Iceland. P: Nordbok, Gotenborg.

185 Sword-hilt. From Snarkemo, Norway. Late 19th c. Universitetets Oldsaksamling, Oslo.

186 *Left:* Bracteate. Gold. From Hammenhög, Skåne, Sweden. 4th c. Statens Historiska Museer, Stockholm.
Right: Fortified village of Eketorp, Oeland. 5th c. Statens Historiska Museer, Stockholm. P: Rune Hedgren, Sweden.

187 *Left:* God Odin riding to Valhalla. Picture-stone. From Gotland. 9th c. Statens Historiska Museer, Stockholm. P: Claus Hansmann, Gauting.
Right: Bridle mount. Bronze, gilt. From Bood, Hella, Gotland. 6th c. P: David Wilson, London.

188 Cart. Wood. From the Oseberg ship. 9th c. Universitetets Oldsaksamling, Oslo.

188/189 Tapestry. From the Oseberg ship. 9th c. Water colour reconstruction. Universitetets Oldsaksamling, Oslo.

189 *Top:* Bracteate. Gold, filigree. From Gerete, Gotland. 6th c. Statens Historiska Museer, Stockholm. P: Claus Hansmann, Gauting.

190 *Top:* Silver ornaments, coins and hacksilver. From Birka, Sweden. A.D. 975. National Museum of Stockholm. P: Sören Hallgren/ATA, Stockholm.
Bottom left: Figure. Bronze. From the tomb of a warrior. Froyhov, Akerhus, Norway. 3th c. Universitetets Oldsaksamling, Oslo.
Bottom right: Diorama of Haithabu. Schleswig-Holsteinisches Museum für Vor- und Frühgeschichte, Schleswig.

191 *Left:* Head of a corpse from Osterby. Schleswig-Holsteinisches Museum für Vor- und Frühgeschichte, Schleswig.
Right: Ladies wear. From Huldremose, Denmark. Nationalmuseet, Copenhagen. P: Lennart Larsen, Copenhagen.

193 *Left:* Belt mount. From Sweden. Frankish. P: Ronald Sheridan, London.
Center: Prow of the Oseberg ship. A.D. 800. Universitetets Oldsaksamling, Oslo. P: Robert Harding, London.
Right: Arm-ring. From Rathedan, County Carlow, Ireland. 9th–11th c. National Museum of Ireland, Dublin. P: Claus Hansmann, Gauting.
Top: Viking attacking with swords and axes. Picture-stone. Lindisfarne, Northumbria. 8th–9th c. P: Robert Harding, London.
Below: Stamping dies from Sweden. 5th–7th c. Statens Historiska Museer, Stockholm. P: ATA, Stockholm.

194 Invasion of Russians into Bulgaria. Illumination from "Chronicle of Manasses". 14th c. From Bulgaria. Biblioteca Apostolica Vaticana, Vatican City.

195 Grave guardian. Figure, clay. 7th–10th c. From China. Royal Ontario Museum, Toronto. P: Leonard von Matt, Buochs.
Right: Master of ceremonies of the royal court. Statue, terracotta. From China. Royal Ontario Museum, Toronto. P: Leonard von Matt, Buochs.

196 *Above:* Spurs. Bronze, gilt. From grave no. 64, Mikulčice, Moravia, Czechoslovakia. Narodní Museum, Brno.
Bottom: Pottery. Cemetery at Přítluky, Moravia, Czechoslovakia. Narodní Museum, Brno.

196/197 *Top:* Semi-subterranean house. Novotroitskoe, Russia. Reconstruction after Ljapkushin. P: Thames and Hudson, London.
Bottom: Hilltop village of Novotroitskoe, Russia. Reconstruction after Ljapkushin. P: Thames and Hudson, London.

197 Tongue piece from the cemetery, Nové Zámky, Slovakia. P: Marija Gimbutas, USA.

198 *From left to right:* Ring with solidus. From a Croatian princess' grave, Dalmatia. 8th c. Museum of Archaeology, Split. A falconer. Plaque. Silver. From a grave, Stare Mesto, Moravia, Czechoslovakia. Narodni Museum, Brno.
Tongue piece. From Nagysurany, Hungary. 8th c. Hungarian National Museum, Budapest.

198/199 Warrior grave. From Holiare, Slovakia. 8th c. Archeologicke Museum, Nitra, CSSR.

199 *Above:* Ear-rings. Silver and gold. From the Princess' grave, Great Moravia, Mikulčice, Narodni Museum, Brno.
Below: Foundations of the palace of Mikulčice, Moravia, Czechoslovakia. 9th c. Narodni Museum, Brno.

200 Drinking cup. Gold. From the treasure of Nagyszentmiklos, Rumania. 9th c. Kunsthistorisches Museum, Vienna.

201 German rider with a prisoner. Detail from a vessel. Treasure from Nagyszentmiklos, Rumania. Kunsthistorisches Museum, Vienna. P: Lichtbildwerkstätte Alpenland, Vienna.

202 *Left above:* Axe of a Khazar warrior. Iron. Museum of National History, Belgorod, USSR.
Left below: Silver coin. Byzantine. Staatliche Museen Berlin, GDR.
Right: Vessel. Clay. Museum of National History, Kertsch, USSR.

203 *Left:* Ships of Russians. Illumination from the Radziwill chronicle. After Artamanov. P: Publisher's Archives.
Right: Jewish gravestone. Phanagoria. After Artamanov. P: Publisher's Archives.

204 An attacks by Huns. Illumination. Ms Periz. F. 17, fol 15v. From St. Gallen. A.D. 975. University Library, Leiden.

205 *From left to right:* Stone image found at Sagly, USSR. 7th–9th c. Two stone images found at Ulaatai, USSR. 7th–9th c. P: Publisher's Archives.

206 *Left:* A musician. From Lungmen, Honan, China. Early 6th c. Victoria and Albert Museum, London.
Right: Emperor Yang Chien of China. A.D. 589–618. P: Cultural Relics Publishing House, Beijing.

206/207 An Ji Bridge, Zhaoxian County Hebei, China. A.D. 605–616. P: Cultural Relics Publishing House, Beijing.

207 *Left:* Buddha. Votivstele. 5th or 6th c. Rietberg Museum, Zurich. P: Claus Hansmann, Gauting.
Right: Confucius. Manuscript illustration. Cultural Relics Publishing House, Beijing.

208 *Left:* Pedestal bowl. Gold. From Ho-chia Shensi, China. Mid-7th c. P: Robert Harding, London.
Center: Spittoon. Porcelain. From China. Late 9th c. P: Robert Harding, London.
Right: Merchant. Pottery. 8th c. From China. Eugene Fuller Memorial Collection. Seattle Art Museum, Washington.

209 *Left:* Wild Goose Pagoda. 7th c. From China. Siren Archives. Ostasiatska Museet, Stockholm.
Center: Boddhisattva flying on a cloud. Painting. 8th c. Shosoin Collection, Nara, Japan.
Right: Pottery. From the tomb of Princess Yung T'ai. A.D. 706. From China. P: Robert Harding, London.

210 Pottery. From Ch'ung P'u, Shensi, China. Early 8th c. P: Robert Harding, London.

211 Tomb guardian. Pottery. From Ch'ung P'u, Shensi, China. Early 8th c. P: Robert Harding, London.

212 *Left:* Standing Vahara. Sandstone. From Sarnath, Gupta, India. 5th or 6th c. P: Claus Hansmann, Gauting.
Right: Standing Buddha. Granite. India. 6th or 7th c. Private Collection, Switzerland. P: Claus Hansmann, Gauting.

213 *Left:* Shiva-Lingam. Stone. India. 7th c. Private Collection, Switzerland. P: Claus Hansmann, Gauting.
Right: Lokhanata-Relief. Stone. North India. 7th c. P: Claus Hansmann, Gauting.

214 *Top:* Temple. Mahâwallapuram/Tamilnadu. India. 7th c. P: Claus Hansmann, Gauting.
Below: Parvati and lions. Mathura-Stone. India. 8th c. Private Collection, Switzerland. P: Claus Hansmann, Gauting.

215 Monolithic rock-sanctuary. Mahâmallapuran/Tamilnadu. India. A.D. 630. P: Claus Hansmann, Gauting.

216 Coronation sword of French kings. Gold. 11th c. Musée du Louvre, Paris. P: Claus Hansmann, Gauting.

217 Odin. Relief. Detail of tombstone from Hornhausen, Germany. 7th–8th c. Landesmuseum für Vorgeschichte, Halle. P: Robert Harding, London.

INDEX

Page numbers in italics refer to illustrations

Aachen (Aix-la-Chapelle), 10, 15, *125, 130ff.,* 132, 147f., 161
Abbasids, 76, 79, 84–90, *84–90,* 92, 144, 147f.
Abd al-Malik, 78–81
Abd al-Rahman I al-Dakhil, 90, *90*
Abd al-Rahman II, 90, *90*
Abd al-Rahman III, 90
Abd al-Rahman al-Ghafiki, 86
Aboba, *see* Pliska
Abraha, 68
Abu Bakr, 76
Abu Hanifa, 88
Abu Issa, 144f.
Abu Kariba As'ad, 142f.
Abu'l Abbas, 86, 147
Abu Masher (Abulmassar), 144
Abu Muslim, 86
Adamnán, 171
Adrian I, 167
Aetius, 14
Afghanistan, 77f., 204
Africa, 7f., 14, 18, 30f., 34ff., 39, 62, 68, 70, 78f., 89f., 112
Agathias, 49
Agilulf, 103, 106, *107f.,* 108
Ahenny, 178, *179*
Aidan (king), 182
Aidan, St., 160, 183
Ailbhe, St., *178*
Aistulf, 106
Ajanta, 212
Akhmim, *54*
Aksum (Abyssinia), *see* Ethiopia
Alamanni, 114, *116*
Alani, 19
Alaric I, 18, 102, 110
Alaric II, 110, 115
Al-Baida, 203
Al-Biruni, *73*
Alboin, 104
Alcuin, 95, 133, 151, 161
Aldeigjuborg, *see* Staraya Ladoga
Alexandria, 24, 44, 46f., 56, 101
Alfonso I, 112
Alfonso II the Chaste, 112
Alfred, *9, 167*
Al-Fustat, *see* Cairo
Al-Hajjaj, 78f.
Al-Hakem I, 90, *90*
Al-Hariri, *88*
Ali, *71,* 77f., 84f.
Al-Mahdi, 84
Al-Mamun, 89
Al-Mansur, *84,* 86, 88, 167
Almoqueira, *92*
Al-Mutasim, *92*
Al-Mutawakkil, *88,* 92
Al-Walid I, 79, *79f.,* 81
Amalfi, 106
Amalsuntha, *98*
America, 7, 150, 188, 193, 216
Anahita, *65*
Anan ben David, 145
Anastasius I, 6, *11,* 17, *29,* 99, 157
Ancyra (Ankara), *29*
Angles, 109, 126, 128, 150, 152f., 158
Anglesey I., 158
Ansgar, St., 187
Antae, 199
Anthemius of Tralles, 50, 52
Antioch (Antakya), 66
Aquileia, 14
Aquitaine, 116, 125
Arabia, 8, 15, 62, 68–76, 78ff., 92, 142f., 216
Arabs, 8, 10, 15, 33, 36–39, 47, 49, 57, 60, 63, 66, 68–93, *68–93,* 110, 112, 121, 124f., 143, 167, 178, 187, 189, 191, 193f., 198f., 202f., 208, 213f.
Aral Sea, 189, 203f.
Ardagh, *176*
Ariadne, *17*
Arianism, 14, 30, 46f., 96f., 99, 102ff., 108, 110ff., 114f., 130
Arles, 146
Armenia, 30, 35f., 38, *43,* 50, 64, 116, 208

Armorica, *see* Brittany
Arnegunde, 116
Arthur, 153, *153*
Asa, *192*
Asia Minor (Anatolia), 23, 29, 36–39, 44f., 48f., 60f., 77ff., 199
Asparuch, 200
Astrakhan, 203
Asturias, 8, 79, 111f.
Athalaric, 98
Athanaric, 7
Athanasius, St., 44, 101
Athelstan, 167
Athens, 15, 38, 50, 65
Athlone, *170*
Attila, *14,* 19, 102, 200, 204
Augustine, St. (Canterbury), 15, 102, *103,* 154, *155,* 159
Aurelian, *18*
Aurelius Ambrosianus, 153
Austrasia, 124
Authari, 106
Auvergne, 146
Avars, 9, 15, 36, 60, 194, 197f., 200, 202
Ayodha, 212
Azov, Sea of, 189, 200

Babylon, 86, 136, 140
Badonicus, Mons, 153
Baghdad, 60, *84,* 86, 88ff., 92, 144, 147, 188f., 213
Baikal, Lake, 204f.
Balanjar (Khir-Zurt), 202f.
Balkash, Lake, 204
Balkh, 88
Baluchistan, 78
Bamburgh, 158
Bamyan, 204
Bangor, 183
Bani Hashim, 70
Baños de Cerrato, *110*
Barbete, R. (Wadi Bakka), 79
Bashshar ibn Burd, 88
Basil I, 60
Basil II Bulgaroktonos, 60, *60*
Basil, St., 44
Basques, 90
Basra, 76, 79, 88
Bavaria, 103, 106, 109, 116, 125, 130
Bayan, 200
Bede, 10, 155, 168
Bedouin, 15, 68f., 88
Belisarius, 14, 28–31, 34, 98f.
Benedict, St., Benedictines, 10, *10,* 15, 100ff., *101,* 103, 129, 160f., 181, 216
Benedict Biscop, 160f., 163, 168
Benevento, 104
Beowulf, 157, *168*
Berbers, 78, 90, 112
Berenda, *61*
Bergamo, *109*
Bernicia, 158ff.
Berytus (Beirut), 43
Beth Alpha, 137
Beth Shearim, 136
Bhubaneswar, 213
Bilge, 205
Black Sea, 16, 22, *23,* 41, 140, 188f., 202
Bobbio, 13, 108, 183
Boddhisatva, *213*
Boethius, 10, 100, *100,* 103
Bokhara, 79, 208
Bolgar, 200
Bologna, 33
Bombay, 140
Boniface, St., 115, 129, *129*
Boyne, R., 176
Brittany, 118, 176, 183
Bro, *187*
Broddenbjerg, *128*
Brude, 183
Brunhilda, 118, 120
Buddha, Buddhism, *9,* 194, 206–209, 212f., *212f.*
Bulgars (Bulgaria), 8f., *12f.,* 31, 36, 38, 60, *61,* 199ff., *200f.*
Bulgars (Russia: proto-Bulgars, Black Bulgaria, Old Great Bulgaria), 188f., 194, 197, 200, 203
Buraq, *71*

Burgundy, 19, 114ff., 118f., 125f
Bustani, 144
Byzantine (east Roman) empire, 6, 8, *9, 14,* 15–66, *16–61,* 68f., 76–81, 90, 92, 96, 98ff., 102, 104–108, *114,* 116, 121, 125, 130f., 134, 140, 142f., 146f., 158, 176, 197–204, 208, 216
Byzantium, *see* Constantinople

Caedmon, 168
Caesarea in Cappadocia (Kayseri), 44
Caesarea Marittima, 34
Cairo, 76, *76*
Calabria, 100
Callinicus, 37
Canterbury, 103, 151, 154f., *155,* 160f., 167
Canton, *see* Kuang-chou
Carloman, 15
Carolingians, *see* Franks
Carthage, *31,* 36, 78f.
Cashel, 178
Caspian Sea, 188f., 202f.
Cassiodorus, 10, 100f., 103, *168*
Castellum, 100
Castelseprio, 109, *109*
Castel Trosino, *116*
Castile, Old, 110, 112
Castalaunian Plains, 14
Caucasus Mts., 200, 202f.
Cesena, *9, 98*
Ceylon (Sri Lanka), 35
Chalcedon (Kadiköy), 27, 44, 46
Chalukyas, 212f.
Champa (Vietnam), 208
Ch'an (Zen), 207
Chandra Gupta II, 212
Chang Seng-yu, 207
Chang Hsuan, 41
Charlemagne 10f., 13, *15,* 38, 94f., 105, 107ff., 120, *120f.,* 124ff., *125,* 128–133, *130–133,* 146ff., 161, 167, 191, 198, 200, 216
Charles Martel, 37, 86, 115f., 124, 126, 129, 216
Charles the Bald, 126
Chelles, *119*
Chen dynasty (Southern), 207
Ch'i dynasty (Southern), 207
Childeric I, 114, *115,* 116
China, 7, 9f., 13, *13,* 15, 41, 62, 65f., 79, 88, 140, 162, 189, 194ff., 200, 204–209, 212f., 216
Chosroes, *see* Khosrau
Ciaran, St., 171
Cividale, *105f.,* 108, *108*
Clichy, 120
Clonard, 171
Clonmacnois, 171, *171,* 178
Clotilde, 114
Clovis, 110, 114ff., 118f.
Cochin, 148
Cologne (Köln), 114, 116, *146*
Columba (Columcille), St., 174, 182f., *183*
Columbanus, St., 108, 119, 181, 183
Comacchio, *107*
Comneni, 60
Conall, 178
Confucius, 207f.
Connaught, 170, 174
Constans II, 36
Constantine I the Great, *12, 22,* 41f., 50, 107, 115, 136, 140, 146
Constantine IV Pogonatus, 36f., 200
Constantine V Copronymus, 38, 48f., *198,* 200, 202
Constantinople (Byzantium), 8, 10, *11f.,* 13, 16, 19, 22f., *22f.,* 26f., *26,* 29, 30, *32,* 36ff., *36f.,* 39, 41ff., *42,* 47, *47f.,* 49, 54, *55,* 57, *57,* 60, 65, 78, 86, 95, 100, 102, 104, 109, 111, 130, 133, 140, 189, 199–202, 216
Constantius II, 140
Cooley, *see* Táin Bó Cúailnge
Coombe, *153*
Copts, *54, 77,* 154, 176
Corbie, 187
Cordoba, 8, 13, *78,* 90, 92, 110
Cornwall, 276, 183
Coroticus, 171
Cosmas Indicopleustes, 10, 26, 34f., *35*
Cotiaeum (Kütahya), *38*
Covadonga, 112

Crimea, 9, 41, 202
Croats, Croatia, 198f., *198*
Cruachan, 174
Ctesiphon, 15, 64ff., 140
Cynethryth, 167
Cyprus, *55,* 77
Cyril, St., 199
Cyrus, 136
Cyzicus, 36
Czechs, 198f.

Daghestan, 202
Dagobert I, 147
Dalmatia, 14, 30, 43, 130
Dalriada, 160, 181f.
Damascus 57, *57,* 63, 66, 78, *79,* 80f., 86
Damgan, *86*
Danevirke, 191
Danube, 18, 22, 28, 31, 98, 104, 198ff.
Dara, *29*
Deben, R., 156
Deccan, 213
Dee, R., 167
Deira, 158ff.
Denmark, Danes, 128, 150, 161, 167f., 184, 188, 190–193, 216
Desana, *97*
Desiderius, 105, 107, 125
Dhu Nuwas, *see* Yusuf Ashab
Diaspora (Dispersion), *see* Jews
Dnieper, R., 118f., 196, 202
Dniester, R., 202
Dobrogea (Dobruja), 200
Don, R., 189, 202f.
Donegal, 182
Dorestad, 128, 191, 193
Dvina, R., 188
Eadfrith, 163
East Anglia (Sutton Hoo) 151, 154, 156f., 168, 187
Ecclesius, 56
Echternach, 128, 163, *163*
Edwin, 158f.
Egbert, 167
Egfrith, 160f., 183
Egil, *152*
Egypt, 36, 39f., 47, 54, 66, 76ff., 101, 116, 140, 144f., 154, 171, 176, 178
Ekerö, *see* Lillon
Eketorp, 186, *186*
Elbe, R., 104, 130, 153, 198, 200
Elephanta, 213
Ellora, 213
Emly, 168
England, 7f., 10, 102, 116, 125, 128, 151–167, 170f., *192f.,* 216
Essex, 153
Ethelbald, 166
Ethelbert I, 154ff.
Ethelfrith, 158, 160
Ethiopia (Aksum, Abyssinia), 35, 68f., 78, 143
Euphrates, R., 18, 22, 66, 86, 88f., 138, 140

Faroe Is., 183, 192
Fergus Mor, 182
Finn, 174
Finns, Finland, 188f., 200, 203
Firuz (Peroz), *9, 66,* 140, 204
France (Gaul), 10, 18, 28, 86, 90, 94, 99, 108, 112, 114–133, 146, 162, 183, 216
Franks (Merovingians, Carolingians), 8f., 13, 15, 19, 90, 94f., 99, 106ff., 109f., 114–133, 150, 152f., 156, 168, 171, 176, 184, 191ff., 198ff., 202
Fredegund, 120
Frisians, 128ff., 149ff., 153, 188, 191, 193
Fulda, 129, *129,* 133

Gabars, 65
Gaiseric (Genseric), 18f., 21
Galicia, 112, 176
Galilee, 137, 140
Gall, St., 181
Galla Placidia, *17*
Gallehus, 190
Gamara, 138
Gascons, 90
Gaul, *see* France
Geatas, 157
Gelasius, *119*
Gelimer, 30
Gemistus Plethon, 60f.
Genghis Khan, 89
Genoa, 106